- DID YOU KNOW THAT... -

STAFFORD, CANNOCK & RUGELEY

MALTHOUSE PRESS.
GRANGE COTTAGE, MALTHOUSE LANE,
BARLASTON, STAFFORDSHIRE, ST12 9AQ

D1437681

MALTHOUSE PRESS.
GRANGE COTTAGE, MALTHOUSE LANE,
BARLASTON, STAFFORDSHIRE, ST12 9AQ

ISBN 978-953-9018-6-9

Introduction

From time to time local historians and the general public may need to consult a book of claims, firsts, lasts etc for their area. Here is such a book. I have chosen ancient parishes as the chapter perimeters because they are static for when we have statistics. For population ratings Staffordshire had 166 ancient parishes; for dimension ratings 169. This book is one of five volumes in the series 'Tim Cockin's Staffordshire Did You Know That...' There are two more volumes planned, Volumes 1 (Potteries), and 4 (Lichfield, Burton, Tamworth). Volumes 2 (Moorlands) and 5 (Black Country) are already published. For their help with this volume many thanks to: Joan Anslow for kind permission to use illustations from her 'Stafford: A Little Book' (1996) (see Marston and Penkridge); Elizabeth Quick of Barlaston for the loan of her copy of 'The Staffords' by JM Robinson; Margaret Neal and Dorothy Bradbury of The Landor Society, the local history society for Rugeley; Julie Shires at Cannock Chase Museum; Chris Copp at County Museum, Shugborough; Terry Gilder, and Roy Lewis of Castle Church.

Obviously claims in themselves do not tell a proper story of the parish, but what I found by chance as information randomly accumulated (and was not searched for) unforeseen themes emerged. For instance:

Adbaston, freedom and constraint
Berkswich, the county town's parade and pleasure ground
Blymhill, gentry flourish, poor flounder
Bradley, the county town's rural sanctuary
Brewood, parish of prowess
Cannock, amid grime, crime and wildness is music and community spirit
Castle Church, the county town's fort, academy and workshop
Cheslyn Hay, low external reputation, high self regard
Church Eaton, parish that takes the honours
Colton, close-knit backwater yet with foreign and exotic associations
Colwich, peculiar road accidents
Creswell, external forces impact on the ordinary
Ellenhall, pastural and secretive
Forton, tiny sirens
Gayton, parish obsequiously giving and receiving
Gnosall, puritanical wanderlust
High Offley, watchful
Ingestre, ostentatious
Lapley, robust

Marston, the county town's dump
Norbury, persistent and eerie
Penkridge, helpful, healing, holy
Rugeley, in the limelight for a multitude of unexpected reasons
Ranton, things untoward
Seighford, industrious despite its rural setting
Shareshill, sweet and sour
Stafford, parish of multifarious activities one would expect associated with a county town
Stowe-by-Chartley, striving and courageous
Teddesley Hay, dutiful
Tixall, parish of little and large technological wonders
Weston-under-Lizard, public ostentation, private disappointment
Weston-upon-Trent, the top-that-if-you-can parish!

Abbreviations for references are not listed - readers can consult The Staffordshire Encyclopaedia, or The Staffordshire Encyclopaedia Website at http:// www.the-staffordshire-encyclopaedia.co.uk/

Tim Cockin. Barlaston. 2009.

Adbaston
1. Did you know that...

Adbaston's top folklore That Knighton was free from rates and taxes because the villagers helped Charles II to escape after the battle of Worcester (1651), but the truth is Knighton became exempt from rates and taxes because the village formed part of an estate of William Adams of Newport, Shrops, which he gave to charity. And because he had lent Charles II money, an Act of Parliament exempted the estate from all taxes. **Last relic of Noah's Flood** Traditionally, Bishop's Offley Pool (BPS p155) (ROT p18). The **name Adbaston first appears** in Domesday Book, 1086. **What Adbaston is famous for** Cadbury's milk factory at Knighton, since 1920s. **Briefest troop of volunteers in Staffordshire** Batchacre Troop totalling 40, as mentioned in the Army list in the early C19; existed for only six years and little is known about it (FSP p63). **Highest point of the Roman road from Stretton (Penkridge) to Ternhill, Shrops** Camp Farm. **'The longest surviving village show in the county' 2006** Knightley, Adbaston Haberdashers Annual Show, this vegetable/ produce show was founded in 1946 (SN Sept 21 2006 p26). **'Ellerton Brown Julia 16th', 'Ellerton Blue Jet'** Ayrshire cattle of GH Dodd & Sons of Ellerton Grange. The first, a four year-old cow-in-calf obtained the Staffordshire Advertiser & Chronicle Trophy 1960 for an exhibitor gaining the greatest number of points in the dairy cattle section of the Staffordshire County Show 1960. The latter, a bull, came 2nd in the class for Ayrshire Bulls born on or after Jan 1 1959 in the Royal Show 1960 (SA & Chron June 2 1960 p4. July 14 1960 p11p).

2. Church...

At Adbaston is St Michael and All Angels, **one of 12 such county dedications** (of AP churches); **7th oldest county church** dating from 1095.

Most interesting thing in the church A plaque commemorating William Wakeley who died Nov 28 1714 aged 125. **One of only two pre-Reformation Churchwardens' accounts to survive in Staffordshire** Adbaston covering 1478-88 (SHC 1999 pp83-96).

3. People...

Adbaston's most famous old worthy Charles Bowker Ash (1781-1864), poet, born Adbaston, son of George Ash of Adbaston Farm. He is said to have travelled widely and lived for a time at Eccleshall, and Hodnet and Hinstock in Shropshire. His 'Hermit of Hawkestone' appeared in 1816. Two volumes of poems, published in 1831, are said to have pleased Coleridge. His best remembered poem at Adbaston is 'Adbaston, or the Days of Youth' (early C19) which extols the charms of his native village. In the Preface to the poem, written by Coleridge, Coleridge compares it with 'The Deserted Village'. He provides the **choicest quote** on the village, this is from his 'Adbaston, or the Days of Youth':

'Dear, native Adbaston! - remote from care,
Thy tranquil fields would mitigate despair;
In thy sweet vales a balsam I could find,
When naught on earth could calm my troubled mind.'

Adbaston's hero Segt A Ridgway, Machine Gun Corps, of Adbaston, awarded the M.M. for conspicuous gallantry and devotion to duty whilst under artillery and machine gun fire. He not only rallied the infantry but brought his own subsection of two machine guns into action, and himself worked a captured German machine gun, with the result that a heavy German counter attack was repulsed (SA Oct 5 1918 p7 col 8). **Staffordshire's 5th oldest man ever** William Wakeley of Outlands who lived to the age of 125. **Strange but true!** In 1837 a notice in The Staffordshire Advertiser placed by the father of William Lea, the younger, of Doley, offered one Sovereign reward for information about the whereabouts of his son. William Lea, the younger, was of 'unsound mind', aged about 28, and wearing a white smock-frock, a moleskin jacket, a yellow waistcoat, and striped moleskin trousers when he went missing (SA Dec 16 1837. Dec 18 1937 p11 col 3). **Adbaston's kindest** John Smith gave £12 to be dealt to the poor in bread the second Sunday in every month, according to a benefactions board in the church, dated Aug 26 1718, but lost by the 1830s. **Adbaston's poorest** From at least 1836 Adbaston poor may have been housed at the old workhouse at 34-38 Vineyard Road (formerly Workhouse Lane), Newport, until the new workhouse was built 1855~6, in Audley Avenue (formerly Longmarsh Lane). This building became Audley House, an old people's home, and then private flats (the infirmary of 1908, still adjoins). **Adbaston's earliest recorded will** Belongs to Elizabeth Salt, and is dated March 25 1595. **First person in the parish register** Margaret, daughter of John, husbandman, and Elizabeth Gervice, buried Oct 5 1600.

4. The area...

Adbaston is the **county's 56th largest parish**, consisting of 4,638 acres; **48th= closest parish to the county town**, 8.9m W; **extremist length** 4m; **extremist width** 4.5m. **Parish's chief settlement** The scattered farming village of Adbaston. **Geology** ADBASTON - Permian (most), Keuper Marls (Adbaston village), Bunter (extreme S); BISHOP'S OF-FLEY - Bunter (N), Keuper Sandstones (SE to intrusions in the N); TUNSTALL - Keuper Marls (most), Keuper Sandstones (NW); FLASH-BROOK - Bunter (W), Keuper Marls (E). **Highest point** 433 feet at Outlands. **Lowest point** 239 feet at Whitleyford Bridge. Adbaston was **108th most-populated Staffordshire parish in 1801** with 407 people; **94th= in 1811** with 536; **96th in 1821** with 596; **96th in 1831** with 601; **97th in 1841** with 610; **98th in 1851** with 591; **99th in 1861** with 593; **102nd in 1871** with 562; **101st in 1881** with 539; **98th in 1891** with 568; **99th in 1901** with 533.

SUBJECT INDEX *0 to Ar*

Berkswich
1. Did you know that...

'Stackton Trussell' The imaginary village immortalized by Hinge and Brackett (*see above*), derives its name from Acton Trussell; Dame Hilda Brackett, alias Patrick Fyffe, used to live in the village (MR2 p10) (Stafford: A History & Celebration. Roger Butters & Nick Thomas 2005 p111). **Berkswich's top folklore** That a 'cup' or 'saucer' shaped burial mound on Spring Hill in the north part of Cannock Chase is the grave of three kings slain in a battle on this spot. **First documentation of the Muscus Multiformiter Pyxidates, Capitbus five apicibus coccine (alias chalice moss or scarlet headed cup)** Probably by Dr Plot on various parts of Cannock Chase (NHS p199 tab 14, fig 1). **Staffordshire's only 'saucer' burial mound** Perhaps The Bury on top of Spring Hill. **Oldest settlement in Staffordshire** Earthworks of possible Mesolithic period have been found at Acton Trussell (John Hunt, University of Birmingham - Staffs Archaeology Day 2006). The **names Acton, Baswich, and Walton first appear** in Domesday Book, 1086. **Parish's chief settlement** Baswich, with the parish church. **What Berkswich is famous for** Having the north, gentle, interesting end of Cannock Chase. **Staffordshire Yeomanry's first public order duty** To quell a corn riot at Radford Bridge, Stafford, Aug 6 1795 (The Uniforms of the British Yeomanry Force 1794-1914. 15: Staffordshire Yeomanry. Smith & Coogan. 1993). **First comprehensive school in Stafford borough** Walton High School, 1967 (VCH vol 6 pp260,264). **'The Milford'** The name for a style of 3-bedroomed house built by Messrs George Wimpey and Company on Weeping Cross estate, and costing £2,325 in 1958 (SA & Chron March 13 1958 p6p). **One of the first Beacon Schools in Staffordshire** Oakridge Primary School, Silvester Way, and Barnfields Primary, Lansdowne Way, Wildwood; two of the initial 75 schools in UK, expected to work in partnership with others sharing their excellence from Sept 1998 - each could received up to £50,000 (BBC Midlands Today

est public maize maze Perhaps that at Moors Covert Farm, Cock Lane, Bednall founded 2003 (Staffordshire's Farm Attractions 2006) (SN Aug 10 2006 p30). **One of the best 52 dog walking routes in Britain** That between Shugborough and Milford Common, as shortlisted for one of the UK's top 21 top dog walks, organised by Hill's Pet Nutrition (E&S Aug 8 2008 p6). **Staffordshire Best Kept Village South Staffordshire District winner (small village category) 1989** Bednall.

2. Churches...

At BASWICH is Holy Trinity, **one of 4 such county dedications** (of AP churches); **61st= oldest AP county church** dating from the C13 or roughly 1250. **In the churchyard** - The grave of Richard Burton's children; five died within 11 days of each other in March 1835. **Berkswich's longest-serving vicar** Thomas Leveson Lane who served 47 years, 1836-83. At ACTON TRUSSELL is St James (Late C13, 1562). **Berkwich's most famous old worthy** James Richard Alsop (1816-80), poet, born Bonehill, near Tamworth. He was vicar of Acton Trussell-with-Bednall 1867 until his death. Rosemary Toeman in Voices of Five Counties says "His thoughtful, kind-hearted poetry, much of it based on classical and biblical stories, was published posthumously in 1880 as 'The Prayer of Ajax and other Poems.'" Arthur Mee in his 'Staffordshire' says he was something of a character, claiming descent from a Norman family of Alsopen-le-Dale in Derbyshire, and "we have a picture of him conning over the sermons he preached.." His son, Arthur Richard, succeeded him as vicar, and his grandson Philip also wrote verse. At WALTON-ON-THE-HILL is St Thomas (1842). At BEDNALL is All Saints (1846). **Oldest grave in Bednall churchyard** Perhaps that inscribed 'M.E. 1681' (Mary & Edward Woolley) in the SE corner. The **first christening at Brocton Mission Room** took place on Sept 17 1939; the baby was the son of Mr & Mrs L Cooper of Brocton (SA Sept 23 1939 8 col 1).

3. Military Camps...

First troops at Brocton Camp The Royal Army Service Corps, who organised supplies for the subsequent WW1 troops (BERK2 p82). **Last regiment to leave Brocton Camp** New Zealand Rifle Brigade who left at end of WW1 (SPT Nov 2006). **Only German military cemetery in Great Britain** The WW1 German Military Cemetery at Broadhurst Green.

4. People...

Brocton's villain John/ David Easthope, 32, of Huntington, Cannock, who recruited Michael Walke, 24, Robert Williams, 20, to kidnap Emily Dewhurst of Old Coach Lane on Sept 12 1979 and blackmail her husband William, a director of the British Reinforced Concrete factory in Stafford, out of £36,000 for her release. Mrs Dewhurst was kept in a secret place for 24 hours. The judge described Easthope as 'an evil man', whilst neighbours described him a Jekyll and Hyde character (E&S March 3 1980. March 4 1980). **1st= hung using the 'New Drop' on the Lodge of the New Gaol at Stafford** John Hackett, 22, a cordwainer, who burgled the house of George Caithness of Brocton, executed 17 Aug 1793; the previous place of execution was Sandyford Meadows, Foregate. **'oldest businessman of the town (Stafford)'** 1898, last surviving burgess who signed the oath of allegiance to Queen Victoria, one of the founders of the 'First' Staffordshire Knot Lodge James Marson (1810-98), born Acton Mill, where his father had been a miller. Ran a chemist shop in Greengate Street, Stafford. Elected capital burgess of Stafford in 1834. The Staffordshire Knot Lodge formed July 2 1836. His funeral took place at Acton Trussell (SA April 2 1898 p4 col 7). **1st Little Miss Stafford** Eileen Jones, aged 7, daughter of Mr & Mrs E James of Low Farm, Bednall, awarded at the 1935 Stafford Pageant, and open to girls between the ages of 6 and 10 (Stafford Pageant: The Exciting Innovative Years 1901-1952. Gordon Henry Loach. 2007). **'Miss Milford'** Affectionate reference to character Miss Jane Alderson, born Milford 1879, confectionary and tobacco seller from her cottage in Milford in 1958. The cottage, on the corner of Milford Common, was one of the oldest in Milford (SN Oct 25 1958 p14). **Miss Staffordshire 1940** Miss Connie Birks of Walton-on-the-Hill, Miss English Electric 1940 (Stafford Pageant: The Exciting Innovative Years 1901-1952. Gordon Henry Loach. 2007). **33rd President of Royal Photographic Society** Bertram Sinkinson, 1953-54, of Caprilla, 58 Cannock Road, Baswich, Stafford Borough councillor for Baswich ward 1953-54. In 1948, when residing at Thorneyfields Lane, Castle Bank, Castle Church, he was made President of British Photographers (SA May 29 1948 p5 col 5 p) (SLM May 1953 p8p). **Most outstanding contribution to the preservation of canals 1967** David Tomlinson, 31, of The Crescent, Walton, awarded by Inland Waterways Association (SA & Chronicle April 18 1968 p1). **Amongst first in the country to gain the Reading Development diploma** Michael Winkle, PE teacher of Leasowes Junior School, Weeping Cross, one of the 250 cohort, first to pass in 1980. The diploma came about from a Government Report in 1975, calling for more courses to help teachers improve their methods (SN March 7 1980 p20). **'Staffordshire's garden guru'** Mitch Westwood, 53, Brocton-based garden designer, an expert on BBC Watchdog, Rogue Traders; made an RHS judge in 2007. He was born and bred at Lichfield (SLM June 2007 p11pc).

Baswich's heroine Alison Kelly received a silver medal at the Association of Chief Police Officers' (Acpo) annual provincial awards ceremony for bravery when four armed robbers raided the Co-op store in Baswich where she worked in May 2007. She and colleagues were pistol whipped during the raid. Forced to open a safe Mrs Kelly stalled and set off the panic alarm. Assaulted, she bravely tried to remove the perpetuator's mask so she could identify him. The offender then struck her over the head with the gun causing a serious head wound. Despite this Mrs Kelly chased the men (SN June 26 2008 p28). **Bednall's hero** Capt Philip Alsop of Bednall was awarded the M.C. for 'conspicuous gallantry, and devotion to duty' on the Western Front in 1918 (SA Aug 10 1918 p7 col 4). **Bednall's heroine** Emily Brookes, 59, of Vicarage Lane, Bednall, who coolly gave breakfast to escaped prisoner, Alex Clarke, 29, serving a three year sentence at Featherstone Prison for robbery and burglary, when he presented himself at her door armed with an axe on July 11 1980. He had not returned to the prison after home leave, and was shortly caught in woods opposite Mrs Brookes' home. She said later "I got up and opened the door and as I opened it he jumped up. He had an axe in one hand... he put his other hand out and said to me "Don't be afraid, I am not going to hurt you, I just want something to eat"." (SN July 18 1980 p5p). **Brocton's hero** PC Cliffard Alan Madelin, of 63 Old Croft Road, Brocton, awarded the BEM when he used the patrol car he was driving at Hanford to ram the vehicle containing escaped prisoners, Ronald Hancock, 22, and Malcolm Campbell, 21, from Wakefield Jail, on Nov 21 1954 (incidentally Madelin's 33rd birthday) so facilitating their capture (SA & Chron Feb 24 1955 p1p). **Berkwich's saddest** A poor travelling woman discovered in a barn at Weeping Cross on the Monday morning before Aug 27 1796. She seemed dead - strangled - with 'her child, which she had carefully wrapped in straw,' sleeping by her side. But the woman was revived with medical aid. She later told, 'that a halfpenny being all the money she possessed, and not having any means of procuring more, she had determined upon putting an end to her existence'. She subsequently had care of sorts, for she was committed to prison for perjury (SA Aug 27 1796 p4 col 4). **Baswich's kindest** Esther Harding of Weeping Cross, by will of 1830, left £50, the interest to be used to purchase warm clothing for the poor of the parish (VCH vol 5 p11). **Bednall's kindest** A Miss Stokes was supplying free coal to families in Bednall village at the New Year in the 1880s; in 1890 40 families received from her a ton of coal each (SA Jan 11 1890 p5 col 1). **Brocton's kindest** Dorothy Bridgeman (d1697), by will dated 1694, made provision to raise money to educate poor children and for dole for the poor in Brocton township. She was the former wife of George Cradock (d1643) of Caverswall Castle and Brocton Hall, Brocton (VCH vol 5 pp10,11). **Walton's kindest** Thomas and Roger Twist of Walton, by their wills of 1683 and 1726 respectively, made provision for clothing and bread dole for the poor of Walton liberty (VCH vol 5 p11). **Berkswich's poorest** In 1797 the parish agreed to sell Deepmoor common to pay for the building of a house of industry. In 1800 it was resolved to open a house for the poor. In 1802 bricks, whitewash and thatch were needed for the workhouse. In 1803 £5,19,7 was paid for 'Repairing and thatching the old Poor House'. In 1806 there were more repairs at the old workhouse. In 1810 there was a new floor at the (new) workhouse. In 1837 an annual meeting of ratepayers was held at the workhouse at Forebridge (SRO D114/A/PC/3. D946/15. D946/17). From 1837 the poor could be housed at Stafford Union workhouse at Marston. The poor Acton Trussell and Bednall township unable to sustain themselves were accommodated at Penkridge Union workhouse 1836-72, thereafter at Cannock Union workhouse. **Staffordshire's 2nd wills proved in a civil District Probate Registry** Belong to Jeremiah Hudson of Brocton, born c1784, a labourer, and a man from Stafford, both proved on Jan 19 1858. Wills before Jan 12 1858 were proved in an ecclesiastical court. **First person in the parish register (Bednall)** Mary Wooley, wife of Edward Wooley, was buried Aug 17 1681. **(Berkswich with Walton)** John, son of Richard and Anne Harrison, baptised March 26 1601. **Earliest recorded**

wills, for **Acton Trussell** Thurston Glover, dated May 22 1588; for **Baswich** Anne Handley, May 18 1648; for **Bednall** Richard Clarke, 1650; for **Berkswich** Richard Twigg, April 20 1666. **Choicest quote** Richard 'Dick' Byrd Levett of King's Royal Rifle Corps in a letter of 16th November 1917 to his parents of Milford Hall in case of his death (he was killed in action 10th March 1917 aged 19 on Loupart Wood on the Bapaume Ridge), wrote 'Tonight is probably the last night I shall be at Milford before going to the front and I am writing this in case I don't come back.'

5. Sport...

The Acton Trussell strongman Nicholas Cooper, who had extraordinary strength in the C17. He could lift a sack of wheat of four strike with his teeth, which amounted to 50 lbs to the strike, and amounts of 200 lbs in weight. He once lifted three men, one under each arm and the the third in his teeth (NHS p293). **Staffordshire's first motorcycle hill-climb competition** Perhaps that held at Satnall Hill, Milford, on Wednesday evening June 5 1907. This was Mid-Staffordshire Automobile Club's first motorcycle (handicap) hill-climb competition. Eight cycles competed and the winner of the first club prize was Arthur Scott on a three-horse-power Raleigh. The following year on May 13 1908 the event took place at Sandon Bank, Salt (SA June 8 1907 p4 col 5. May 16 1908 p4 col 6. May 23 1908 p4). **'one of the finest short holes to be found on any English inland course'** The 9th hole of Brocton Golf Course, 180 yards long; its green has the lake running along on the left and a deep ditch surrounding the other sides. Within the oval space enclosed by the lake and ditch, a bunker on the right eats into the surface of the green, still leaving an ample target for the right shot (SCP July-Aug 1949 p25). **Eleys Charity Cup winner 1921, I.W. Bailey Cup winner 1923, British Crown Green Coronation Cup winner 1935, President of the British Crown Green Bowling Association 1956-57** Mr E James (b1886) of 'Rocklands', Weeping Cross, originally of Wolverhampton (SA & Chron Feb 9 1956 p1p. April 2 1959 p14p. Oct 28 1959 p14p). **Midland Counties Junior Mile champion 1951, National Junior Mile finalist 1951, Staffordshire Senior Mile champion 1954** Matt Whittaker (b1933) of Witney Road, Baswich, PE teacher at Hagley Park CSM School, Rugeley, second eldest of the Whittaker brothers, athletes (see Castle Church) (SA & Chron April 21 1960 p12p). **Moonraker Rally (National Rally Championship 7th Round) winner 1980** Mike Hutchinson of Wildwood, motor racer, in his first season in the national circuit (SN May 16 1980 p72). **National AAA's Youth under-17s high jump champion 1980** Michael Powell, aged 15, of Brocton, member of Wolverhampton and Bilston AC (SN Aug 8 1980 p53p). **Top English scorer at Mind Games 2008** Lawrence Cooper, aged 38, of Sandringham Close, Baswich, playing many opponents ranked higher than him, including several Grandmasters; the English team finished with four wins (E&S Oct 27 2008 p5).

6. The area...

Berkswich is the **county's 35th largest parish**, consisting of 6,971 acres; **6th closest parish to the county town**, 1.3m SE; **extremist length** 5.2m, making it **30th longest parish in the county**; **extremist width**

3.7m. **Geology** ACTON TRUSSEL - Alluvium (Penk plain), Keuper Red Marls (centre), Keuper Sandstones (extreme E); BASWICH - Keuper Red Marls surrounded by Keuper Sandstones (Newtown), Bunter (Brocton, Chase highlands); BEDNALL - Bunter (Bednall village, E), Keuper Red Marls (W fringe). **Best veteran woodland in Staffordshire** Brocton Coppice, west of Brocton, on Cannock Chase, according to Jonathon Webb, Staffordshire's first Biodiversity Officer (Staffs Wildlife No. 77 Sept 1999 p7). **Highest point** Warren Hill at 729 feet. **Lowest point** 239 feet by the Sow at Milford. Berkswich was **52nd most-populated Staffordshire parish in 1801** with 1,096 people; **58th in 1811** with 1,111; **55th in 1821** with 1,376; **58th in 1831** with 1,329; **60th in 1841** with 1,438; **55th in 1851** with 1,623; **61st in 1861** with 1,555; **68th in 1871** with 1,335; **67th in 1881** with 1,378; **68th in 1891** with 1,327; **63rd in 1901** with 1,457.

SUBJECT INDEX *Ar to Ba*

A cottage in the village, and the little girl born with two teeth (see People).

Blymhill

1. Did you know that...

Blymhill's top folklore That Wrestlers Inn nearly a mile north east of Blymhill was famous for gaming, cock fighting and wrestling which took place here, apparently, on account of its closeness to Shrops which could be easily entered to evade the Staffs authorities. The inn has since become Wrestlers Farm House. The **name Blymhill first appears** in Domesday Book, 1086. **What Blymhill is famous for** Motty Meadows, the most northerly habitat in British Isles for the Snake's head-fritillary. **First brick house in the W of Staffordshire** Perhaps Laurels Farm, dated 1678 (SL p100). **The parish that wanted to leave Staffordshire** Blymhill, along with Weston-under-Lizard, petitioned in 1926 to be incorporated in Shifnal RD and thus in Shropshire, as recommended in the Boundaries Commission report of 1888 (SA May 15 1926 p7). **First Staffordshire parish published by the VCH** Blymhill (on account of it being alphabetically first) appeared first in the first topographical volume of the Staffordshire Victoria County History (volume 4), covering Cuttlestone West hundred. Published by Oxford University Press on Thursday Sept 18 1958, at Cloth £4 4s, or half-leather £6 6s. Work on the Staffordshire VCH was resumed in 1950 (SA Nov 26 1954 p2 col 3. SA & Chron Sept 18 1958 p6 cols 3-4).

2. Church...

At Blymhill is St Mary, **one of 23 such county dedications** (most common dedication in the county); **Staffordshire's 88th= oldest ancient parish church** dating from the C14 or roughly 1350. **Most notable things** The parish chest (covered with some good old ironwork) (LGS p87); the north aisle window to the memory of Lady Lucy Caroline Bridgeman d1858 aged 32, and her sister Lady Charlotte Anne Bridgeman d1858 aged 31, both died by fire in the library of Weston Hall, Weston-under-Lizard. It was put up by their friends in the county and neigh bourhood (SHC 1899 p288). **In the churchyard** The founder's tomb in an arched recess containing a coffin lid and thought to be that of the first rector, lies by the south wall of the chancel. The churchyard was **Lichfield Diocese Best Kept Churchyard winner 2004, 2006**; won silver in 2005. **Blymhill's most famous old worthy** Rev Samuel Dickenson (1753-1823), botanist. His obituary in the Gentleman's Magazine 1823 reads "At the Rectory of Blymhill, co. Stafford, aged 90, the Rev Samuel Dickenson, Rector of that place, and a learned and ingenious naturalist. He was presented to the above Rectory in 1777, by J Heaton, J Fowler, Esqrs. To the Rev. Stebbing Shaw's valuable History of Staffordshire he was of great assistance, by kindly exerting his classical abilities, and throwing much light upon the various vestiges of the Romans in that county; and by communicating a catalogue of plants found in the county, rendered essential service in the botanical and agricultural departments. His son, who is a zoologist, communicated to the same work the article on Zoology." **Choicest quote** The author of the Random Notes column in The Staffordshire Advertiser wrote in 1934 'The Rev. Samuel Dickenson, who was rector of the parish for 46 years, was a son of the Rev. John Dickenson, who held the living for thirteen years. Samuel, the elder, compiled a list of indigenous plants of Staffordshire which found a place in Shaw's "History of Staffordshire," and John Horace wrote on the zoology of Staffordshire for the benefit of the same county historian. Samuel Dickenson died in 1823 at the age of 90, John Horace Dickenson died in 1854 at the age of 78, and there was another clerical Dickenson who died at Blymhill in 1805, at the age of 97. These facts appear to be sound proof that Blymhill is a fine health resort, and an ideal place in which to flourish in physical and intellectual strength. The longevity record of the rectory in recent years is another corroboration of the conclusion' (SA Sept 15 1934 p7 col 2). **Blymhill's longest-serving vicars** Preb ERO Bridgeman, serving 50 years, rector 1883-1933, to whose memory a processional cross was given by subscription (SA Oct 14 1933 p11 col 1), is just eclipsed by the incumbency of Ralph Masfen, who served 51 years, 1555-1606.

3. People...

She was born with two teeth Sarah Wood of Brineton, Blymhill, born 1670 with two teeth, considered then a bad omen in life (NHS p271). The parish register actually mentions her two teeth, saying "1670 Oct 6 (baptised) Sarah daughter of John and Priscilla Wood, she had two teeth when born, and when baptised one!" Her father was buried in 1726, and perhaps as a testament to the prophesy she was unlucky and unable to find a husband, for a Sarah Wood is buried on June 4 1742: There are very few Woods at the time in the register. **Blymhill's villains** In 1798 John Norris of Blymhill, a substitute in the Old Militia for Moses Smith, was unable to serve as he was to be transported for theft, causing the parish to pay £10.0.0 to provide another substitute (SRO 1044/4/2). **He believed he owned all Blymhill** In 1830 John Cowley was advised by one Joseph Holman, a dealer in shoes at Dudley, he was heir to the whole parish, because his ancestors had been awarded it by Charles II for help given him by them after his escape from the battle of Worcester, 1651. This was taken to be a principal manorial estate of Blymhill, consisting of High Hall and Bent Farms, which then belonged to the Stubbs family. Instead, of proving his right through the courts, Cowley tried to extract ownership by intimidating George Bradnock Stubbs at his home at Walsall. Failing this he gathered a mob to try and gain possession of High Hall Farm. It was turned away by the tenant who had assembled an equal force. Mrs Tolfree, tenant of Bent Farm, was then intimidated. On Sept 2 Holman gained possession, keeping her practically hostage until the sheriff's men came on Sept 10. The men fled, some were captured; Holman escaped. Cowley and the others received gaol sentences of up to three months and were bound over to keep the peace (SA Oct 30 1830 p3 col 5). **Blymhill's kindest** Rev John Taylor of Dudley, but a native of Blymhill, by his will dated 1671, made fiance available for the repair of the schoolhouse, and to teach two poor children to read. William Adams, by his will dated 1718, made provision for the purchase of cloth for coats for poor children of the parish; his charity formed part of the Blymhill Clothing Club in the C20 (VCH vol 4 pp72,73). **Blymhill's poorest** Parish accounts in 1756 record £2.4.0 was paid to the 'ye workhouse'; and there are references to a workhouse in 1757. The parish house mentioned in 1775 may be the 'House for ye Poor' mentioned in 1777 (SRO D1044/4/1). In 1791 a public meeting was held at Church Eaton workhouse at which it was agreed to take the poor of Blymhill (SRO D3377/48). Parish officials took the Brews family to Shifnal parish workhouse, Shropshire, in April 1795 (SRO D1044/4/1). From 1836 the poor were housed at Shifnal Union workhouse, Park St, Shifnall, built 1817. **Blymhill's most needy** Brotherton women in Blymhill and Brineton liberties were often in need of parish relief in the earlier C19. Brotherton's wife was taken to Gnosall workhouse in 1813, Rachel Bootherton to Wheaton Aston workhouse in 1814, Elizabeth Brotherton of Blymhill to Wolverhampton workhouse in 1825, and Brewood poorhouse in 1830; whilst money was needed for the burial of Mary Brotherton of Brinton in 1834. Brothertons often appear having relief in the 1820s and early 1830s in both liberties (SRO D1044/4/2, 3). **First person in the parish register** Alice Cott'n baptised April 5 1561. **Blymhill's earliest recorded will** Belongs to Thomas Turner, and is dated May 10 1533.

4. The area...

Blymhill is the **county's 88th smallest parish**, consisting of 3,024 acres; **40th= closest parish to the county town**, 7.8m SW; **extremist length** 2.9m; **extremist width** 3.8m. **Parish's chief settlement** Blymhill, a small rural village; Brineton to the N is of the same size. **Geology** BLYMHILL village (E side) and E half - Keuper Red Marls; BLYMHILL (W side) and Brinton villages - Keuper Sandstones; BLYMHILL Common - Bunter. **Highest point** 454 feet on the boundary at Ivetsey Bank. **Lowest point** 291 feet on the boundary by Dawford Brook. Blymhill was **98th most-populated Staffordshire parish in 1801** with 475 people; **98th in 1811** with 513; **94th in 1821** with 604; **99th in 1831** with

566; **96th in 1841** with 633; **96th in 1851** with 622; **100th in 1861** with 591; **97th in 1871** with 608; **104th in 1881** with 503; **101st in 1891** with 532; **100th in 1901** with 522.

SUBJECT INDEX *Ba to Be*

It was tradtiion in Bradley parish for a maid to bow when she passes the Webb Stone.

Bradley
1. Did you know that...

Bradley's top folklore That three glacial boulders in a rough line in and near Bradley village were stolen by the Devil from the church to build up hell, but as he ran with them they became heavier and he tripped and fell, and they rolled away down to their present position. It is believed if spinsters and or maidens don't bow to the largest stone, the Webb Stone, by the side of the road leading to Mitton, as they pass it, they will never marry. And that on the night of Oct 31 and in the early morning of November 1 maidens might know the name of their future husbands if they bring little gifts of cakes to the stone. Apparently, this stone turns completely round at one minute to midnight. **What Bradley is famous for** Berry Ring, an Iron Age fort of 7 acres. The **name Bradley first appears** in Domesday Book, 1086. **First 'caput' of the de Stafford family** May have been at Littywood (SL p88) (SSAHST 1982-3 p36). **'The village which never grew up'** Bradley, according to the Stafford Newsletter columnist, Terence Kirtland, in his 'Around Our Villages' series in 1958 (SN Nov 1 1958 p14). **Record calving for a British Friesian** 14 calves by Marshgreen Ruth 2nd 169900 RML, by June 1948, owned by Mr WH Bowers of The Grove Farm, Bradley. The cow was bred by Mr H Brown of Woodseaves to autumn 1947 (SA June 5 1948 p2p). **Stafford and District Car Club's first 'autocross'** Held on a 910-yard grass track circuit at Littywood Farm on Sunday June 11 1961, organised in conjunction with the English Electric (Stafford) Club, and Wolverhampton and South Staffs Car Club (SA & Chron June 15 1961 p16 col 2). **What Bradley did for the Millennium** Bradley W.I. made about 12 embroidered images representing community activities that may be held in a village hall. They hang on a wall in Bradley Village Hall. **Staffordshire Best Kept Village winner (small village category) 1965, 1974, 1977, 1982, 1983, 1984** Bradley.

2. Church...

At Bradley is All Saints, **one of 19 such county dedications** (of AP churches); **23rd= oldest county church** dating from the C12 or roughly

1150. **In the church** A C13 coffin lid in the tower, that was found among the foundations of the south porch (VCH vol 4 p 89), and the monument to Thomas Browne (d1633) consisting of two kneeling figures facing one another, with detached columns left and right (BOE p76). **In the churchyard** Against W chancel wall N side - The six children (2 girls, 4 boys) of Rev Thomas & Elizabeth Browne, who all died 1807-1844 between the ages of 3 to 27, before their parents. About 40 yards S of E end of the church - Ann Trickett d Nov. 26 1885 aged 73 erected as a token of affection by M ... M Gibbs of New York City. **Bradley's longest serving vicar** Rev Walter Collins who served 55 years, 1727-82. **He likened parish councils to 'the Cinderellas of local government'** Rev Harry Hadley Fox, vicar of Bradley 1927-68 (the last vicar, subsequent incumbents being priests in charge), in his capacity as chairman of Bradley PC in 1965, at a meeting of Staffordshire Parish Councils' Association, rapping Stafford RDC for not informing parish councils concerned about planning applications received by the RDC (SA & Chron Jan 28 1965 p7).

Sir Thomas Browne.

3. People...

Bradley's most famous old worthy Sir Thomas Browne (1562-1633), London merchant; Proctor of the Canterbury Court of Arches and a governor of Charterhouse School. In later life he came to live at Shredicote, possibly deserting the capital because of religious and political troubles. In 1619 the vicar of Bradley procured for him a license to eat flesh on Fish Days to combat infirmity in his joints and knees. He died on the fifth day of April "mourned by all: his wife, his children and the people of the parish." His alabaster wall tomb in Bradley church consists of painted kneeling figures of a bearded man in a long cloak, and a woman in a tight-waisted dress, with a ruff and flowing head dress (*see above*). **'one of the pioneer breeders of Shropshire Sheep'** Charles Byrd (d1896) of Littywood, a well-known agriculturist (SA Nov 21 1896 p4 col 7). **A founding member of the Staffordshire branch of the National Farmers' Union** John C Holme (1871-1952), born Earl Sterndale, Derbys, as a boy he came with his father to farm at Hill and Burley Fields, Stafford. From 1923 he farmed at Billington, having bought the farm in 1919; member of the Staffordshire Agricultural Society, for whom he acted as judge and grader (SA May 23 1952 p4p). The Staffordshire branch of the NFU was formed 1919 (SA Sept 24 1954 p1 col 4). **Fancy that!** The death of Air-Marshall William Arthur D Brook, CB, CBE, aged 52, Air-Officer Commanding No. 3 Group, Bomber Command, Mildenhall, Suffolk, in a horrendous air crash at Littywood Farm on Aug 19 1953. Brook was carrying out manoeuvres over the parish (which were not part of the exercise for which he had been briefed), when the Meteor jet-fighter he was piloting crashed into a Dutch barn, killing himself. A verdict of misadventure was declared. He was to become Air Vice-Marshall in two weeks time (SA Aug 21 1953 p4p). **Stafford's first 'musician in residence'** Jonathan Price (b1957), cellist, of Bradley, brought up in Audley, for 2 years from July 2008-10. The residency is in partnership with the Manchester Camerata and Arts Council England (SN Sept 4 2008 p4pc). **Bradley's kindest** Humphrey de Hastang, former rector of Bradley, Archdeacon of Coventry, became inadvertently the kindest, when his 1344 endowment of a priest to sing daily mass in a lady chapel at Bradley got converted at the Reformation into the Bradley Trust fund, which has since provided charity in various ways to the village. In addition, Mrs Ann and Mrs Appoline Brown (both d1691), of Shredicote, and a number of others have given to the poor (VCH vol 4 p 90) (A Chronicle of Bradeley. William & Anne Wilkinson. 1999. p9). **Bradley's poorest** The 'Old House' mentioned 1809 in parish accounts, may have been a poorhouse. It was re-thatched in 1813, 1814. In 1810, 1812-19 Bradley was using Church Eaton workhouse. There may have been a workhouse in Bradley. In 1814 and 1816 the overseers of the poor paid for sheeting and chaff "Bed' at the workhouse; in 1822 they incurred £2,15,6 to repair the workhouse; in 1828 they incurred £1,7,6 for alterations to it. In 1818 James Leese ran away from it but was apprehended (SRO 9/A/PO/3-5). From 1837 the poor were housed at Stafford Union workhouse at Marston. **First person in the parish register** Dr Roger Dingley, parson, buried Aug 10 1538. **Bradley's earliest recorded will** Belongs to Roger Jenyns, and is dated Oct 20 1538 (but this could relate to another Bradley in Lichfield diocese). **Choicest quote** John Hadfield in The Shell Book of English Villages, 1980, a book which does not contain too many Staffordshire entries, wrote 'It can be taken to represent many mid-Staffordshire villages not overwhelmed by recent growth. The church stands on a slight ridge, with views W over the valley of the Church Eaton Brook and the course chosen for the Shropshire Union Canal....The country round has a thin scattering of brick farmhouses and cottages,'

4. The area...

Bradley is the **county's 47th largest parish**, consisting of 5,594 acres; **9th closest parish to the county town**, 2.2m SW; **extremist length** 5.6m, making it **22nd= longest parish in the county**; **extremist width** 4.2m. **Parish's chief settlement** Bradley, a small compact rural village. **Geology** Entirely Keuper Red Marls. **Highest point** Butter Hill at 503 feet. **Lowest point** 273 feet at the boundary by Church Eaton Brook. Bradley was **83rd most-populated Staffordshire parish in 1801** with 593 people; **82nd in 1811** with 627; **85th in 1821** with 723; **88th in 1831** with 731; **95th in 1841** with 649; **95th in 1851** with 628; **98th in 1861** with 597; **96th in 1871** with 614; **107th in 1881** with 496; **105th in 1891** with 474; **113rd in 1901** with 399. ly

SUBJECT INDEX *Be to Bi*

The legend of how Sir John Giffard shot dead a panter in the 16th Century.

Brewood
1. Did you know that...

Brewood's top folklore It is said a wooden cross, by the lodge to Chillington Hall at the junction of Upper Avenue and Port Lane, is the spot where Sir John Giffard shot dead a panther, which had escaped from their menagerie and ran wild in nearby Brewood Forest. Sir John with his young son, Thomas, went in search of it. The two discovered it just in time to save a woman with a baby in her arms onto whom it was about to pounce. As Sir John shot the beast dead with his bow and arrow his son reputedly cried 'Prenez haleine, tirez fort' (take breath, pull hard). The event became Giffard family legend and Giffard's Cross was set up to commemorate the site where the event took place. **What Brewood is famous for** Chillington Hall, seat of the old county family of Giffard. The **name Brewood first appears** in Domesday Book, 1086. **First brick house in west of Staffordshire** Perhaps that of 1679 in Coven village (SL p100). **'a gem of a village'** Brewood, as claimed by 'Geraldine', columnist for the 'Female' page in Staffordshire Advertiser and Chronicle June 15 1961 p10. **'the meeting is, to use an expressive term, the most "aristocratic" as well as the most friendly little affair in the neighbourhood'** A correspondent of Staffordshire Advertiser 1839 on Brewood races, held in later September (probably associated with the Sept 19 fair) (SA Sept 16 1939 p10 col 5). **When Brewood became 'Brewood, Stafford' instead of 'Brewood, near Wolverhampton' for postal reasons** 1853 when Brewood was added to the Stafford district, according to an note in the Staffordshire Advertiser July 9 1853 p4 col 3 which stated that letters should be directed in such a way, or else suffer a 24 hour delay in delivery. Coven in the same parish, appears to have remained 'Coven, near Wolverhampton'. **'The Best One Day Show in England'** Advertising slogan for the Brewood Show in The Staffordshire Advertiser 1949; it was genuinely thought to be 'one of the best one-day shows in England'. The show began as the Brewood and District Agricultural Show in 1899, was revived after WW2 (SA June 18 1949 p8. July 30 1949 p8 col 8. Aug 8 1952 p6. Aug 6 1954 p6) (SA & Chron Aug 9 1956 p9. Aug 2 1957 pp1,4) (BDH2 pp302,304,305, in error saying the last show was on Aug 6 1953). **TH Green's best**

grammar school in Staffordshire 1864-8 Brewood with a good range of subjects, well staffed, regular candidates sitting exams, growing pupil numbers (LHSB No. 14). **One of Staffordshire's first 'Quality' parish Councils** Brewood and Coven Parish Council as awarded by Staffordshire's County Accreditation Panel. The scheme was launched in March 2003; there are two other Staffordshire parish councils awarded this Status, as well as one town council; there are only a hundred other councils with Quality Status in the country (info Mary Booth). **'The noted ham 'n' eggery'** As self-styled by The Bell Inn on A5 near Horsebrook, by c2006. **'one of the largest and most contemporary collections of art in the UK'** Art collection of Manchester businessman Frank Cohen (b1943), at Initial Access Gallery, 10,000 feet exhibition space converted from two industrial sheds at Units 19 and 20, Calibre Industrial Park, Laches Close, Four Ashes. The Gallery opened in Jan 2007 to exhibit three shows a year from his collection - one of the largest and most contemporary collections of art in the UK. Frank Cohen has been dubbed the 'Charles Saatchi of the North', 'Medici of the North', 'one of the most famous art collectors in the world' (Wikipedia, 2008, and other websites). **Bridge that tore off the top of a double decker bus** That carrying the railway over Station Drive-Road, Four Ashes, April 17 2008, when a learner driver with National Express West Midlands tried to pass under it (The Daily Telegraph April 18 2008 p11ps). **Staffordshire Best Kept Village County Village of the Year 1999, 2000, 2004; winner (large village category) 1981, 1996, 1999, 2000, 2004; South Staffordshire District winner (large village category) 1995, 1996, 1997, 1998, 1999, 2000, 2001, 2003, 2004** Brewood; **South Staffordshire District winner (large village category) 2005, 2006, 2007, 2008** Coven.

2. Churches...

At Brewood is St Mary & St Chad, the **only such duel dedication in the county** (for AP churches); **61st= oldest AP county church** dating from the C13 or roughly 1250. **Best things** The Giffard chest tombs. **First lit by gas** For the evening service on Oct 9 1864, and the independent chapel was lit by gas at the same time (SA Oct 15 1864 p4 col 6). **Altar frontals embroidered by an 80-year-old** Those made for Brewood church by Mary E Wakefield (b1879) in 1959 (SA & Chron June 15 1961 p10 col 6). **The church (exterior)** Note the arrow-sharpening marks. **In the churchyard** Colonel William Carlos/ Carless d1689; he sheltered with Charles II in the Royal Oak. William Parke bookseller from Wolverhampton, a friend of Dickens, Harrison Ainsworth & other eminent writers (BDH p144). Gravestone near the S door of John Taylor, sculptor who fell from scaffolding aged 31. He had worked on the Albert Memorial, Lichfield Cathedral, Wolverhampton Art Gallery, and his own gravestone, which he carved as a youth in the form of the Cross covered by flowers. He was born at Uplands in Tinkers Lane (BDH p144, 2nd ed p155). **The best epitaphs** are - John Ellidge

> "Near to this place I do lie
> It was the Stone caused me to die"
> James Taylor, aged 3 years

"Near to this Stone, beneath this earth
Here lies the mildest babe that ever drew breath."
Hon John Byng, 5th Viscount Torrington. 1793 (The Torrington Diaries 1781-94, vol 3 p142).

'This world is full of crooked streets;
Death is the market-place, where all must meet;
If life was merchandise which men could buy,
The rich alone would live, the poor must die'
(SA Dec 31 1932 p4 col 3). **Brewood's longest-serving vicar** Alexander Bunn Haden who served 33 years, 1830-63. At Bishops Wood is St John the Evangelist (1851). At Coven is St Paul (1857).

3. Chillington Hall and the Giffards...

Masefield's least favourite secular houses Brewood's Chillington Hall 'a blatant building of brick' and its Speedwell Castle 'a hideous building' (LGS p91); Hon John Byng, 5th Viscount Torrington, was similiarly scathing about Chillington Hall, 1793 (The Torrington Diaries 1781-94, vol 3 p142). **Hon John Byng's (5th Viscount Torrington) first seen or heard of wayside cross in UK** Giffard's Cross at Chillington, 1793 (The Torrington Diaries 1781-94, vol 3 p144). **'one of the show places of the county'** Chillington Hall, according to G Rickward & W. Gaskell in Staffordshire Leaders: Social and Political, 1907, p129. **'One of the finest pieces of water, within an inclosure, that this Kingdom produces'** How James Paine described The Pool or Lake at Chillington Hall (SHOS vol 1 part 1 p90) (CL Feb 13 1948 p329p) (Chillington Hall Guide). **Longest continuous residency by the same family in one Staffordshire house** The Giffards at Chillington Hall from 1160 to between 1884-8 when Mr WTC Giffard moved to Pendryl Hall, Codsall, and Mr RH Briscoe of Somerford Hall moved to Chillington Hall (SA March 27 1937 p4 col 8). **The pride of the Chillington stables** Euphrates (SA Jan 26 1861 p4 col 4). **Chillington's saddest** John Jenkins, aged about 43, boatman to TW Giffard, a native of Torpoint, Cornwall, and two of his sons, George, 13, and Robert, 9, who lost their lives in a boating accident on Chillington Pool on May 11 1856; Jenkins left a widow with eight children, with no means of supporting them (SA May 17 1856 p2 col 6).

The GIFFARD who: **accompanied Strongbow in his Irish campaign of 1172** Peter Giffard I (fl1170-1203), granted Chillington in 1178; Strongbow was the popular name for Richard fitz Gilbert, Earl of Clare. For his efforts Giffard was rewarded with estates including Tachmelin (SHC 1902 p195) (BDH2 p138): **served in the war in Wales** Peter Giffard III (fl1241-63) (SHC 1902 p87): was **loyal to Simon de Montfort's rebellion 1264-65** William Giffard (fl1263-72), successor of Peter III, for which he was temporarily dispossessed of Chillington (SHC 1902 p88): **the lawyer** John Giffard I (fl1272-1307), who became embroiled in various legal battles against claimants for parts of the Giffard estates (SHC 1902 p89) (BDH2 p138); **remained loyal to Edward II** Sir John Giffard II (fl1310-43), refusing to take up arms with the Dispensers and other barons against the King. He fought for the King in Scotland, and was one of the Commissioners of Array for Staffordshire (SHC 1902 p96) (BDH2 p138): **served in the war in France** Sir Edmund Giffard (fl1355-77), in the retinue of Ralph, Earl of Stafford: was **first of his family to be sheriff of Staffordshire** Thomas Giffard (d c1420) in 1409-10 (SHC 1902 p107) (BDH2 p139) or 1411 (Staffs Schools Resource Book 1992). He accompanied Henry V during the invasion of France, but was apparently forced by illness to return to England (BDH2 p139): was **over 70 before he succeeded to Chillington, five times sheriff of Staffordshire (1509, 1518, 1526, 1531, 1542), Ranger of the Seven Hays of the Forest of Cank, kept a menagerie from which a panther is said to have escaped** Sir John Giffard III (c1466-1556), unable to succeed his father, Robert Giffard (d1486), until the death of his mother Cassandra (d1537); present on the Field of the Cloth of Gold; he has a chest tomb memorial in Brewood church (SHC 1902 pp111,115): was **the first of the family to be recusants, Elizabeth I visited him 1575** John Giffard IV, fl1560-1613. He suffered various periods of imprisonment before the threat of a Spanish invasion at the time of the Armada united the country, and he took the oath of allegiance, although even then his states were not returned to him. He has an altar tomb in Brewood church: was the **Jesuit priest and double agent** Gilbert Giffard (d1590/1), a younger son of John Giffard IV; he betrayed his Jesuit friends and Mary, Queen of Scots. After involvement in the Babington conspiracy, he fled to France and died miserably in a French prison (BDH2 p139): **garrisoned Chillington Hall for the royalists** Peter Giffard (d1663), grandson of John the recusant. He rode with his sons to join Charles I's army at Nottingham. Chillington Hall was soon captured, changed hands several times, and he spent most of the Civil War a prisoner at Stafford and Eccleshall (BHD2 pp139-140): **helped Charles II escape after the battle of Worcester 1651** Charles Giffard (d c1691), youngest son of Peter (d1663), conducting the King first to Whiteladies and then Boscobel (BDH2 p140): **administered pensions to those who had helped Charles II after the battle of Worcester** John Giffard (d1696), Peter's grandson, appointed one the of the three Trustees in the Letters Patent dated 1675 recording the pensions (BDH2 p140); he was the last survivor of the original trustees (SHC 1902 p191): was the **last Giffard of Chillington before the estate passed to another branch of the Giffards** Thomas Giffard (d1718), great-grandson of Peter (BDH2 p140): was **first Giffard of Blackladies to hold Chillington** Peter Giffard (d1746), descended from a younger son (John) of Peter (d1663): **began the remodelling of the hall** Thomas Giffard (d1776), son of Peter of Blackladies, in the early 1770s: **finished the remodelling of the hall** Thomas Giffard (d1823), son of Thomas (d1776), employing Sir John Soane as architect: was **2nd wife of 'Mad Jack' Mytton** Caroline Mallet (d1841), 6th daughter of Thomas Giffard (d1823), son of Thomas (d1823), in 1821. 'Mad Jack' was a notorious Shropshire sportsman and eccentric (BDH2 p140) (DNB): was **Lieutenant Colonel of Staffordshire Militia** Thomas William Giffard (1789-1861) (SHC 1902 pp194,199): was the **first non-Catholic Giffard at Chillington** Walter Peter Giffard (1796-1877), brother of Thomas Wil liam Giffard (d1861): was **23rd Giffard of Chillington, resided at Pendyrl Hall, Codsall** Walter Thomas Courtenay Giffard (1839-1926), eldest son of Walter Peter (d1877) (Staffordshire Leaders: Social and Political. G Rickward & W. Gaskell. 1907. p129); was **24th Giffard of Chillington** Thomas Arthur Walter Giffard (1882-1971), son of Walter Thomas (d1926) (Staffordshire Leaders. p129). **25th Giffard of Chillington** Peter Giffard (1921-1998), son of Thomas (d1971); however, The Daily Telegraph obituary, July 29 1998 p29p, has him 28th of his family to possess the estate: was **26th Giffard of Chillington, England and Wales' longest-serving chief constable 2006** John Giffard (b1952), son of Peter (d1998), Chief Constable of Staffordshire 1996-2006; chief constable contracts are usually for seven years; in 2003 he won a three year extension (SN March 16 2006 p7) (ES April 3 2006 pp6-7).

4. People...

Brewood's most famous old worthy, one of the last royalists to escape the battle of Worcester 1651 Colonel William Carless (c1620-89). His family had been Broom Hall tenants since at least 1556 and there he might have been born. In 1651 he hid with Charles II after the battle of Worcester in the Royal Oak. After the Restoration he was taken into his service, given a grant of wine, one-third of the London straw tax, and a coat of arms. He died in London. Although Brewood parish register has no baptismal entry for him his burial is recorded. A memorial stone with an arched top containing a carved sprig of oak leaves, near his unmarked grave in Brewood churchyard, reads:- '

Near here lieth
the remains of
Col William Carless
whom the King did call
Carlos
he died Mary 28 1689.'

On the west wall of the chancel is a plaque commemorating him. (Wikipedia 2006). **'one of the best-known residents of Brewood' 1911** Thomas Clifford (1840-1911), originally of Hanley, landlord of the Swan Hotel, and then the Lion Hotel, Brewood, and a representative for Brewood on the Cannock Board of Guardians, an overseer of the parish, and member of the Town Lighting Inspectors (SA Oct 7 1911 p7 col 1). **Birchfield Harriers most famous athlete by 1933** William Whiteway Alexander (1852-1933), born Hampshire, one of the finest long distance runners in the country of his day, and something of a doyen of sportsmen thereafter. Resided Brewood from 1869, in which year he gained his first athletic success by winning the Strangers' quarter mile race at the Brewood Grammar School sports. Removed to Birmingham in the late 1870s (Birmingham Despatch Oct 6 1933). **Miss Staffordshire 1937** Miss Barbara Onion, Miss Brewood 1937; she was the 5th Miss Staffordshire ever (Stafford Pageant: The Exciting Innovative Years 1901-1952. Gordon Henry Loach. 2007). **When the High Sheriff of Staffordshire appeared before the bench** When RF Monckton, appeared on Jan 17 1938, before Penkridge magistrates for temporary music and dancing licences for the new village hall at Brewood, and an extension to the normal hours for one night, the opening night, in his capacity as chairman of Brewood Village Community Council (SA Jan 22 1938 p11 col 5). **'The Woman Who Saved a City', 'Mara'** Mary E Wakefield (b1879), author of 'Ancient Brewood' (1932), whose action in WW1 saved Wolverhampton from disaster by five minutes. From the post office at Brewood, kept by her husband, she sent a morse code warning that she believed Zeppelins, bombing in the distance, were on their way to the town. Wolverhampton then imposed a blackout, and escaped a second time when the Zeppelins returned. When writing for local newspapers her non-de-plume was Mara. Her son, AJ Wakefield, was Director of Agriculture in Tanganyika before 1939, and dismissed with another man by Mr Strachley from the Overseas Food Corporation Groundnuts Scheme. He was then appointed UN representative for technical assistance to Haiti (SA Jan 14 1933 p5 col 6. June 18 1949 p7p) (SLM May 1950 p133p. March 1953 pp5-6). **First national recipient of 'The Queen's Prize' for student gaining highest marks in National Diploma in Agriculture** Albert Derek Sadler of Fair View, Horsebrook Lane, Brewood, aged 22, in 1955. The prize, as instituted by the Royal Agricultural Society of England in Dec 1954, in association with Elizabeth II, was worth £100 (SA & Chron Sept 8 1955 pp4 col 3, 6p).

Brewood's villain David Morris, 54, who once lived at Brewood Hall, where he kept pornographic paedophilia. In 1987 he was jailed for four and half years for possessing and distributing child abuse videos which so sickened female jurors at Nottingham Crown Court it made them physically sick. Brewood Hall was raided by a vice squad while Morris was living at his other address in Mansfield. Police found suitcases stuffed with pornographic magazines and videos, along with a child-sized doll dressed as Little Red Riding Hood. Peter Joyce, prosecuting, warned the jury "As for as obscenity is concerned these films are of the hardest core pornography." The material was brought over from Amsterdam. Miss Jan Ford, owner of Brewood Hall, was called by the defence as a character witness (SN Nov 21 1987 p3). **Brewood's bravest** Sophie Young (b1991), of Brewood who saved her mum, Jane, when she collapsed due to an unidentified seizure on Feb 1 2003. Sophie put her mother in the recovery position and phoned for an ambulance. She is one of the youngest recipents of a bravery award given by Staffordshire Ambulance Trust (E&S March 7 2003 p1pc). **Brewood's kindest** Mostly gentry: the Giffard family of Chillington Hall, co-founded Brewood Grammar School, c1550; in the C19 the Moncktons of Somerford Hall supported charity schools in Somerford and Brewood town (VCH vol 5 p47). Mrs Briscoe (d1901), wife of RH Briscoe of Chillington Hall (their son-in-law Mr Giffard being the owner), formerly of Somerford Hall. Her obituary in the Staffordshire Advertiser states 'To the poor she was always kind, and she will be greatly missed in Brewood.. The Vicar referred in his sermon to the great kindness which he and the parish had received from Mrs Briscoe and to the interest which she took in all matters concerning the welfare of St Luke's. He said no fewer than three of the parochial buildings in connection with St Luke's bore her name on the foundation stones...' (SA March 2 1901 p7 col 4). **Brewood's poorest** The parish workhouse stood in the lane leading to Kiddemore between the Church-fields and Hockerill. It was moved c1795-1801 to premises in Bargate. In 1836 the building became the workhouse for Penkridge Union (renamed Cannock Union 1870s). It remained so until inmates were moved to the new Union workhouse at Cannock in 1872. In 1878 Brewood workhouse was put up for sale and sold in 1879 (SA March 16 1872 p4 col 7. Aug 17 1878 p1 col 2. Jan 11 1879 p4 col 7) (VCH vol 5 p18). **Brewood's earliest recorded will** Belongs to Thomas Barnford, dated 1646. **First person in the parish register** Thomas Elkyn baptised Feb 21 1562. **Choicest quote** A correspondent to The Gentleman's Magazine 1797 wrote 'Brewood is a small market town in Staffordshire, situated on a gentle eminence.... the situation of this town (or rather village) is rural, pleasant and retired, and is a proper place of retreat from the bustle of large towns....'

5. The area...
Brewood is the county's 10th largest parish, consisting of 12,152 acres; **40th= closest parish to the county town**, 7.8m SSW; **extremist length** 4.4m; extremist width 6.2m, making it **13th= widest parish in the county. Parish's chief settlement** Brewood, a large residentially-desirable (for Wolverhampton) brick-Georgian village, although Coven to the E is bigger. **Geology** BREWOOD, CHILLINGTON, HORSEBROOK, KID-DEMORE GREEN - entirely Keuper Red Marls; COVEN - Keuper Sand-stones (most), Bunter (E fringes); ENGLETON - Keuper Red Marls (W), Keuper Sandstones (E); HATTONS - Keuper Sandstones; SOMERFORD - Keuper Sandstones (most), Keuper Red Marls (W fringe). **Highest point** 485 feet at Bishop's Wood. **Lowest point** 283 feet at the boundary by the Penk. Brewood was **21st most-populated Staffordshire parish in 1801** with 2,867 people; **24th in 1811** with 2,860; **27th in 1821** with 2,762; **26th in 1831** with 3,521; **27th in 1841** with 3,641; **27th in 1851** with 3,565; **34th in 1861** with 3,399; **36th in 1871** with 3,237; **40th in 1881** with 2,948; **46th in 1891** with 2,667; **50th in 1901** with 2,535.

Arthur Conan Doyle was involved with the Wyrley Gang series of horse mutilations in Cannock parish.

Cannock
1. Did you know that...

Cannock's top folklore The folklore that has evolved surrounding the Wyrley Gang, an unknown group, who carried out the mutilation of farm animals, mainly horses, in Great Wyrley 1903-15. Arthur Conan Doyle, creator of Sherlock Holmes, secured the release of George Ernest Thompson Edalji of Great Wyrley, wrongly convicted. Meanwhile the mutilations carried on and Staffordshire Police struggled with what remains their most perplexing case. In 1934 Enoch Knowles was captured and convicted. **Oldest-known carvings on stones** About 90 ironstone stones shaped liked animals' heads with images of men, animals (horses, bear, cattle, brontosaurus), fish, trees and ferns, found over 15 years from c1900 by a miner and farmer, Henry Rigby, on land at Great Wyrley. They were kept in secret for some years by Walter Pond of Birmingham. In the period 1922-30 nothing was found in Europe to pre-date the carvings on these stones, believed to be Palaeolithic (Daily Express April 2 1930 illustration). **Staffordshire's largest Iron Age fort** Castle Ring at 8.5 acres. **Most conspicuous feature of central Staffordshire, Cannock Chase** Telecom Tower, Pye Green, built 1970, which is 258 feet high and standing at a height of 775 feet (Staffordshire: Shire County Guide. Peter Heaton. 1986) (WMAG Aug 1979 p21) (BOE p94) (SL p253) (STMSM Aug 1979 p25p) (MR p269pc). **Only Neolithic flint factory of its kind in Staffordshire** Discovered at Courtsbank Covert, 1910. **What Cannock is famous for** Cannock Chase and mining. The **name Cannock first appears** in Domesday Book, 1086; Cannock Forest in 1140s (VCH vol 2 p338). **Greatest advance in population than any other Staffordshire county UD 1911-21** Cannock, according to census figures (Staffordshire County Handbook c1958). **2nd largest number of council houses built for its size in the UK by 1964** Cannock Urban District (CAd March 20 1981). **Worst local authority in country for amount of rubbish recycled** Cannock Chase Council, recycling just 8% of its rubbish (BBC Midlands Today Jan 14 2005). **16th worst place to live in Britain 2007** Cannock Chase Council, according to a survey for Channel 4's programme Location, Location, Location. **'biggest parish council in Staffordshire' 1977** Great Wyrley (E&S March 31 1977). **One of the most celebrated court cases of the C19** The prosecution of Lord Hatherton by the Marquess of Anglesey over coal mining on the Rumer Hill estate, an estate held by Hatherton of the marquess by copyhold, 1842 at Worcester. **The 1st telegraphic instrument - a Wheatstone - at Hednesford** Was introduced at the post office in Old Hednesford during the great military manoeuvres on Cannock Chase, 1873 (SA Dec 6 1919 p7 col 1). This would be the invention of Sir Charles Wheatstone (1802-75), English physicist and inventor. **Most perplexing case the Staffordshire Police has ever tried to solve** The identity of the (Great) Wyrley Gang horse mutilator 1903-15. **First parish council to have a Badge of Office** Possibly Huntington Parish Council, for the office of chairman; in early 1953 it was presented to the then Chairman, Mr S Harris (SLM March 1953 p5). **When Cannock appeared in The Daily Telegraph crossword puzzle** In The Daily Telegraph weekend section Dec 9 2006, in answer to 38 Down in the GKcrossword, the clue being 'Staffordshire town that is south of an Area of Outstanding Natural Beauty that shares its name (7)'. **Staffordshire tapestry which took most hours to make** Probably the Cannock Tapestry depicting scenes of Cannock, made 2001-07. Chadsmoor Tapestry Group took 50,000 hours over the project, which cost £9,000. It went on display at Cannock Council Offices in Nov 2007 (BBC 1 Midlands Today. Nov 27 2007). **Cannock mutton superior to any other** In the opinion of the Duke of Richmond in the mid C19, himself a sheep breeder on the South Downs, on the 'famous' flock of Shropshire sheep of Thomas Darling, land agent to the Earl of Uxbridge and farmer of Chestall, owing to their being grazed on the heights of Cannock Chase. The flock were dispersed in summer 1888 (SA Aug 4 1888 p2 col 3). **Cannock Excelsion, Cannock Revival, Cannock Pride, Cannock Smiler, Cannock Enterprise, Cannock Nabob, Cannock Tom, Cannock Conqueror, Cannock Nut** The first two were stallion horses of the Cannock Agricultural Company advertised to sire mares in the locality; the first was foaled in 1895, the second in 1890 (SA May 5 1900 p8 col 7). The others were all stallions in the Longhouse Farm Stud of Cannock Agricultural Company Ltd advertised to pregnate local mares; the latter was a Hunter Sire belonging to AB Forsyth of Cannock 1901 (SA April 14 1888 p8 col 6. May 4 1901 p8). **Britain's 10th top pumpkin 1983** An 'Atlantic Giant' pumpkin grown by David Shaw of Station Road, Great Wyrley, measuring 18 inches high and 83 inches round, weighing 164 lbs (CAd Oct 21 1983 p3p).

2. Buildings ...

Oldest inhabited farmhouse on the Chase Probably Bean Farm. **Oldest building in Cannock** The Green, dating from the C16. **'one of Staffordshire's most noted sporting inns in the first half of the nineteenth century'** The Cross Keys, Hednesford (Best of Cannock Chase. p84). **'as snug a house as any gentleman could wish for'** Hednesford Lodge, later Anglesey Hotel, built by Edmund Peel, in the opinion of General William Dyott of Freeford Hall in his diaries 1781-1845 (CAd April 20

1984 p4). **'village school without a village'** Brindley Village Primary School, in the period after the rehousing of residents from Brindley Village to Brindley Crescent housing estate, Hednesford in 1955, to the closure of the school in summer 1959. The school was one of the few in England where wild deer could sometimes be seen from the classroom windows (CAd July 27 1984 p5). **First Job Centre in Cannock** The Unemployed People's Centre at 27 Park Road, officially opened Feb 6 1984, run by the Cannock Town Committee, People's Campaign for Jobs (CAd Jan 27 1984 p2). **'one of the best (of 15) pedestrian-minded transport schemes in the country'** Hednesford town centre, officially opened Aug 20 1993, as chosen by Transport 2000 (Chase Post Aug 5 1993) (Cannock Chase Chronicle Aug 13 1993).

3. Transport ...

'one of the last narrow lock flights to be built', longest flight of locks on the Birmingham Canal Navigations 13 locks of the Churchbridge Branch, five eighths of a mile long, built 1858/9 and first used when the Cannock Extension was completed in 1863 (Waterways World. March 1990 pp82-85 ps). **Pioneers of a private local bus service** Harper Brothers Ltd of Hednesford Road, Heath Hayes, in c1924. In 1925 two 14-seater American Chevrolet vehicles were purchased, and in 1928 services from Cannock to Brewood, Brownhills and Aldridge began. The company closed in 1975 (CAd Jan 15 1959. Nov 13 1975). **First petrol made in England** At a unique distillation plant at Leacroft Colliery, set up in 1933, in operation from July 28 1934 using coal mined locally. Around 150 tons of coal was used to produce 30,000 gallons of petrol each day (CAd Jan 13 1984 p4). **3rd in United Kingdom Bus Driver of the Year 1978, Midland Red Driver of the Year 1977, 1978** Paul Roberts (b1949) of Ajax Close, Great Wyrley (CAd Sept 22 1978 p3p). **"World's worst street"** James Street, Chadsmoor, according to Mr AE Beddow at Cannock Urban Council meeting on Feb 1 1938, requesting its urgent attention under the Private Street Works Act. Later in the meeting it was reported that works were proposed to be carried out on Foster Avenue, Chadsmoor, which Mr Beddow, declared "the world's second worst street" (SA Feb 5 1938 p9 col 7). **'worst road in Staffordshire' 1981** The A460 through Wedges Mills for congestion, with a 24-hour daily average of 17,500 vehicles, calculated by an automatic traffic count (CAd Oct 23 1981 p6). **Worst of the worst speed humps in Britain** A specific hump in Tower View Road, Great Wyrley, as noted by Continental Tyres. Meanwhile, Great Wyrley is blighted by too many speed humps in some residents' opinion, with 146. The road with the most is Anson Road with 11 (info Research Institute for Transport Futures, 2007) (BBC 1. The One Show. Jan 17 2008). **England's most photographed highway** A34, Walsall Road through Great Wyrley with seven speed cameras (The Sunday Times April 21 2002) (E&S Dec 31 2002 p39 - news round-up).

4. Cannock Chase ...

First-known chief forester Richard Chenven, appointed by William I. **Last highwayman on Cannock Forest** Was caught, hung, and buried near the South Staffs Waterworks tower at Pye Green (CAd Feb 15 1985). **Last besom (broom-maker) of the Chase** Liz Hodgkiss, the 'Besom of Spring Slade', working after 1880s (PCC pp80-82). **Smallest Area of Outstanding Natural Beauty in mainland Britain, largest country park in Staffordshire** Cannock Chase Country Park (Staffordshire Breaks 2006. Staffordshire Tourism). **One of the two largest Christmas tree producers in the UK** The Forestry Commission on Cannock Chase; the other is the Forestry Commission at Delamere Forest, Ches (SLM Dec 2006 pp7-9). **First blast furnace in the Midlands** At ironworks of Lord Paget on Cannock Chase, 1560s (Staffordshire County Guide 2006/7 p39). **Founder of The Friends of Cannock Chase** Councillor Meshach Wright (1878-1937), JP, of 'Highfield', West Hill, Hednesford, journalist, in 1934. The Society's aim was to link together all those who appreciate the beauties of the Chase, and wish for its amenities to be preserved. Wright served on Cannock UDC 1920-, Chairman 1927-. Author of 'The Best of Cannock Chase' and 'The Friendship of Cannock Chase' (Rugeley Times Feb 27 1937). **First purpose-built Cadets' Centre of Adventure in the country** Fort Muller (named after the county commandant, Col Muller) on Cannock Chase, the first stage of which was officially opened May 9 1959 by General Sir Montagu Stopford, chairman of the Army Cadet Force Association, as a cadet training headquarters (SA & Chron May 14 1959 p9p). **England's last herd of fallow deer, Britain's largest herd of fallow deer** Roam Cannock Chase. The first claim, which goes on to state, at least, they are one of England's last herds of fallow deer, was made by SA & Chron March 19 1959 p5 col 5; the second claim was made by Staffordshire Breaks 2006, published by Staffordshire Tourism. **Most southerly point in England on which the red grouse breeds** Cannock Chase (LGS p12). **Last grouse shoot on the Chase** 1952 (exhibition of Patrick Lichfield's photographs, Shugborough, 2006). **2nd longest interlude between sightings of Staffordshire wildlife** Perhaps the 84 years between sightings of the Welsh Clear Wing Moth not seen on the Chase (Staffordshire's only habitation) between 1922 and 2006 (BBC 1 Midlands Today. Nov 1 2006). **Home to the UK's largest colony of Welsh Clear Wing Moth** Possibly Cannock Chase (Staffs Wildlife Trust no 102 April 2008 p17).

5. Churches ...

At CANNOCK is St Luke, **one of 2 such county dedications** (for AP churches); the other is Sheen; **41st= oldest county church** dating from 1190. **Least interesting church** According to Vivian Bird he had seldom seen a less interesting church than Cannock parish church (VB p122). **England's 3rd most popular church for weddings 1990** St Luke's, Cannock, based on returned given to the Archbishops' Council (The Sunday Telegraph July 8 2007 p9). **In the churchyard** Grave near to the S door of Samuel Lord (1800-57), racehorse trainer to Edmund Peel, at Hednesford (CCF p75). **Cannock's most famous old worthy** Henry Sacheverell (1674-1724), religious controversialist and preacher of fiery high-church sermons with a 'stentorian-voice', of Marlborough, Wiltshire. He was ordained deacon 1695, but in 1697 the bishop of Lichfield refused to ordain him a priest, claiming he didn't know enough Latin. But he was successful with the support of the high-church dean of Lichfield Lancelot Addison (Sacheverell was a friend of his son Joseph, at Magdalen) and took up the living of Cannock - this was **Dr Sacheverell's first curacy**. He returned to be a Fellow at his old college, Oxford, in 1701. Famously impeached for sedition before the House of Lords 1710; found guilty, but through Queen Anne's leniency he was only forbidden to preach for three years. At BRIDGETOWN is St Paul (c1899). At CHADSMOOR is St Chad (1892). At GREAT WYRLEY is St Mark (1845), and St Andrew (1966), Hilton Lane. **First couple married in the church** Victoria Sheperdson and John Aston in early Jan 1983 (CAd Jan 7 1983 p3p). **'The Morris dancing curate'** Bob Swallow (b1953), curate of St Mark's and St Andrew's from 1979; when he celebrated his first communion the Cannock Chase Morris team surprised him by coming along in full costume, forcing him to join in a dance after the service (E&S July 10 1979 p8p). At GREEN HEATH is St Saviour (1888). At HEATH HAYES is St John the Evangelist (1903). At HEDNESFORD is St Peter, built 1868, extended 1906; its oldest possession, and **earliest chalice in the Archdeaconry of Stafford** A silver-gilt medieval chalice, possibly Flemish, pre C14 (BAST vol 73 1955 p6) (Staffordshire: Shire County Guide. Peter Heaton. 1986). At HUNTINGTON is St Thomas (1872). At MOSS WOOD is St Barnabas (c1960). At WEST CHADSMOOR is St Aidan (1956).

NON-CONFORMIST Cannock Wood Methodist Church 1834 (CAd Jan 20 1984 p3). **'The Chapel in the garden'** Wesleyan chapel, Shaws Lane, Great Wyrley, built c1926, on account of its well-kept gardens in the vicinity (Great Wyrley Millennium Souvenir. p259). Jacobs Hall Lane Methodist Church, Great Wyrley, built 1934, demolished after a fire in 1984 (E&S Dec 17 1984 p21). ROMAN CATHOLIC **'The English Lourdes', first church in England dedicated to Our Lady of Lourdes, 'first of its kind in this country to be built on principles which are adopted abroad for earthquake areas'** The Church of Our Lady of Loudres, Hednesford, in the French Gothic style, to protect it from mining subsidence. The building was initiated by Father Patrick J Boyle, priest at Cannock from 1911 to his death in 1921. The first sod of the church was cut on August Bank Holiday 1927, the foundation stone laid on Sept 12 1928, and the Pilgrim's Grotto in the grounds was opened on June 5 1934. **Biggest religious gathering ever held on the Chase to 1933** When over 15,000 Roman Catholics from all over the Birmingham diocese came to the 2nd Eucharistic Conference, held in the grounds on June 12 1933. The first service in the church took place on Wednesday, Nov 1 1933, conducted by Father JP Healy (CAd Sept 8 1929. July 1931. June 15 1933. April 28 1934. June 2 1934) (LiMe Nov 10 1933 p10 col 2).

6. Youth & schools...

Oldest (youth) club in the country 1959 Perhaps Heath Hayes Brotherhood Youth Club, which started in 1911 under the leadership of Mr G Marriott. It had three sections, one for scouts, one for gymnastics and one for sport. It accepted girls in 1953 (CAd May 2 1959). **Staf**

fordshire's first state elementary school to install a 'cinema' Perhaps Heath Hayes Boys' Council School, Cannock, in 1932, by headmaster R Evans. In 1934 it installed sound equipment (SA April 21 1934 p6 col 7). **One of the first schools in the country to take up the American idea of safety first patrols** Chadsmoor C of E Boys's School in 1933. Specially chosen boys wearing distinctive safety first armlets patrol on duty at certain points 10 minutes before and after school time (CAd April 29 1933). **'one of the best equipped (nursery schools) in Staffordshire' 1978** Landywood nursery school, opened Aug 1977 (E&S Aug 3 1978 p6). **Country's only school split by a main trunk road** Perhaps Huntington Primary School, split by the A34 when the former secondary school closed, leaving the junior school to take over the buildings (CAd July 27 1984). **First steel pan ensemble to take the London College of Music Ensemble exams** West Hill Primary School, Hednesford, 2007, by Year 5 and 6 pupils; and passed with an overall score of 93% (Life magazine for Staffs CC employees. April/ May 2007 p26-27pc). **First Gospel Aerobics club in the Midlands** That at Cannock by autumn 2007 (BBC Midlands Today Oct 16 2007).

7. Heroes and villains...

Cannock's villain James Hawkins, an under gamekeeper, who murdered Matthias Wellington, a labourer, in the kitchen of the Crown Inn, Cannock in 1836. Such was the indignation in Cannock against Hawkins the constables wisely removed him swiftly to Stafford for trial (SA Oct 24 1936). **Cannock's bravest** Henry Merritt, fireman at No. 9 Cannock Chase Colliery, who with a man called Stokes (who lost his life in the attempt), went to rescue five men from a distant part of the pit where an underground fire had broken out on Dec 14 1911. One man got out by holding on to Merritt. Merritt made repeated searches for the others, who didn't follow him, but they had suffocated. He reached the surface exhausted. In July 1912 he received the Edward Medal of the first class from George V at Buckingham Palace (SA July 6 1912 p9 col 3). **Cannock's war hero** Simon Davison of Cannock, 22, Grenadier Guards, killed in Helmand province, Afghanistan, buried 15 May 2007 (BBC Midlands Today 15 May 2007). **Hednesford's war hero** John Baker 1/6th South Staffs Regt, 24, only son of John Baker JP, member for Hednesford on Staffs CC, for conspicuous bravery in the brilliant exploits of the 46th North Midland Division in capturing the Nord Canal Sept 29 1918 (SA Dec 14 1918 p3p). **Hednesford's boy hero** Shane Cannon of Brindley Heath, 15, who braved freezing conditions to help Karen Tillotson, 14, of Hednesford from a water-filled quarry in Rawnsley Road, Hednesford, and stayed in the water as firemen lowered a rope to life Sharon Nutting of Chadsmoor, to safety. In 1984 he was awarded a testimonial from the royal Humane Society (CAd Sept 7 1984 p4). **Hightown's heroes** Edward Capewell and Ernest Bailey, who tried to save two fellow miners trapped in a roof fall at West Cannock Colliery on May 13 1935. In 1936 they each received a certificate for bravery from the Carnegie Heroes Trust Fund. **Hednesford's hero** William Benton, also awarded for the same gallant act. **Hednesford's**

heroine Mrs G Goldby of 340 Hill Street who saved the three babies (twins aged two, and a 9-month old) of her neighbour Mrs W Gallett of 338 Hill Street from a fire in her kitchen on March 21 1938 (SA March 26 1938 p3 col 3). **Chadsmoor's hero** John Hubbard, also awarded for the same as William Benton, and lost his life in the rescue attempt (SA Jan 18 1936 p5p). **Chadsmoor's villain** Simon Cowley, 31, who strangled his wife Tracey, 24, of Larchwood Drive, in early June 1993, apparently during a bizarre sex act, and at first pretended to be a grieving husband desperate to find his wife's killer. He received a life sentence (Chase Post June 10 1993, June 13 1993). **Hednesford's villain** Henry Thomas Gaskin, 27, miner at West Cannock Colliery, who strangled and then cut off the head of his wife, Elizabeth, aged 23, and mutilated the rest of her body, near Hednesford Pool on Feb 19 1919. All her remains were deposited in a water tank at Victoria Street gasworks. So macabre was the crime a souvenir postcard was produced commemorating the murder. Gaskin was executed at Winson Green prison on Aug 8 1919, despite 6,000 signatures on a petition asking for a reprieve on the grounds that he was provoked by the admitted unfaithfulness of his wife (CAd March 1 1919. March 8 1919. Aug 16 1919). **Cannock's villainess** Debbie Clifton, 33, of Cannock, who fraudulently collected money house-calling in her neighbourhood for the Madeleine McCann Fund (a little girl famously abducted on holiday in Portugal in May 2007), in order to feed her heroine addiction. She was sentenced on two counts of theft and one of criminal damage to three months in prison (BBC Midlands Today July 9 2007). **Fancy that!** In 1837 Richard Cooper, late of the Royal Oak, Cannock, gave himself up to Mr Wood, constable of Rugeley, saying he had stolen a goose from J Crudgington of Hatherton, and sold it for want, stating that he would sooner be transported than apply to the parish for relief. He had indeed committed the crime and was sent to trial (SA June 17 1837 p3 col 3).

8. People...

Staffordshire's oldest mother ever In Staffordshire Advertiser Oct 15 1796 p4 col 3 it was recorded 'BIRTH - A woman aged between 70 and 80, the wife of a labourer, was safely delivered of a child, on Monday last, at Cannock, in this county!!' (SA March 31 1888 p5 col 5). **'King of Hednesford'** Title 'Old Jacky Wright' of Hednesford gave himself in the mid C19. **'The Collier Poet'** George Wilkes of Rawnsley (TB Feb 24 2000 p18). **Cannock's poetess** Nancy Foster (1913-33) of Hednesford, telephone operator in the offices at West Cannock Colliery, dying aged 21. Her 'The Collected Poems of Nancy Foster' appeared in 1935, the proceeds from the sales going to the erection of a memorial stone on her grave (CAd March 30 1935 p3) (TB). **'Jack the Rag Man'** Alias for the occupier of a small farm at Hill Top, Hednesford, in c1920, who kept his premises in such a filthy condition it was a haven for vermin (CAd March 10 1960). **Patentee of an Improved mowing and reaping machine** S Jellyman, engineer, of Cannock, exhibited in early June 1869 at Shire Hall (SA June 5 1869 p4 col 6. June 26 1869 p4 col 5). **Miss**

Staffordshire 1934 Miss Marjorie Jarvis, aged 16, Miss Charity of Cannock; she was the 2nd Miss Staffordshire ever. **1st ever Deputy Miss Staffordshire** Miss Joan Carnell in 1946, in which year she reigned as Miss Cannock (Stafford Pageant: The Exciting Innovative Years 1901-1952. Gordon Henry Loach. 2007). **First woman vice-president ever of the Methodist Conference** Mrs David Lewis of Heatherleigh, Shoal Hill, daughter of Rev H Babb of Swan Bank Methodist Church, Bilston, elected 1947; widow; known in Staffordshire for her educational work and for her special interest in mental welfare (SA Aug 2 1947 p5 col 1. July 17 1948 p5 col 1p). **Miss West Midlands 18-Plus 1977-78** Jane Moxon of Cherrington Drive, Great Wyrley (CAd Nov 11 1977 p3p). **The Naughty Nudes of Cannock Chase** Three young men - Peter Kosoros, Steven Dace, and Kevin Fowler - when at a party in Heath Hayes did a nude dash at 2.30am Boxing Day 1983. A passer-by wrote a jovial letter to Cannock Advertiser saying he would not reveal the locality of the dash if the men sent a contribution to charity, which they duly did (CAd Jan 20 1984 p1p). **First girl in the country to win the**

CANNOCK PEOPLE - Jennie Lee, Albert Dando, Fred Pritchard. Bottom row - John Wakefield, Nancy Foster, Maria Aston.

Duke of Edinburgh's gold award by taking physical fitness as part of the course Miss Susan Chmielewski, a policewoman, from Cannock, in 1970; the rules having changed in 1969 so girls could take fitness as part of their course (Staffs Illustrated. March 1970. Staffs Scene). **Great Wyrley 'miracle' baby** Tracey Irving of Gorsey Lane, born 1967, with a hole in the heart and other complications, only discovered at the age of two. After four operations, and by the age of ten she was fit and healthy (CAd Aug 8 1977 p3p). **Last baby born at Cannock Chase Hospital maternity unit** Victoria Ann Lally on Feb 29 1984, of Beech Tree Lane, near the hospital in Wolverhampton Road (CAd March 2 1984 p1p). **Staffordshire's first recipient of a Royal Society for the Prevention of Accidents award** David Carr of Walsall Road, Great Wyrley, teacher at Landywood Middle School (CAd Oct 8 1976 p8p). **Youngest private secretary in the country** Teresa Cutler (b1964) of Great Wyrley when she became a fully qualified member of the Institute of Private Secretaries in 1982, aged 17, but could not receive her diploma until the age of 20 (CAd Oct 29 1982 p1p). **Young Inventor of Great Britain 1992, 'one of the country's youngest ever stage managers'** Lucy Westnidge (b1978) of Cannock. Attended Blake High School, Cannock. The invention was a waterporter, a gardening device for the elderly and disabled (E&S May 24 2008 p8pc). **Staffordshire's most prodigious public embroiderer** Sylvia Everitt of Rawnsley who created the county's Millennium Embroideries 1995-99. **Julian Barnes' finest novel** Claimed in a review in the Irish Times of 'Arthur & George' (2005), about The Great Wyrley Gang; P.D. James in The Times wrote 'This novel is Barnes at his best' (dustjacket of 'Arthur & George'). **Paul McDonald's strangest book ever read** Kathleen O'Leovan (1896), the first novel of William Henry Robinson (Maurice Grindon) (1847-1926), born Cannock, son of the founder of the Walsall Advertiser, John Russell Robinson. His other works include 'Man Immortable' (1902), 'Till the Sun Grows Cold' (1904) (BCM Winter 2006 pp49-50). **TV's Junior Stars in their Eyes 2002** Charlotte Gethin, a teenager from Cannock, for her portrayal of Eva Cassidy, in Oct 2002 (E&S Dec 31 2002 p39). **Cannock's saddest** George Ernest Jones, aged 10, of Platt Street, Hightown, killed on a tramline of the West Cannock Colliery, Hednesford, in Aug 1904 having got into a tub of coal being transported. He subsequently fell off falling in between other tubs. When he was pulled from underneath the last tub his body was found to be dreadfully mangled. His jaw, left thigh, and arm were fractured, and, he had an extensive scalp wound and similar injuries on arms and legs. He died 10 minutes after admission to the Hednesford Accident Home (SA Aug 20 1904 p4 col 5). **Cannock's kindest** Mrs Walhouse of Hatherton Hall built a school and teacher's house in 1828 in New Penkridge Road, Cannock. In addition, she paid for the education of approximately 200 children there herself. By her will proved 1843 she bequeathed £800 to the school; thereafter successive female Walhouses gave financial gifts (VCH vol 5 pp71-72 p of facing p53). **Cannock's poorest** A parish workhouse was built at Snout's Gap, Walsall Road, in 1743 (VCH vol 5 p52). In April 1814 Widow Huballs' pay was stopped, and in May she was entered into the workhouse along with her children. In 1817 the vestry resolved to have twice monthly inspections of the workhouse. A governor of the workhouse is recorded in 1812, and Mrs Trubshaw is recorded as governess in 1826. In 1814 and 1820 there were proposals for a new workhouse on a piece of Lord Uxbridge's waste land (SRO D1054/7/4). From 1836 Cannock was in Penkridge Union, renamed Cannock Union from 1870s, but the Union workhouse was at Brewood. In 1872 a new workhouse was opened for this Union on Wolverhampton road, Cannock (VCH vol 5 p52). **Cannock's earliest recorded will** Belongs to William Deykyn, dated Nov 30 1604. **Great Wyrley's earliest recorded will** Belongs to John Alport, dated Dec 2 1562. **Choicest quote** In his Forties' Child, 1980, Tom Wakefield portrays the Cannock of his boyhood 'The town centre of Cannock was approximately one mile from where we lived. It had all the appearance of a country market town. There was a clock, a war memorial and an imposing church whose surrounding land and greenery took up a large slice of the commercial shopping centre. The church had a grand appearance - so grand that we never went in it. It was the 'Cathedral' of the area and I don't think that many miners worshipped there. Joey was not afraid of its stature.'

9. People in politics...

MP with biggest majority in history to 1945, Open University's first Vice Chancellor, Britain's first Arts Minister 1964, 'the bonniest of fighters' Jennie Lee (d1988), when she won the Cannock Division seat 1945 (TB May 4 2003 p4p), then she served for Cannock county constituency 1950-70. The quote is from Michael Foot writing her obituary in The Guardian, Nov 18 1988 p39, in which he states her most important single achievement was her indispensable role in the creation of the Open University, finding the money for the project. **Oldest serving poor-law officer in the country, certainly in Staffordshire 1934** AH Buck (probably Alfred H Buck, poor law clerk in 1901, born Hednesford c1872) served with Cannock Union 1884-90, 1893-1905, Caistor Union, Lincs, 1890-93, Newport Union, Shrops 1905-11, Master of the Lichfield Poor-Law Institution 1911-34. By 1934 his wife had served 40 years as a Poor Law officer, and their combined 90 year service to date was deemed probably unique in the history of the Poor-Law service (SA Sept 15 1934 p10 col 6). **First time Cannock UDC had a female chairman and vice-chairman together** 1952, when Mrs M Hotchkiss, a Hednesford schoolteacher, took the chair (for a second year), and Mrs E Jones of Chadsmoor, became vice-chairman (SA May 23 1952 p4 col 3). **Youngest ever chairman of South Staffordshire District Council** Graham Jones (b1941), teacher of Poplar Road, Great Wyrley in 1983 when aged 42 (E&S May 18 1983 p5p). **Youngest ever Alderman on Staffordshire County Council** James Eric Roberts (b1911), of Broomhill, from May 1947, when aged 35, former Labour member for Chadsmoor and Heath Hayes 1945-47. In 1935-37 he was awarded Cassel and Trade Union scholarships to Ruskin College, Oxford. His publications on his local dialect 'Bilberry Pie' (1963), 'More Bilberry Pie' received international recognition (CAd Feb 17 1939. May 23 1947). **Longest serving clerk to Cannock Local Board (later Cannock UC)** Charles Adshead Loxton (1855-1950), of Shoal Hill House, Cannock, appointed May 12 1882, retired 1933, serving over 50 years (CAd Dec 16 1950 p1p).

10. Music & musicians...

Composed the tunes for the hymns 'I gave My Life for thee' and 'Lead, Kindly Light', invented the machine for making twist augers Cornelius Whitehouse (1825-99), born Wedges Mill, later edge tool manufacturer of Churchbridge and then Bridgtown. Staunch Non-conformist. The former hymn was written by Frances Ridley Havergal of Shareshill, the latter received praise from Cardinal Newman. His auger maker was a double action floor cramp, later used to make garden shears (Cannock Chase Courier. Feb 27 1953 p4. March 8 1953 p4). **Oldest cornet player in the country 1951** Claimed by James Mason, aged 87, of 163 Wolverhampton Road, Cannock. He had played in almost every church, chapel, and hall in the Cannock district over the past 70 years (SA Sept 21 1951 p5p). **'Musical Marie', 'Cannock's musical marvel', 'the world's only lady marathon pianist'** Maria Aston of Cannock who in summer 1955 contested the world record for non-stop piano playing at the Dudley Hippodrome, playing for 133 hours ten minutes non stop (over 5 and a half days); when she needed the call of nature, a screen was discreetly pulled around her (TB March 4 2004 p13p). **'Chase Mr. Music'** Howard Benton (1908-81), of Shaws Lane, Great Wyrley, musical director of Chase Orpheus Males Voice Choir (which he founded in 1952), and Cannock and District Ladies' Choir; former member of Landywood Sextet (which he also founded), and Cheslyn Hay (from 1922), Rubery Owen, Essington, Cannock Servicemen's, and Harrison's Colliery Male Voice Choirs; the Howard Benton Subscription Fund to honour him was launched in 1973. During his career he won 70 first prizes at major music festivals and Eisteddfods (CAd July 29 1977 p28p. Feb 6 1981 p11p). **Staffordshire's first accordion festival** That organised by the British Accordion Federation at Coniston Hill, Cannock, on Nov 26 1960 (SA & Chron Nov 10 1960 p5). **Britain's 2nd-best home organist 1981** Mrs Jean Parker of Great Wyrley, aged 29, at the Commonwealth Institute, London (E&S April 28 1981 p5p).

11. Mining & work...

Unique feat Harrisons Colliery, top end of Hazel Lane, Great Wyrley, staged an underground 'sing a long' concert in 1943, recorded by the BBC. About 300 mines attended. The tenor, Trevor Jones, had himself been a stallman in a Welsh pit. The other three artists were Mary Lake (soprano), Joan Davis (pianist), and Harold Fairhurst (violin), who was well over six feet tall and had difficulty in finding a place where he could wield his bow without hitting the roof (Great Wyrley Millennium Souvenir. p23). **One of the largest collieries in the Cannock Chase Coalfield 1954** Coppice Colliery Heath Hayes (VCH vol 5 p62). **One of the first purpose-built computer centres in British Industry** The National Coal Board's computer centre at Cannock (Staffordshire Hand book c1966 p73). **Digging world record** A 824.8 feet, 12.5 feet wide, 6.5 feet high coal-hewn roadway at West Cannock Colliery No. 5 dug by 35 miners in 1981 (CCAP p158) (GBR 1990 p98). **Staffordshire's last longest serving collier** Perhaps William John Wilkes of Bridgtown (born Calf Heath) who worked the pits from the age of 7 in 1875 to his death in 1946, 71 years (TB May 4 2000 p8). **West Midlands Area Coal Queen 1955** Sylvia Evans, 19, of Platt Street, Hednesford, crowned at the N.U.M. gala at Tamworth in June 1955 (SA May 26 1955 p6p). **'Mr Cannock Chase'** Fred Pritchard (b1943), property developer, Chairman of Pritchard Group plc based at Anglesey Lodge, Market Street, Hednesford. Former Director of Business Link Staffordshire and Southern Staffordshire Chamber of Commerce and East Mercia Chamber of Commerce; Director of Chase Chamber of Commerce, c2007; very active in local community and arts initiatives, as well as the regeneration of the Cannock Chase area; builder of The Ramada Birmingham North hotel, Watling Street, Cannock, and the proposed Avon Plaza, a leisure and retail development in Cannock (various websites) (The Sunday Times April 27 2008) (BBC Midlands Today Oct 13 2008). **National home of the Institute of Vitreous Enamellers incorporating the Vitreous Enamel Association (IVE, 1934)** 39 Sweetbriar Way, Heath Hayes in 2008. The Institute exchanges technical information on vitreous enamelling.

12. Sport...

'the most noted place for training available to persons in the Midland Counties' Hednesford as described in the Sporting Magazine, June 1839 p106 (VCH vol 5 pp49,52). **Grand National winners 1861** Jealously trained by John Wilkins, landlord of, and at Cross Keys Inn; **1907** Eremon; **1910** Jenkinstown; **1931** Grakle, last three trained by Tom Coulthwaite (d1948) at Hazelslade or Flaxley Green (SSE 1990 pp87-100). **Featherweight champion of the Midlands c1923, 'one of the best featherweights in country'** Albert Dando, born Brindley Heath 1904, former miner who worked in the West Cannock Colliery, by 1935 was licensee of the Star and Garter Inn, Wedges Mills. He 'is probably the finest boxer ever bred in the Cannock Chase area' (CAd March 30 1935. Jan 2 1981), the second claim is a quote from Sporting Star - E&S Feb 1938. According to the Star he had about 300 contests, was never knocked out, never lost on a foul, or ever claimed a foul. **The 'Midlands richest individual (bowling) competition' 1980** The Olympia. This Midlands Crown Green Bowls championship first took place at the Heath Hayes Constitutional green in 1975. From 1976-79 it was staged at the Hilton Recreation Ground, Featherstone; between 1980-91 it was staged at G.E.C. bowls club, Stafford. In 1981 Bass took over sponsorship and the event went on to become one of the richest and most prestigious open events, ending when Bass withdrew sponsorship in 1991 (SN Aug 15 1980 p53) (TB July 17 2008 p29). **Bowls club who had not suffered defeat in 200 years** Cannock Bowls Club, as recorded by the Morning Leader of Sept 17 1907 (TB June 21 2007 p33). **British Crown Green Amateur Bowling Association Individual Merit Com-**

petition runner-up 1958 John 'The Cap' Wakefield of Somerset Place, Broomhill, Cannock, aged 40 (SA & Chron Aug 7 1958 p10p). **Dutch Open Ten Dance (junior ballroom dancing) champions 1980** Alan Young (b1965) of Shaw's Lane, Great Wyrley, and partner Rachel Cottrell (b1966) of Cannock Road, Blackfords; together they had already amassed over 1,000 medals, trophies, plaques and certificates for dancing (CAd Nov 21 1980 p23p). **First Cannock Chase People's Marathon** See Rugeley. **First Wyrley 10 Kilometre Road Race** 1983, the first winner was Arthur Freer of Hammerwich in 31 mins, 47 seconds (Chase Post Sept 29 1983 p20p). **'more Olympic medals than any other British athlete in history'** Kathy Cook (b1960), sprinter of Churchbridge, with a total of 19 at the 1984 Olympic Games. Earlier in 1984 Kathy won the TSB 'Golden Girl' award, for winning the national championship in 100 metres for the 2nd time, and the 200 metres for the first time, when she gave a championship best performance of 22.27 secs (CAd June 29 1984 p15p. Aug 28 1984 p28p). **Olympic 4x400 metres relay silver medalist** Gary Cook, husband of Kathy (see above) of Churchbridge, at the 1984 Olympic Games (CAd Aug 17 1984 p28p). **'UK's state-of-the-art hockey centre'** At Cannock (Staffordshire County Guide 2006/7 p50). **Great Britain's youngest Olympic hockey player ever** Charlotte Craddock of Wolverhampton, aged 17 at the 2008 Olympics; she plays for Cannock Hockey Club (BBC Midlands Toady July 7 2008). **West Midlands Masters powerlifting champion 1984** Colin Gethin (b1943), of Hall Meadow, Wedges Mills. To take the title he had to lift 155 kilos squat; 95 kilos bench and 205 kilos deadlift (CAd Nov 2 1984 p26p). **Midlands Strongest Man 2003, Britain's Strongest Man 1999, 2000, 2003, runner-up 1998, 2001, World's Strongest Man competitor** Richard Gosling (b1974) of Wellington Drive, Cannock (E&S Aug 27 2003 p10p) (ES May 10 2006 p12). **'top lady bowler in the country', first lady team member in winning Staffordshire side in British Crown Green Senior County Championships** Lynn Pritchatt of Chadsmoor Progressive WMC in 2004 final. The first claim was made by Bowls journalist Mike Wakelam in 2007 (TB May 6 2004 p29. Sept 9 2004 p29p. June 21 2007 p33). **British Mixed Pairs winners 2008** Mel Evans and Lynn Pritchatt, of Chadsmoor Progressive, organised by the British Crown Green Bowling Association (E&S Oct 18 2008 p52p).

13. The area...

Cannock is the **county's 11th largest parish**, consisting of 10,961 acres; **33rd closest parish to the county town**, 6.1m SSE; **extremist length** 6.5m, making it **13th= longest parish in the county**; **extremist width** 6.2m, making it **13th= widest parish in the county. Parish's chief settlement** Cannock, a large (former) mining town. **Geology** CANNOCK - Bunter (Church Hill, Cannock and Hednesford, rest of W half), Middle Coal Measures (S and E), Keuper Sandstones (extreme E); GREAT WYRLEY - entirely Middle Coal Measures; HUNTINGTON - entirely Bunter. **Highest point** 746 feet at Pye Green. **Lowest point** 367 feet near Wedge's Mills. Cannock was **33rd most-populated Staffordshire parish in 1801** with 1,700 people; **43rd in 1811** with 1,639; **34th in 1821** with 2,232;

33rd in 1831 with 2,468; **32nd in 1841** with 2,852; **32nd in 1851** with 3,081; **30th in 1861** with 3,964; **22nd in 1871** with 7,749; **15th in 1881** with 18,377; **15th in 1891** with 21,959; **15th in 1901** with 26,012.

SUBJECT INDEX *Bo to Ch*

The legend of the Staffordshire Knot, with Stafford Castle in the distance.

Castle Church
1. Did you know that...

Castle Church's top folklore There are a number of traditions how the Stafford Knot, the emblem of the Stafford family of Stafford Castle, came to be. The most famous is, it was devised so three people could be hung at the same time. Another tales tells that quarrelling between north and south Staffordshire was only settled when a chieftain proposed each party should bring a length of cord and tie it in an indissoluble knot to bring peace to the north and south of the county. **What Castle Church is famous for** Stafford Castle. **Only Selchemore in Domesday Book** Duignan believed Selchemore (modern Silkmore) to be unique. The **name Castle first appears** in 1208, Castle Church in 1562-6; Burton, Rickerscote and Silkmore in Domesday Book, 1086. **Extraordinary mature calf** A sturk of the short-horn breed of Mr Cordwell of Burley Fields when at only 16 months old produced a very fine calf, a 'circumstance almost unprecedented'; it was bred by George Green of Lane Delph (SA April 21 1838 p3 col 4). **Staffordshire's 2nd railway accident** When an axle on 'The Stentor' engine going between Birmingham and Stafford broke in the early evening of Sept 14 1837 at Rickerscote. The first accident was near Whitmore in Aug 1837 (SA Sept 16 1837 p3 col 1). **Staffordshire's first railway injury** Robert Oliver, jeweller on his way to Dublin, on the GJR from Birmingham, in a state of drunkenness fell as a standing passenger onto the carriage links 0.25m south of Stafford, in which position he sustained severe injuries to his left arm and left side of his head on the wooden sleepers (SA Nov 11 1837 p3 col 1). **Dean's Hill death that could neither be proved murder or suicide** William Thompson, aged 23, groom to Mr Buxton of Castle Cottage, Dean's Hill, in peculiar circumstances on May 24 1871 in which Thompson had been in a minor altercation with Mr Buxton's cook, Sarah Ann Kibble. But at the inquest it could not be proved whether he had taken his own life with a knife, or she had murdered him in a struggle, there being no witnesses, present at the time (SA May 27 1871 p2 col 5). **Stafford's first flying display** Gustav Hamel in a monoplane flew at La-mascote on Oct 12 1912 (EAS p20) (SAIW pl. 52). **5th parish registers transcribed and published by Staffordshire Register Society** Castle Church, 1903. **Earliest photograph of a property in a sale advertisement in the Staffordshire Advertiser** Moss Pit House, in many editions from June 15 1912. **'Queensville Pride'** A shire stallion of CJ Nevitt of Bailey Street, Stafford, foaled in 1901 toured in 1904 to impregnate local mares (SA June 11 1904 p8 col 7). **'Moss Pit Jan Joan'** Was a Friesian cow belonging to Mr T Goodyear, which came first and was champion in the North West Friesian Society's show and sale 1959 (SA & Chron Feb 5 1959 p1 col 6). **Winner of The Daily Mirror Gugnunc Collar for bravery** Peter (d1937), a black-and-white Collie belonging to the licensee of the Crown Inn Lichfield Road, Queensville, William Jones, who saved Howard Picken, aged 8, from drowning in the Sow. Peter went on to appear at many shows and in parades, travelling over 2,000 miles to events in 1936 (SOPP pl 41p) (ROT p42). His first appearance at Crufts was in 1931 (SA Jan 23 1932 p6 col 5. Jan 23 1937 p6p). **London Bulldog Club championship prize winner** Candy's Golden Boy, a bulldog belonging to John Kelsall of 61 Queensville, aged 16, who took 4 first prizes and a 'very highly commended' prize at the championship in 1962 (SA & Chron March 22 1962 p9p). **First offence on first stretch of motorway in Staffordshire** A 16-year old learner driver fined £10 by Stafford Court on Nov 20 1962 for driving a scooter on the Stafford by-pass near Stafford Castle, while only having a provisional license, his passenger, a 15 year old boy, was fined £4 (SA & Chron Nov 22 1962 p15 col 8). **First offender brought before Stafford borough magistrates for walking on the M6** John Kay, aged 39, of 59 Browning Crescent, Fordhouses, was fined £2 for walking along the hard shoulder of the southbound carriageway in Dec 1963 (SA & Chron Dec 12 1963 p6). **Staffordshire Best Kept Village winner (medium village category) 1980** Hyde Lea. **Largest collection of Staffordshire postcards in private hands** 23-24,000 cards collected by and in the custodianship of Roy Lewis, local historian of Rowley Park, and presently of Western Downs, but belonging to his granddaughter Jennifer Lewis. The **earliest known Staffordshire picture postcard (printed) of the collection** is postmarked 24th Aug 1895 - a view of Lichfield Cathedral; **earliest card is postmarked** Jan 1899; **earliest known photographic postcard** Perhaps Stafford main street in 1901 with the initials E.T.A (info Roy Lewis, 2006).

2. Churches...

At CASTLE CHURCH is St Mary, **one of 23 such county dedications** (most common dedication in the county); **76th oldest AP county church** dating from 1252. **St Mary's longest-serving vicar** John Peplor or Peploe, who may have served some 56 years, c1673 to c1729. At CASTLETOWN is St Thomas (1866-1972), known as the **railwayman's church**. It was built by James Tyrer of Tixall Hall, a large shareholder in the LNWR, and it was intended mainly for the railway workers living in the area, with all sittings free; it was endowed with shares in various railway companies, and the stone for it was carried free where it passed over the LNWR line (VCH vol 6 p249). At FOREBRIDGE is St Paul (1844), Lichfield Road, where took place **Stafford's 1st military wedding of WW2** between Sergt E William Turner of Queensville Ave, of 241-61st Field Regt RA, and Miss Doris Adderley of Marston Road, by Sept 16 1939 (SA Sept 16 1939 p5p). At RICKERSCOTE is St Peter (1957), S side of Rickerscote Road.

3. Buildings...

Staffordshire's last monastic house founding before the Reformation Austin Friars, Stafford Green, Forebridge, 1343 (HOS p25). **First maintained girls' high school in the administrative county** Stafford Girls' High School, The Oval, off Lichfield Road, 1907 (VCH vol 6 p264). **Earliest flat-roofed house in England** Upmeads, Newport Road, built 1908 (SOPP pl 56p). **Pevsner's most interesting house of 1908 in the country** Upmeads, Newport Road, was one of them (BOE p250). **Best new housing estate in the Midlands 1951** Kingsway designed by E Bower Norris for Kingsway Housing Association, formed by English Electric, near Burton House Maternity Home (SN May 18 2006 p12). **2000th Stafford (Borough) council house** In Steadman Crescent at Moss Pit, July 1954 (SN May 18 2006 p12).

William Howard (1621-80).

4. Stafford Castle & The Staffords...

'heap of stones' How Stafford Rural Councillor DH Hitchen described Stafford Castle, recommending it be turned into a recreational area with a zoo, 1972 (SN May 18 2006 p8). **'more original papers survive than for any other English medieval family'** The Stafford estate and household papers from the C15 when they were Dukes of Buckingham (STAFFS p31).

The STAFFORD who was: **Staffordshire's largest landowner c1086** Robert de Toeni (d1088) (STAFFS p2); **benefactor of Kenilworth Priory** Nicholas de Stafford (d1138), son of Robert de Toeni (d1088) (STAFFS p3); **in the Holy Land with Richard the Lionheart on a crusade when he died** Robert III de Stafford (d c1193), great grandson of

Robert de Toeni (STAFFS p3); **the heiress who married a Bagot** Millicent (d c1225), sister of Robert III, married Hervey Bagot, a sub-tenant of the Staffords (STAFFS p4); **the Bagot who took the Stafford name** Hervey Bagot (d1237), son of Millicent; **killed under a falling wall at the siege of Deresloyn Castle, Wales** Nicholas de Stafford (d1287), great grandson of Millicent (STAFFS p6); **'established the Stafford family in the peerage of England'** Edmund Stafford (1273-1308), 1st Lord Stafford, son of Nicholas. He received a writ of summons to Parliament in 1299 (STAFFS p6); **1st Earl of Stafford, abductor of Margaret Audley, 'one of the richest men in England' 1347, took part in the first major English victory of the Hundred Years War, most prolific of the medieval Staffords of Stafford Castle, is Castle Church's most famous old worthy** Ralph Stafford (1301-72), son of Edmund (d1308), 2nd Lord Stafford; Knight Banneret 1326~7; frequently a JP; summoned to Parliament 1336-50; served in Scotland 1327, 1332, 1336-7; returned from France with the King 1339; battle of Sluys 1340; steward of the King's Household 1340/1; granted a market at Madeley 1341; temporary possession of the Great Seal 1342; sailed to Brittany and took part in the siege of Vannes 1342, captured, escaped; in action in Gascony 1344; licensed to make castles of his seats at Stafford and Madeley 1347~8; Knight of the Garter 1348 as one of the founders; expedition in France 1355; founder of St Augustine's Priory, possible benefactor to St John's Hospital, both at Stafford Green. Margaret Audley became his 2nd wife, whom he abducted c1336 from her house at Thaxted, Essex. Edward III surprisingly allowed the marriage. The victory was in 1339 at Cadsant in Flanders. He was created Earl of Stafford in 1351 (STAFFS pp7,9,11); **'Seneschal of Gascony'** Sir Richard de Stafford, younger son of Edmund (d1308); **89th & 92nd Lord Chancellor of England** Edmund Stafford (1344-1419), 2nd son of Sir Richard. He served 1396-99, 1401-03; he was Bishop of Exeter; **first holder of the office of Keeper of the Privy Seal and Lord Chancellor to be styled 'Lord Chancellor' (102nd Lord Chancellor of England), 79th Archbishop of Canterbury** John Stafford (b c1385), a cousin of the main line of the family, serving as Lord Chancellor 1432-50; and as archbishop of Canterbury 1443-52 (STAFFS p14); **ceremonial carver at the coronation of Richard II** Hugh Stafford (1342-86), son of Ralph (d1372), 2nd Earl of Stafford (STAFFS p14); **'one of the richest and most powerful landowners in England' 1438, 'premier duke of England'** Humphrey Stafford (1402-60), great grandson of Ralph (d1372), 6th Earl of Stafford, 1st Duke of Buckingham, who inherited an income of £4,500 (gross) p.a., in addition to that of £1,500 p.a. from his father (STAFFS p19); **first Stafford who was Lord High Constable of England, the 'most untrue creature living'** Henry Stafford (1455-83), grandson of Humphrey (d1460), inherited 1460. 2nd Duke of Buckingham. This hereditary title was granted as a reward for services to Richard III, as well as inherited through the Bohun family. Later, he betrayed Richard III who accused him of being the 'most untrue creature living' (STAFFS p31).

The STAFFORD who was: **last (hereditary) High Constable of Eng-**

land Edward Stafford (1478-1521), 3rd Duke of Buckingham, forfeited Stafford Castle on his execution 1521; future Lord High Constables being appointed for the day of the coronation (The Guinness Book of Lasts. Christopher Slee. 1994. p142); **'one of the best educated members of the Tudor peerage'** Henry Stafford (1501-63), 1st Baron Stafford, son of Edward (d1521), having attended both Oxford and Cambridge Universities, and enrolled at Gray's Inn, mastering French and Latin completely (STAFFS p50); **estranged wife of 3rd Duke of Norfolk** Elizabeth Stafford, daughter of Edward (d1521) (STAFFS p50); **one of the first Englishmen to do the Grand Tour of Europe** Thomas Stafford (1531-57), a younger son of Henry (d1563) (STAFFS pp52-53); **Mistress of the Robes to Elizabeth I** Dorothy Stafford, daughter of Henry (d1563) (STAFFS p53); **a 'lewd, miscontented, young person'** William Stafford (1554-1612), son of Dorothy. He upset the Earl of Leicester, Elizabeth I's favourite, and thus was so considered at court. He was onetime prisoner in the Tower of London (STAFFS pp53-54); **Ambassador to France** Sir Edward Stafford, serving 1583-90, brother of William (d1612). He was a suspected spy (STAFFS p54); **presided over the trial of Mary Queen of Scots** Edward Stafford (1535/6-1603), 3rd Baron Stafford, son of Henry (d1563), at Fotheringhay in Oct 1586, along with 23 other nobles (STAFFS p54); **'not a man beloved, especially by his own family', beheaded for alleged involvement in the Popish Plot, martyred, 'last Catholic Englishman to die for his faith'** William Howard (1621-80), 1st Baron and Viscount Stafford, who married the Stafford heiress, Mary. He ascended the scaffold on Tower Hill on Dec 29 1680, and was granted the title 'Blessed' in 1929 by Pope Pius XI (Blessed William Howard High School, Stafford, is named after him). The first claim is by John Evelyn, diarist (STAFFS pp66,75), the second by Staffordshire Advertiser & Chronicle May 16 1963 p6 (*see illustration above*); **the Countess of Stafford created in her own right** Mary, heiress of Edward (d1625), 5th Baron Stafford, wife of William Howard (d1680), created 1688; **with James II in exile, 1st Earl of Stafford** Henry (1647-1719), son of Mary & William Howard (d1680). He was at James II's death bed and a witness to his will (STAFFS pp75il,76); **sold the Arundel Collection** William (1690-1734), 2nd Earl, son of Henry (d1719). He inherited the collection from Countess Aletheia and it was preserved at Stafford House, London (STAFFS p77); **last Earl of Stafford** John Paul (1700-62), 4th Earl Stafford, younger brother of William (d1734), 2nd Earl; **were 'Blue Nuns' in Paris** Louisa and Xaveria, younger sisters of William (d1734), and Anastasia and Anne younger daughters of John Paul (d1762), 4th Earl. 'Blue Nuns' were the Order of the Immaculate Conception, and so called because of the colour of their habits (STAFFS p77); **'The Poet', "a mighty delicate gentleman"** Fanny Burney on Edward Jerningham (1737-1812), poet, son of Mary Plowden, granddaughter of Henry (d1719), 1st Earl Stafford. He apparently became an Anglican after witnessing the coronation of George III (1761), and was on intimate terms with the later George IV, cataloguing his library at Brighton Pavilion. Socialite and effeminate;

he never married (STAFFS pp85il,86); **reclaimed the Stafford barony, had Stafford Castle rebuilt as a folly** Sir George William Stafford-Jerningham (1771-1851), grandson of Mary Plowden. Fought and beat a rival claimant for the Stafford barony, Richard Stafford Cooke, 1825, becoming 8th Baron Stafford and 2nd Viscount Stafford, assuming the surname Stafford-Jerningham 1826; **designed Stafford Castle** Edward 'Ned' Jerningham (1774-1822), amateur architect, younger brother of Sir George (d1851) (STAFFS p94); **'the most beautiful in person, the most powerful in mind, the most commanding, graceful and attractive in manners'** Frances (nee Sulyard) (d1832), wife of Sir George (d1851), 8th Baron (STAFFS p99il); **'very amiable, good-looking and gentlemanlike'** Edward Stafford-Jerningham (1804-49), younger son of Sir George (d1851), according to Mrs Fitzherbert, 'wife' of George IV, whose niece (and adopted daughter from age six) Marianne Smythe, he married (STAFFS p123il); **declared insane** Augustus Stafford-Jerningham (1830-92), 9th Baron Stafford, son of Edward (d1849) (STAFFS p123).

5. People...

First person known to have drawn longitudinal lines on an atlas globe for the guidance of ships at sea William Perkins (d1774) of Forebridge House, Lichfield Road (SAC pp123p,124). **Nobel Prize winner for physics 1933** Dr Paul Adrien Maurice Dirac (b1903), Lucasian Professor of Mathematics at Cambridge University, for research into atomic theory. He was son of Mons Charles Dirac, of Switzerland, French master at King Edward VI School, Stafford, to c1904 (SA Jan 6 1934 p6 col 4). **2nd in LMSR signalling exam 1933** F Savage of St Leonard's Ave, Forebridge; first place went to a Wakefield signalman with a score of 97% (SA Jan 20 1934 p6). **Miss Staffordshire 1939** Miss Mary Mitchell, Miss English Electric Company 1939; she was the 7th Miss Staffordshire ever. **Miss Staffordshire 1952** Miss Maureen Cave, aged 17, Miss English Electric 1952; she was the 14th Miss Staffordshire ever (Stafford Pageant: The Exciting Innovative Years 1901-1952. Gordon Henry Loach. 2007). **Miss England 1973 regional winner** Sue Rutty of Nelson Way, Rising Brook (E&S Feb 22 2003 p8). **Photographed next to the tallest woman in the world** Joyce Lake of St John's Road, Rowley Bank, when on holiday in 1980 she met Sandy Allen, 25, at a museum in San Francisco (SN Aug 22 1980 p11p). **Carol-Ann Duffy's first play performed** The poet who attended Stafford Girls' High School, and resided at Poplar Way, Rising Brook, made her playwright debut with 'Take My Husband' at the Playhouse Theatre, Liverpool, 1982 (SN Dec 27 2007 p6). **Castle Church's WW1 hero** Sgt Percy Powell, of the Royal Army Medical Corps (attached 80th Field Ambulance), of 126 Newport Road, who achieved the double honour of the Greek Military Cross (3rd class), awarded for gallantry and distinguished service in Salonica, by the King of the Hellenes 1919, and the Serbian Silver Medal for zealous service, awarded by the King of Serbia 1920 (SA Jan 31 1920 p5p). **Castle Church's WW2 hero** Capt CE Morgan, son of C Morgan of Moss Pit Lodge. In Nov 1940 he took command of HMS Valiant. On the night of March 28 1941 Valiant discovered the strong Italian fleet lying 100 miles off Cape Matapan, Greece. The naval engagement that followed has been described as 'The most sweeping British Naval victory since Trafalgar'. HMS Valiant, Warspite and Barnham blasted and sunk in 20 minutes three Italian cruisers, two destroyers and seriously damaged several warships, including the battleship Vittorio Veneto. The gallantry of Capt Morgan, DSO, and searchlight operator Midshipman Prince Philip of Greece, was offically recognised by a mention in despatches. Later Morgan was raised to the rank of Admiral (Stafford At War. an SN publication. 1995. p8). **Youngest major in the WRAC (TA) 1951** Possibly Miss Lucy Elizabeth Jupp of Moss Pit Lodge, aged 27, on being promoted to command in the women's territorials No. 323 (Staffs) Battalion WRAC. The normal age for majors is 35 (SA July 13 1951 p1p). **Founder of the MG Octogan Car Club** Harry Crutchley (1942-2008) of Queensville Ave, Queensville, in 1969 for fans of the pre-1959 MG models (SN March 20 2008 p3pc). **First person in UK to be made subject of an interim ASBO** (Anti-Social Behaviour Order) Natasha Marshall (b1988) of Silkmore after she breached a full ASBO which was in preparation, for a catalogue of harassment, abuse and violence against neighbours on Silkmore estate (ES Feb 21 2003 p14). **Staffordshire's 1st= fatality of the Iraq War** Trooper David Clarke, 19, of Bedworth Ave, Littleworth killed in 'friendly fire' in Basra on March 24 2003. Former Weston Road High School pupil, in the Queen's Royal Lancers. Cpl Allbut of Stoke-on-Trent was also killed in the same Challenger 2 tank (E&S March 26 2003 pp1,7. March 20 2008 p24).

Castle Church's villain Charles Moore, Irish labourer and pathological liar, who casually worked at Ashflats farm. Believing the farmer John Blackburn, aged 78, a miser who hid his wealth there, Moore and accomplices broke in and murdered him and his wife, Jane, aged 73, on Oct 24 1852. They gained a mere five shillings - hence the case has been called the Five Shillings Murder. There was no appeal for Moore, as for another accomplice, and he was hung. **Castle Church's saddest** Christine Heffernam, of Merrivale Road, Silkmore, and Louis Stevens of St Peter's Gardens, Rickerscote, both aged 9, who lost their lives when their train, dubbed the 'Lollipop Special', derailed at Cheadle Hulme Station on May 28 1964. They were part of a party of 230 children from four schools (at Stone, Gnosall, Seighford and Stafford) on their way to York on a day trip. The inquiry declared the train was going too fast (SA & Chron May 28 1964 p1. June 4 1964 pp10-11ps. Feb 11 1965 p1). **Castle Church's kindest** Dorothy Bridgeman (d1697), by will dated 1694, made provision to raise money to educate poor children in Forebridge township. She was the former wife of George Cradock (d1643) of Caverswall Castle and Brocton Hall, Brocton (VCH vol 5 pp58-59). **Castle Church's poorest** The almshouse mentioned in parish accounts in 1755 may have been a poorhouse. There was a fire there in 1759, and it was thatched in 1760. A workhouse is mentioned in 1775 (SRO D946/16), and stood in Forebridge township on the corner of Lichfield Road and White Lion Street (VCH vol 6 p231). From 1837 the poor were housed at Stafford Union workhouse at Marston. **Castle Church's earliest recorded will** Belongs to Ranulph Croxton, and is dated Oct 4 1550. **First person in the parish register** Joyse, daughter of John Norris and Annes, baptised Dec 28 1568. **Choicest quote** Godfrey Sittig on archaeological excavations at Stafford Castle in the Staffordshire Magazine Nov 1979 writes 'Over the years many people have wondered and thought about the treasures that may lie hidden and buried under all that rubble around the castle or under the trees surrounding it. Tales of an underground passage leading into town (Stafford) have been circulating for years. Unfortunately, no two people seem to agree on the site of its termination in the town, and so far no trace of it has been found at the castle. But who knows what might be discovered yet?'

6. Trade...

Patentee for steering gear relating to ships Mr H Wright formerly of Ferndale, Lichfield Road, Stafford, in 1908 with tiller-rods operated by hydraulic rams supplied with fluid under pressure by a single pump, operated by a rotary motor (SA June 27 1908 p4 col 5). **Largest locomotives for metre-gauge lines 1935** Amongst a few others, those produced for tender in 1935 by Messrs WG Bagnall Ltd of Castle Engine Works, for San-Paulo Parana Plantations, Ltd, Santos, South America, weighing in working order 95 and half tons, designed to haul trains of 400 to 500 tons at 15mph on grades of 1 in 55 (SA Dec 7 1935 p7p). **Bagnall's first diesel locomotive built** 0-6-0 type, finished Jan 23 1951, designed for shunting and weighing 55 tons, one of four ordered by the Steel Company of South Wales, for use at their new steel works (the biggest in Europe) near Port Talbot (SA Jan 27 1951 p5 cols 5-6). **First Stafford company to completely computerise their business** Jen Shoes (formerly RT Jennings & Son) shoe distributors, Newport Road, 1972 (SN May 18 2006 p13). **'one of the greatest concerns of its kind in the world'** Dr Reeve, Bishop of Lichfield, on the English Electric Company, Lichfield Road, Forebridge, on the death of its chairman Lord Nelson in 1962 (SA & Chron July 26 1962 p10 cols 7-8). **Heaviest electrical load transported in the country by 1959** Probably the stator for the first 200,000 kw, 3,000 r.p.m. turbo-generators for the High Marnham power station of the Central Electricity Generating Board, transported from English Electricity Company, where it was made, on May 30 1959 (SA & Chron June 4 1959 p7 cols 4-5).

7. Sport...

Winner of South Africa's Dalrymple and Hollins Cups 1903, Grand Aggregate and Rifle Championship of London and Middlesex 1912, Bisley King's Prize (equally) 1934 (all marksmanship) Capt J Sedgewick, MC, of Rising Brook, originally of Durham, tieing in 1934 with Capt JA Barlow of W Yorks Regt with a score of 288, only one point below the record score in the competition under the then current conditions (SA July 28 1934 p5p). **Britain's strongest man 1913** Edward Aston, claimed he was. On Dec 9 1913 he visited Siemens' Institute (part of Siemens Bros. Dynamo Works Ltd, later English Electric, Lichfield Road, Forebridge) to give a lecture on the value of systematic course of physical culture, and subsequently performed feats of strength (SA Dec 13 1913 p6 col 5). **Bowler who beat the President of the Staffordshire Bowling Association on his own green** TS Bailey of Lichfield Road, Stafford, president of the Stafford Bowling League, when he defeated AH Paulton in 1920 at Wolverhampton by 21 points to 19 (SA July 17 1920 p9p). **Northern Command Middleweight Champion 1941** Stanley Woodward (b1920), former pupil of Rickerscote and St Leonard's Schools. In WW2 he was awarded the Military Medal and bar for bravery as a non-commissioned officer in the 3rd Tank Regt in action at Bras, Normandy in the Liberation of France, 1944 (Stafford At War. SN publication. 1995 p11p). **WRAF Singles Tennis champion 1949, 1950, 1951, 1952, 1953, 1954** Flight-Officer Mrs Judy Wallace of the Stafford Castle Tennis Club, and the Staffordshire women's tennis team; selected to play in the All-England championships at Wimbledon in 1954 (SA Aug 13 1954 p3p).

Midlands Mile Champion 1954, AAA Championships Mile event 1954 2nd, Great Britain Team 'C' in the the world 4x1500 metres record 1954 Mike Whittaker (b1934) of West Way, Highfields, an English Electric Co Ltd employee. Youngest of the Whittaker brothers, atheletes (see Berkswich), a third brother, Doug, was also of Stafford AC; the three took first three places in a mile race at Aldersley Stadium, Wolverhampton, in 1961 (SA & Chron April 20 1961 p14 col 9). In Midlands Mile 1954 Mike set a new record of 4 mins, 13.6 secs; in the AAA Championships Mile event he achieved the first time anyone had bettered 4 mins, 10 secs to qualify for the final (SA Sept 10 1954 p3. SA & Chron Jan 28 1960 p14p). **First Staffordian to reach the final of the British chess championship** Tony Sutton of 28 Newport Road, Stafford, aged 23, in 1963 (SA & Chron June 27 1963 p13 col 6). **Stafford Town FC's first game** When they played away to Rushall Olympic on Saturday Aug 24 1963 in the County League championship. They drew 0-0. The club were formerly Rickerscote FC, changing their name for the 1963-64 season (SA & Chron Aug 8 1963 p15. Aug 29 1963 p14). **Staffordshire Lawn Tennis Association premier division winners 1963** Stafford Lawn Tennis Club (men's team - JE Barresclough, B Store, FJ Sandy, and JD McColl), Newport Road, Stafford. This was the first time the club men had won this title (SA & Chron Oct 3 1963 p18). **Stafford's first Festival of Sport** Sunday Aug 21 1977 at Rowley Park, organised by the Stafford Sports Advisory Council; guest of honour was David Morgan, aged 13, the youngest person to swim the Channel (SN Aug 26 1977 p46). **Midland Pool Champion 1980** Andrew Wadham, aged 26 or 28, of Queenville (SN May 23 1980 p64p). **Staffordian of the past 100 years, St George's Hero 2007, 'The Running Paramedic'** Ray Edensor of Castlefields, 49, charity fund-raiser in long distance runs, running 26 marathons in 26 days, and 260 miles in a decontamination suite. In 2006 he was voted by Staffordshire Newsletter readers 'Staffordian of the past 100 years' to celebrate 100 years of the newspaper. In 2007 he was picked as one of the five heroes for the St George's Heroes award, instigated by the English Beef and Lamb Executive for English heroes (BBC 1 Midlands Today 21 March 2007) (SN March 22 2007 p19. April 19 2007 p12pc).

8. The area...

Castle Church is the **county's 70th largest parish**, consisting of 3,933 acres; **3rd closest parish to the county town**, 0.2m W; extremist length 3.4m; **extremist width** 3.5m. **Parish's chief settlement** Castle Church, a hamlet, now entirely engulfed by some of the wealthiest and poorest Stafford suburbs. **Geology** MOST - Keuper Red Marls; SOW and Penk basins - Alluvium; NE TIP - Bunter. **Highest point** Stafford Castle at 472 feet. **Lowest point** 239 feet by the Sow below Kingston Hill. **Very rare plant** Astragalus Glycyhyllus (Wild Licorice) found growing by roadside near St Austin RC chapel, Forebridge (SHOS vol 1 part 1 p99). Castle Church was **87th most-populated Staffordshire parish in 1801** with 563 people; **90th in 1811** with 566; **62nd in 1821** with 1,118; **55th in 1831** with 1,374; **59th in 1841** with 1,484; **42nd in 1851** with 2,315; **35th in 1861** with 3,362; **28th in 1871** with 4,746; **26th in 1881** with 5,923; **27th in 1891** with 6,384; **30th in 1901** with 6,455.

SUBJECT INDEX *Ch to Co*

*Chartley
Wild Cattle
in front of
Chartley
Castle.*

Chartley Holme
1.Did you know that...

Chartley Holme's top folklore The families who have held Chartley have believed a black calf born in the herd of Chartley Wild Cattle portends a death in the family, or, and, some disaster will befall them. The first-known such case was when a black calf was born prior to Robert de Ferrers' defeat at the battle of Chesterfield in 1266. **Rare breed of cattle** The Chartley Wild Cattle, the descendants of an indigenous breed who once roamed Chartley Park. The **name Chartley first appears** in Domesday Book, 1086; 1586 for Chartley Holme. **Parish's chief settlement** None, but Chartley Hall and Castle (transferred at some point from Stowe to be exempt from rates). **What Chartley Holme is famous for** Chartley Castle, and Chartley Old Hall, the seat of the Devereuxs who have famous associations with Elizabeth I. As well as being the hunting ground of Mary, Queen of Scots during her imprisonment at Chartley Old Hall. **One of the most extraordinary legal actions on record** According to Masefield was the case of breach of promise heard at Westminster Hall, 1846, between plaintiff, Mary Elizabeth Smith, and defendant, Rt Hon Washington Sewallis Shirley (1822-1859), Earl Ferrers, owner of Chartley. The judge found the plaintiff's ardent love-letters purporting to be by Shirley to be fabrications, possibly written by her, and dismissed the case (SA Feb 21 1846 pp2,4) (LGS p108). **Geology** Entirely Keuper Red Marls. **Highest point** 564 feet in the NE. **Lowest point** 312 feet at Chartley Hall. Chartley Holme is the **county's 126th largest parish** (extra-parochial), consisting of 1,707 acres; **31st closest parish to the county town**, 5.8m ENE; **extremist length** 1.9m; **extremist width** 1.8m. Chartley Holme was **164th most-populated Staffordshire parish in 1801** with 9 people; **163rd= in 1811** with 9; **164th= in 1821** with 11; **164th in 1831** with 9; **148th in 1841** with 71; **153rd in 1851** with 29; **153rd in 1861** with 36; **154th in 1871** with 41; **155th in 1881** with 39; **158th in 1891** with 37; **157th in 1901** with 34.

2. People...

Chartley Holme's most famous old worthy Ranulph 'de Blundeville' (c1172-1232). He succeeded as 6th Earl of Chester in 1180. Builder of Chartley Castle in the 1220s; founder of Dieulacres Abbey at Leek, 1214; sheriff of Staffordshire 1216-22, 1223. On his death the earldom lapsed to the Crown. **First-known to be girded with a sword on his elevation to the peerage** Possibly William Ferrers (d1246) of Chartley, who was so honoured when created Earl of Derby in 1199 by his great friend King John (UTR p38). **Elizabeth I's favourite, 29th Lord Lieutenant of Ireland 1599** Robert Devereux, 2nd Earl of Essex of Chartley Old Hall. He was beheaded near the Tower on Feb 24 1601 (SOSH p187) (Wikipedia). **'the little western flower'** Lettice (nee) Knollys (d1634) wife of Walter Devereux (d1576), and on whom 'the bolt of cupid fell' as described in Shakespeare's 'Midsummer Night's Dream. **Most prolific peer of all time** Sir Robert Shirley (1650-1717), 1st Earl Ferrers, owner of Chartley. By his first wife he had 17 children (10 sons and seven daughters), and by his second wife he had 10 children (five sons and five daughter), making a total of 27 legitimate children; additionally he fathered 30 illegitimate children (GBR 1970 p181). **Last English nobleman to be hanged as a felon** Lawrence Shirley (1720-60), 3rd Earl of Ferrers, for the murder of his steward, a man named Johnson (So you think you know? Stafford. A quiz & miscellany. Francis Frith Collection. 2005. p13). **First father and son to receive V.Cs.** Possibly Major-General Sir Walter Congreve (b1862) of Chartley Hall from 1904, and his son William La Touche Congreve (1891-1916) (newspaper cutting from after 1925 in WSL D323/41/80, Horne's Scrapbook, No. 2 after p210). The latter could be claimed certainly as **Chartley's hero**. In WW1 he received the M.C. and got the D.S.O. early in 1916 for the single-handed capture of 72 Germans. For his gallant conduct in the Battle of the Somme on July 20 1916, only seven weeks after his marriage, he received the V.C.. His heroism is recalled on his memorial in Stowe-by-Chartley church (see). **Staffordshire's highest ranking officer of WW1** Major-General Sir Walter Congreve (b1862), who had by late 1915 commanded the 18th Brigade at the Aisne, and was then commanding a Division. The county's other Major-General was Sir Philip Chetwode of Oakley Hall, Mucklestone (CL Nov 13 1915 p645). **Croix de Guerre medalist** Lady Congreve, wife of Capt WN Congreve of Chartley Hall (who won a V.C. for bravery at Colenso, South Africa), for courage and coolness working in a hospital near Nancy, France, under constant enemy plane bombardment (SA Aug 24 1918 p3 col 5p). **Chartley's poorest** From 1858 the poor could be housed at Stafford Union workhouse at Marston. **Choicest quote** John Leland in The Itinerary, c1540, wrote 'Ther is a mighty large parke. The olde castel is now yn ruine;'

SUBJECT INDEX *Co to Da*

*The Salem
Chapel, High
Street, Cheslyn
Hay, built 1855.*

Cheslyn Hay
1. Did you know that...

Cheslyn Hay's top folklore There is a local legend of a Saxon cemetery at Cheslyn Hay. **What Cheslyn Hay is famous for** The infamy of those original squatters. **Church** At Cheslyn Hay is St Peter, Pinfold Lane, opened c1950 (VCH vol 5 p102). **'one of the last places in England where the custom (of sun wheels) was observed'** Wyrley Bank, alias Cheslyn Hay, according to Jon Raven in his 'The Folklore of Staffordshire' (1978). The custom, common in the mid C18, was observed on Midsummer Eve when the village's young people would make hoops, which were entwined with hay and twigs and lit from the 'bon' fires before rolling down a hill. At Wyrley Bank it consisted of first taking a wheel from a cart to the top of Wyrley Bank and then letting it run down the hill (The Bygone Days of Cheslyn Hay. Roland Ridgway. 2002. p153). **First Staffordshire parish to discuss any kind of WW1 memorial** Cheslyn Hay parish council plans to erect a memorial to those lost in WW1 are the earliest recorded in the Staffordshire Advertiser. It met on Nov 13 1918 to discuss several options - a monument, enclosed, and surrounded with scrubs, a public nursing scheme, public library, and reading rooms, and baths (SA Nov 16 1918 p7 col 2).

2. People...

Cheslyn Hay's most famous old worthies, kindest The Hawkins family are claimed as the builders of modern Cheslyn Hay. Arnold Hawkins had The Park built in the Italianate villa style in Cross Street in 1853, possibly commissioning an Italian artist to design it (CAd May 13 1983 pS3). Joseph Hawkins, coalmaster, was working the Old Coppice Colliery, Cheslyn Hay, by 1872. Thomas A Hawkins presented the fire station in Station Street in 1908 (VCH vol 5 p101). **Cheslyn Hay's villain** Nathaniel (surname unknown), who murdered his parents, or some say his parents-in-law, and wife to gain control of their small estate, was often seen at Cheslyn Hay. He was charged in March 1674-5 and refused to plead. He was executed by being pressed to death by heavy weights, a form of punishment abolished in 1772. **Cheslyn Hay's villainess** Sarah Baker, pit lass, aged 24, of Wyrley Bank, convicted at the Summer Assizes 1853 of murdering her Charles Baker, illegitimate infant, aged about 2, Charles, at Pelsall, on June 12 1853; she had just been in Brewood workhouse (SA July 23 1853 p6). **She lost four husbands in 33 years** Hannah Perry (1877-1966), of Pinfold Lane, Cheslyn Hay. In Jan 1898 she married a young miner Alfred Jenkins. He died of peritonitis on Jan 21. In 1899 she married Bill Stanley, another miner. In 1908 he emigrated to America, leaving her with their two children. Believing herself to be widowed in 1912 she married another miner, Fred Boucher, who was killed on the Somme in 1916. With the return of Bill Stanley after WW1 she 'renewed' her marriage. Bill died of blood poisoning in 1931. Hannah never married again, moving to be close to her sons in the Bloxwich, Rushall areas (Cheslyn Hay: The Golden Years. Trevor McFarlane. 2007 pp60-61ps). **'The Girl with the Tractor'** Patricia Henshaw, daughter of Leslie Hawkins of Cheslyn House in Cross Street, Cheslyn Hay. She was a debutante in the 1938 season; joined the Land Army in WW2 and had the honour of appearing as 'The Girl With The Tractor' on the front cover of 'Picture Post' June 21 1941 (Glimpses of Old Cheslyn Hay & Local Areas. Trevor McFarlane. 2006. p44ps). **One of the first aldermen of South Staffordshire District** Bill Craddock, Cannock Rural District councillor 1955-74, Cheslyn Hay South councillor for South Staffordshire District 1974-2007, made one of the three first honorary aldermen of this local authority in 2007 (SLM Aug 2007 p27pc). **Strange but true!** Shirley Hall of New Horse Road, Cheslyn Hay, gave birth to her daughter Samantha at exactly the same time, place and day as her own birth 27 years earlier (1.06pm, Jan 4 1957, New Cross Hospital, Wolverhampton), in 1984 (E&S Jan 5 1984 p1p) (Chase Post Jan 12 1984 p1p). **Cheslyn Hay's poorest** From 1836 Cheslyn Hay was in Penkridge Union, renamed Cannock Union from 1870s. From 1872 the poor would have been housed at the new Union workhouse on Wolverhampton road, Cannock (VCH vol 5 p52). **Choicest quote** Lord Hatherton of Teddesley Hall noted in his diary, April 24 1840, 'walked with Mr Gilpin and Mr Bright to Cheslyn Hay, that part called Wyrley Bank, formerly the most disreputable place in the neighbourhood, now a village with a few reputable shops in it.'

3. The area...

Cheslyn Hay's is the **county's 147th largest parish** (extra parochial), consisting of 819 acres; **54th= closest parish to the county town**, 9.3m S; **extremist length** 1.5m, making it **22nd= shortest parish in the county**; **extremist width** 1.5m, making it **26th narrowest parish in the county**. The **name Cheslyn Hay first appears** in 1236. **Parish's chief settlement** Cheslyn Hay, a peculiar, large village which evolved out of a roguish squatters' settlement. **Geology** E - Upper Coal Measures; central S intrusion - Permian; W - Bunter. **Highest point** 508 feet S of Cheslyn Hay village. **Lowest point** 367 feet at Wedge's Mills. Cheslyn Hay was **102nd most-populated Staffordshire parish in 1801** with 443 people;

101st in 1811 with 486; **102nd in 1821** with 548; **93rd in 1831** with 648; **84th in 1841** with 774; **81st= in 1851** with 876; **70th in 1861** with 1,177; **64th in 1871** with 1,431; **59th in 1881** with 1,799; **55th in 1891** with 2066; **48th in 1901** with 2,560.

3. Sport...

British Schools Gymnastics Championship under-13 boys pairs gold medalists 1979, under-16 boys pairs gold medalists, 1980 Stewart Wootton and Paul Thistleton of Cheslyn Hay High School. In addition, Simon Smith and Glynn Morgan of Cheslyn Hay Middle School won the under-11 boys pairs in 1979 and the under-13 boys pairs in 1980 at the same event (CAd March 23 1979 p25p. March 21 1980 p2). **First Cheslyn Hay fun run** June 1983. The first winners David Hollingmode, and Irene Gornall, were both of Great Wyrley (CAd June 10 1983 p20ps). **Warwickshire and Midland Counties champion of champions (snooker) 1984** Steve James of Cheslyn Hay WMC (CAd June 1 1984 p20p). **Para-Olympic club throwing gold medalist 1984, 25m backstroke bronze medalist 1984** Lisa Barker of Cheslyn Hay Otters (Chase Post July 19 1984 p3). Another successful Cheslyn Hay Otters member in 1984 was Vicky Dolman, aged 23, who won silver in shot put at the 4th national athletic championship for visually handicapped (CAd June 15 1984 p17). **Paralympic Games Shotput 5th 2005** Martin Crutchley of Westnourne Ave, Cheslyn Hay, aged 25 (E&S Dec 19 2008 p17pc).

SUBJECT INDEX *Da to Du*

Church Eaton's witch reputedly moved its church.

Church Eaton
1. Did you know that...

What Church Eaton is famous for Its witch, Joan Eaton. **Most important WW2 airfield in Staffordshire** RAF Wheaton Aston at Little Onn, along with that of Lichfield. It was an Advanced Flying Unit, part of 21 Group in the parent station of RAF Perton and RAF Tattenhall. Established 1941, closed 1947 (Stafford At War. a SN publication. 1995. p2). **The most advanced Poultry Progeny Testing Station in the country** Opened on former Wheaton Aston airfield Feb 28 1957, serving farmers in the West Midlands, South-West England, and Wales. It had 220 breeding houses, 800 rearing folds, 10 deep litter houses, each 105 feet long and 30 feet wide, 5 brooder houses and 100 sets of three-tier nursery brooders. It was considered more advanced than the Ministry of Agriculture's other two stations, which opened at the same time (SA & Chron March 7 1957 p5ps). **Unique derivation for a surname** Onn will be from Onn in this parish (PDS). **'one of the smallest theatres in the country'** In the Royal Oak Inn, Church Eaton, which holds an annual comedy festival (BBC Stoke & Staffordshire Where I Live website, 2006). **Wood Eaton Hatherton, Wood Eaton Bounder, Wood Eaton Rock, Wood Eaton Blaze, Wood Eaton Regent II, Wood Eaton Monarch, Wood Eaton Warrior, Wood Eaton Kingmaker, Wood Eaton Fashion** Were Shire stallions (save Wood Eaton Fashion, a dam) in the Wood Eaton and Blithford Studs of CE Morris-Eyton of Wood Eaton Manor advertised in Staffordshire Advertiser to pregnate local mares; Wood Eaton Kingmaker won the 1st West Staffs Show 1914; the first two were foaled in the C19; the second in 1902; the third in 1905; the others, save Wood Eaton Fashion, were all foaled in 1915 (SA April 15 1899 p8 col 7. May 16 1908 p8 col 7. May 18 1918 p2). **Staffordshire Best Kept Village winner (medium village category) 1979, 1981, Stafford District winner (small village category) 2008** Church Eaton.

2. Church...

At Church Eaton is St Editha, **one of two such county dedications** (of AP churches); **23rd= oldest county church** dating from the C12 or roughly 1150. **Strange but true!** In 1959, after an inspection by steeplejacks, the spire was found to be over six inches out of alignment. The

Rectory, Preb HW Jones, suspected as much (SN Sept 12 1959 p9p). **Church Eaton's top folklore** The legend of local witch, Joan Eaton, who prevented a church being built by day at Little Onn by repeatedly removing the stones at night to Church Eaton. The builders gave up and the church was built at Church Eaton. She reputedly turned the milk of the Dun Cow of Red House Farm dry and put the cow and calf footprints on the stone by Red House Farm. Tradition has her burnt at the stake at Joan Eaton's Cross, a small triangular green at the fork of two lanes south west of the village of Church Eaton.

3. People...

Church Eaton's most famous old worthy, 41st Bishop of Durham William James (1542-1617), son of John James of Little Onn, born Sandbach, Ches, 1606-1617 (DNB). **Church Eaton's villain** Robert Vernon, aged 16, but looked 20, guilty of 'feloniously assaulting and ravishing Eliza Taylor of Little Onn, 'an interesting looking girl' aged 14, on July 7 1839 on the canal towpath near her home. During the trial the prisoner had 'a most unintelligent and stupid expression of countenance, and seemed to regard the proceedings against him on this capital charge with perfect indifference.' A judgement of death was recorded, but the sentence was one of transportation for life (SA July 27 1839 p4 col 4). **'one of the few girls in England to plough with a team of horses' 1946** Ruby Carrington, aged 18 of Aquamoor, 'farm boy' for Gordon Lloyd of Manor Farm, Church Eaton. She opted to plough using a horse (SA Jan 25 1947 p2p). **Church Eaton's saddest** Cadet Sergeant Geoffrey Harold Lloyd, aged 17, of Codsall Road, Tettenhall, killed practising a forced landing approaching Wheaton Aston aerodrome when his Miles Hawk nosed-dived into the ground on Feb 26 1952. Prior to the crash the plane had circled Red House Farm for about half an hour. Lloyd had been in the Air Training Corps for about 18 months, and had been on a flight to Singapore and back. A verdict of accidental death was returned, assuming the young pilot had got into an unintentional spin and was too low to get out of it (SA March 6 1953 p6p). **Most famous person at Wheaton Aston Polish Resettlement Camp** Probably Zdzislaw Luszowicz, born Cracov 1914, Polish Resistance agent with Special Operations Executive; parachuted into Poland 1944; betrayed to the Russians during their advance in Poland; interned and interrogated, though did not break; escaped to the West. Received the King's Medal for Courage in the Cause of Freedom. Wheaton Aston aerodrome at Little Onn served as a transit depot for the Polish Resettlement Corps from 1947. In 1954 with the end of the National Assistance Board the Camp became effectively a British-Polish housing estate, many of the former prefab huts converted to homes. It closed in 1965. Luszowicz was here in the early 1950s. In 1961 he was appointed an inspector by Staffs CC Education Committee for their Saturday children's classes there, and at the other **'Little Poland'** camps of Seighford and Stafford. Meanwhile, or subsequently he lived at Stafford and taught at Rising Brook High School (SA & Chron Oct 26 1961 p1 cols 2-3) (Stafford At War. a SN publication.

1995. p18p). **Only female in British Isles awarded the Polish Gold Badge of Honour by 1960** Mrs Bolechowski in 1960, Scottish wife of chairman of the Polish Ex-combatants Association, for her work for the Polish community in the Stafford area, where she had lived since 1937. Notably, helping to resettle Free Polish forces at the Polish camps at Seighford and Little Onn (SA & Chron Nov 17 1960 p8). **'The Grand Old Man of Church Eaton' 1961** Morley Winter Osbourne (b1866), former jockey who had ridden many famous horses. His favourite horse was 'Red Walker', which he had ridden for seven years; another was 'Skedaddle' which he rode to victory in a steeplechase in France (SA & Chron Sept 28 1961 p11 col 1). **Shelsley Walsh National Hill Climb record breaker (in Classic cars 1945-68 category)** Richard Dodkins of Church Eaton in 1980 when he set a new reocrd clipping 1.19 seconds off the old record, driving a Ginetta G12 car (SN July 11 1980 p60p). **Bristol Gold Cup winner 2006** Tom Cox, 18, of Manor Farm, Marston, with his Tomcroft Suffolk flock of sheep; he is only the 2nd Midlander to win in the history of the Cup (SN Nov 2 2006 p80pc) (BBC 1 Midlands Today. Nov 2 2006). **Church Eaton's kindest** Thomas Blake, c1685, and Rev Walter Jennings, c1723, rector of Church Eaton, both provided Sunday bread doles for the poor. Lucretia Astley, 1669, Henry Crockett, c1730, Ann Wright (d1855) have also given to the poor of Church Eaton (VCH vol 4 p103). **Church Eaton's poorest** Overseers of the poor were paying the rent for a poorhouse by 1757. In 1791 a public meeting was held at the workhouse to establish rules for the workhouse. It was ordered that William Bettelley of Wood Eaton be Governor. A poor stranger died at Marston in 1781-82 (SRO D3377/48). Apparently, the parish workhouse erected c1798 on land in Wood Eaton, was later converted into a school (VCH vol 4 p103) (SN Nov 29 1958 p14). From 1836 Church Eaton was in Penkridge Union, renamed Cannock Union from 1870s. From 1872 the poor would have been housed at the new Union workhouse on Wolverhampton road, Cannock. **First person in the parish register** Joane daughter of John Adames and Thomasin, his wife, baptised Nov 5 1538. **Choicest quote** Church Eaton Parish Magazine for May 1925 remembered to its readers parish benefactress Miss Edith Lord of Malvern, a relative of the Wyley family, former residents of High Onn House with whom she had lived for some time 'Some of the senior members of the choir will, although they did not know Miss Lord personally, remember her for her kindness, as it was her custom for many years, even after she had left Church Eaton, to send each member a scarf or handkerchief each Christmas, and these were usually handed out after the morning service on Christmas Day.'

4. The area...

Church Eaton is the **county's 61st largest parish**, consisting of 4,283 acres; **29th closest parish to the county town**, 5.4m SW; extremist length 3.7m; extremist width 4.2m. The **name Eaton first appears** in Domesday Book, 1086; Church Eaton 1261. **Parish's chief settlement** Church Eaton, a rural roadside village. **Geology** MOST - Keuper Red Marls; ORSLOW - Keuper Sandstones. **Highest point** 435 feet a little S of High Onn. **Lowest point** 285 feet on the boundary by Church Eaton Brook. Church Eaton was **67th most-populated Staffordshire parish in 1801** with 784 people; **69th in 1811** with 804; **80th in 1821** with 829; **82nd in 1831** with 786; **89th in 1841** with 743; **93rd in 1851** with 654; **94th in 1861** with 643; **95th in 1871** with 638; **94th in 1881** with 655; **95th in 1891** with 616; **95th in 1901** with 587.

SUBJECT INDEX *Du to Ed*

Mourning the slain in medieval Colton.

Colton
1. Did you know that...

Colton's top folklore Two legendary separate incidents from medieval times with similarities. Nicholas, son of William de Colton, who became entangled with Adam, son of Hereward in 1263. In the ensuing brawl, Nicholas is said to have slain his adversary Adam, and then sought sanctuary in Colton church. Legend has it that his father was instrumental in helping him escape before the sanctuary elapsed at midnight. The second murder story is supposed to have occurred in 1271 when John, chaplain of Colton, is alleged to have murdered Christina, wife of Nicholas de Colton. This murder is said to have come about while John was interposing between Nicholas and a stranger. Could the first brawl have been over Christina? (Rugeley Times July 15 1972). **What Colton is famous for** A number of minor things - Old Bellamour Hall ruins (and that the name for the house came from Herbert Aston from Italian Bell amore, because it was finished by the benevolence or good love of his friends), medieval Colton Old Park pale, the settlement of Littlehay only linked recently with the unidentified place Colt in Domesday Book. The **name Colton first appears** in Domesday Book, 1086. **One of the finest gardens in Staffordshire 1880s-90s** Bellamour (new) Hall when in the ownership of TB Horsfall, and as depicted in simple watercolours by Gwendoline Horsfall. **Where the first banana ripened in England, where the first Lichillus Horsfalli orchid grew** At Bellamour Hall by George Morrall (1832-1918), who retired in 1910 after 50 years head gardener at the hall. The orchid is very rare, and evidentially named after the owners of the hall, the Horsfall family (CAd Feb 19 1910 p5 col 2) (Rugeley Times Sept 17 1977 p4p). **Hosts of 420th 'Gardener's Question Time' programme, Colton's first broadcast** Colton Village Produce Guild at Colton on Jan 9 1960 (Rugeley Times Jan 16 1960 p5p). **Unique bridge** Moreton Brook bridge in Colton village, because it is wide enough for vehicular traffic but still has a ford at its side (Rugeley Times April 27 1968). **Colton's biggest ever function by 1962** A two-day event on Friday and Saturday, Sept 14-15 1962, barbecue, fete, and two dances held at Bellamour Hall Farm, the home of Mr JC Price, £150 for the village hall modernisation fund (SA & Chron Sept 20 1962 p5p). **Border Collie Trust GB headquarters** Colton (Wikipedia 2006), and rescue centre (MR2 p97).

2. Church...

At Colton is St Mary, **one of 23 such county dedications** (most common dedication in the county); **55th= oldest AP county church** dating from 1220. **The most interesting thing** Three misericords installed in the chancel c1850. They were picked up in a mason's yard at Tenby. They were then, or had been, sold to the carpenter of a neighbouring village, and placed in a summerhouse, from which they were rescued by Mr Seaton. They show i) a flying wyvern, ii) two seated wyverns back to back, iii) Janus, the double-headed god (JMW p52) (CWF p194). **In the churchyard** The first illuminated gravestone was erected in 1851, so early a date to be remarked upon in The Staffordshire Advertiser. It was in the gothic decorative style with the first letter of the inscription in blood-red lettering, followed by jet black lettering upon a white background (SA April 5 1851 p4 col 5).

COLTON PEOPLE - Frederick Bonney. Mr & Mrs Henry Bradbury.

3. People...

Colton's most famous old worthy Frederick Bonney (1842-1921), photographer and anthropologist, born Rugeley, son of Thomas, Headmaster of Rugeley Grammar School, and Elizabeth Smith, part of the Pegg family of Colton. He was an early recorder of Australian aborigines 1865-81, many at the huge Momba sheep and cattle station in New South Wales. He gave a paper on aboriginal customs and practices to Anthropological Institute 1883; awarded Gold Medal for research. Resided Colton House 1882-1902; thereafter at The Hollies, Church Street, Rugeley. Buried Rugeley Cemetery (information from Bev Croft). **Colton's last May Queen** Miss Lizzie Kate Norman (later Parr) crowned 1902. The tradition of May Queen's at Colton goes back to 1885. They were chosen by ballot, all the school would set out to visit first the rectory, then Bellamour Lodge and the Reading Room, collecting enough money for a tea party at the end. The custom was revived in 1980 with the crowning of Miss Maria Wigley (Rugeley Times May 11 1974 p5p. May 17 1980. Aug 30 1980). **First Colton couple to celebrate their Golden wedding anniversary** Perhaps Mr & Mrs Bradbury (Henry, 74 and Emily, 69) of Colton, who married in St Mary's church on Oct 2 1876. In c1921 the couple moved to Abbots Bromley on Mr Bradbury's retirement (SA Oct 9 1926 p5p). **First Liberal to sit on Stafford RDC** Believed to be William Bourne, headmaster of Colton primary school, who fought Mrs Bertha Bowen (Con), one of the school managers in a by-election; the seat was previously held by Mr DHT Smith (SA & Chron Feb 28 1963 p8 col 3). **National Traction Engine Club award winner 1981** David Bradbury, of Bank Top Cottage, Hollow Lane, Colton, a silver rose bowl for services to the steam engine movement (Rugeley Times June 27 1981 p3p). **Colton's hero** Capt Stanley Upton (b1926), of the Martlin Cottages, Colton, who fought in WW1 with the 1st Worcestershire Regt, volunteered for the Commandos and took part in the D-Day invasion at Normandy. After the war he joined the Royal Military Police, and served at Triest for 4 years, before moving to Hong Kong, West Germany, Kenya, Singapore, and Cyprus (for the UN). He was also briefly a personal bodyguard for Princess Anne (Rugeley Mercury June 21 1974 photo). **Colton's villains** Rev Simon Hudde, vicar of Rugeley, Sir Walter de Ridware and many other well-known gentlemen in the locality who raided Sir John de Gresley's park at Colton in 1359 (SA Nov 5 1904 p3 col 7). **Colton's saddest** Kevin John Whittaker, aged 5, of Blakenall, Walsall, who drowned in the Trent and Mersey Canal near the turnover bridge at Bellamour in Aug 1961. His family were on a fishing trip, camping nearby (Rugeley Times Aug 12 1961). **Colton's kindest** John Spencer of Rolleston Park, Rolleston, gave 500L in 1765, in compliance of the wishes of his late brother, Francis Spencer, to a trust for Colton charities, which got used to pay a schoolteacher and keep a school. Another school for poor female children was set up in the earlier C19 out of the bequest of Thomas Webb, by will, dated 1801. In modern times there have been Alan Hurd and his wife Valerie of Colton, both members of the Salvation Army, who set off in 1975 for three years work in a leper colony in Zambia (Rugeley Times June 7 1975 p6). **Colton's poorest** In 1821 Rugeley received money Colton for board of its poor in Rugeley workhouse (SRO D6447/1/). From 1836 the poor could be housed at Lichfield Union Poor House. From 1840 this was in Trent Valley Road. It became part of St Michael's hospital. **Colton's earliest recorded will** Belongs to John Wiggan, and is dated April 1 1536. **First person in the parish register** Gulium, son of George Baggeley baptised April 7 1647. **Choicest quote** Rev FP Parker in his Some Account of Colton and of the De Wasteneys family, 1897, wrote this early 'account is chiefly taken up with details of some interest perhaps to Colton people, but of little or no importance to their neighbours, it must be pleaded that few public events can be connected with a country village, particularly when it stands retired from a main road, and when, as in the present instance, it has not been the home of any one historical family,'

4. The area...

Colton is the **county's 75th largest parish**, consisting of 3,692 acres; **36th closest parish to the county town**, 6.6m ESE; **extremist length** 3.7m; **extremist width** 3.4m. **Parish's chief settlement** Colton, an isolated, pretty village, with a long twisting main road. **Geology** MOST - Keuper Red Marls; TRENT valley and Bellamour - Alluvium. **Highest point** 384 feet on the E boundary of Colton Old Park. **Lowest point** 216 feet in the Trent valley. Colton was **89th most-populated Staffordshire parish in 1801** with 545 people; **102nd in 1811** with 484; **99th= in 1821** with 569; **92nd in 1831** with 675; **92nd in 1841** with 672; **94th in 1851** with 652; **96th in 1861** with 629; **92nd in 1871** with 657; **92nd in 1881** with 678; **92nd in 1891** with 645; **89th in 1901** with 677.

SUBJECT INDEX *El to En*

*Admiral Lord
Anson and
the garden
ornaments at
Shugborough.*

Colwich
1. Did you know that...

Colwich's top folklore There was the tale that Essex Bridge was built for Elizabeth I by Robert Devereux, but this has been surpassed by national interest in the code on the inscription of The Shepherds' Monument in Shugborough Park. The Monument is set back in a glade along a walk parallel with the river Sow. It is a mystery who built, commissioned, or designed it, but most-perplexing are what ten inscribed letters 'O-U-O-S-V-A-V-V' on it mean. The most popular interpretation was that they contained clues to the whereabouts of the Holy Grail; another is that they allude to the ephemeral nature of wealth, the sentiment of the Monument's probable builder, Thomas Anson; another that are a clue to Thomas Anson's secret lost love (info David J Robbie); another is that they don't mean anything (info Dianne Barre). **What is Colwich famous for** The Ansons and their seat Shugborough. The **name Colwich first appears** in 1166. **Oldest known glass kiln in England** In 1992 a C14 glass kiln found at Lower Furnace. Nearby, at Upper Furnace, Little Birches, Wolseley Park, was found a C16 glass kiln. One or both were taken to the Broadfield House Glass Museum at Kingswinford (ES Aug 10 1994 p11) (info MK Neal, Lander Society). **Longest and best-preserved packhorse bridge in Staffordshire** Essex Bridge over the Trent at Shugborough (Staffordshire: Shire County Guide. Peter Heaton. 1986) (Staffordshire Encyclopaedia). **'the little Dukeries'** Area on the eastern side of Cannock Chase so given for the number of estates such as Shugborough, Blithfield, Ingestre in the vicinity (Staffordshire Illustrated April 1967). **'one of the earliest experiment in rehousing in this country'** The Ring, a former circular row of cottages between Great and Little Haywood. A writer in 1816, describing the experiment said: "It does not consist, like other villages, of a number of scattered houses, but is one building, enclosing a court into which the front doors of all the cottages open" (SA & Chron Oct 11 1956 p6p) (STM March 1966 p24). **'an example of how dignified a midland brick village can be if it tries'** Great Haywood, according to Humphrey Parkington in his 'English Villages and Hamlets' (Batsford, c1934) (SA Nov 24 1934 p10 col 4). **One of Staffordshire's first 'Quality' parish Councils** Colwich Parish Council as awarded by Staffordshire's County Accreditation Panel. The scheme was launched in March 2003; there are two other Staffordshire parish councils awarded this Status, as well as one town council; there are only a hundred other councils with Quality Status in the country (info Mary Booth). **'Wolseley Duke', 'Wolseley Right Stamp'** Shire stallions toured to sire with local mares belonging to Richard Parton of Wolseley 1901 and 1904. There was also a 'Wolseley Berry' a mare (SA May 4 1901 p8. April 23 1904 p8 col 6).

Staffordshire's most extraordinary motor car accident The drowning in early March 1905 of Miss Dorothy Grace Notley, aged 21, chaperoned and travelling in a Gladiator car from South Devon with her aunt Mrs Sarah Challinor, the wife of the Hanley town clerk. The car developed a steering fault approaching a nasty 'S' bend before a bridge over the Trent at Great Haywood, it went out of control and plunged into the river. The chauffeur James Roker, jumped clear and was able to rescue Mrs Challinor, but not Miss Notley. During the excitement, steam engines pumping the river startled a horse. The horse, drawing a furniture van, bolted. The van overturned killing a Mrs Payne, the local brewer's wife. After a two-week search Miss Notley's body was found, not where everybody expected but by the village grocer further down the river, entangled in weeds near Essex Bridge. At Miss Notley's home town of Diptford, Devon, blinds were drawn in every house and hundreds attended the memorial service (SA March 18 1905) (Daily Mail Oct 2 1974 p13). **'most tricky road in England'** A mile and half of road from Colwich to Great Haywood on the then main London to Manchester road, according to Stafford RD councillors. The situation was made worse by the recent improvements to the Wolseley Bridge to Colwich road, allowing vehicles to speed up entering the accident zone; of the 39 road accidents in Stafford RD in a two months period 15 were on this stretch of road (SA & Chron Feb 24 1955 p6 col 3). **Best-kept lock house in England 1959, runner-up 1960** The lock keeper's house at Colwich, kept by Jack Bates (SA & Chron Aug 25 1960 p1p). **'one of the country's earliest revival folksong clubs'** Met at The Lamb and Flag Inn, Little Haywood, c1960 (MR2 p153). **First to cross the new Seven Springs-Sherbrook stepping stones** Pat Exton and Sally Harper of Stafford in 1956. The old stones had been replaced by the Friends of Cannock Chase using stones which had formed part of the wall of Stafford Gaol (SA & Chron July 12 1956 p6p). **Staffordshire's Sale of the decade (1970s)** When Evans & Evans auctioneers sold the contents of Fradswell Hall in a three-day sale in 1976. The hall had been the home of High Court Judge Sir John Ashworth. More than £140,000 was realised (SN May 14 1976 p18). **One of the highest speed rail collisions with the least fatalities** When the Liverpool-Euston and Euston-Manchester trains collided at 100 mph at Colwich Junction at 6.30pm on Sept 19 1986. The driver of the London bound train, Eric Goode, 58, alone died, 72 were injured, with 727 remaining unhurt. **'one of the largest sole owner operators of its type' c2000** Ed Weetman (Haulage & Storage) Ltd based at Pasture Fields Enterprise, specialising in the storage and distribution of animal feed all over the country (Nostalgic Stafford. Alstom. 2002 p92). **Rare modern narrowboat** Maid of Oak, a narrowboat made entirely of English oak, belonging to Peter and Julie Thorn of Great Haywood; since the 1940s nearly all have been made out of steel (SN Aug 10 2006 p8ps). **Isolated farm Prince Charles visited** Swansmoor Farm, Great Haywood, in May 2002. There to meet members of the farmers' Midland Co-operative to discuss rural affairs (Rugeley Mercury May 16 2002). **Staffordshire Best Kept Village Stafford District winner (large village category) 1996** Great Haywood.

2. Churches...

At COLWICH is St Michael and All Angels, **one of 12 such county dedications** (of AP churches); **61st= oldest AP county church** dating from the C13 or roughly 1250. **In the church** Memorial to John Whitby, died 1752 aged 34, has a long Latin eulogy. It is thought to have been written by Dr Johnson, who had been a resident tutor to him when he was a boy (OP p24). Plaque to Sir Graham Balfour (d1922), educationalist who worshipped at Colwich 1902-22, and Robert Louis Stevenson's biographer (VB p117). **In the churchyard** Alan Anson, first bishop of Qu' Appelle, Canada (A Guide to Stafford Rural District c1971 p21). In 1977 a mystery vault with no known memorial was found by accident. In the vault was found a skeleton, the skull had a small hole which appeared to have been made by a blow from above. It was the opinion of the then incumbent that the vault had been robbed (Rugeley Times May 21 1977 p9). **One of the first female lay-readers in the country** Maureen Cheney (1948-2008) of High Chase Rise, Little Haywood, RE teacher, church warden and lay reader at St Michael's, in the early 1970s (SN May 1 2008 p25pc).

At GREAT HAYWOOD is St Stephen (1840). **In the church** The processional cross was designed by Owen Spencer aged 15 of Graham Balfour Trinity Fields Comprehensive School, Stafford, in 1972, and is not made from traditional oak but mahogany and pine (Rugeley Times May 30 1972 photo). **Strange but true!** Rev Arthur Thomas Phillips, aged 83, vicar of Great Haywood from 1934, who was returning from a rural deanery meeting at Cannock as a passenger in a car driven by Rev Bertram Matthews, vicar of Colwich. At the Etching Hill crossroads, where Shooting Butts and Chaseley Roads cross, they collided with another car driven by Brigadier Sidney Albert Westrop. Although, Rev Matthews and the Brigadier were unhurt, Rev Phillips died, due to rib and lung injuries, and shock (SA & Chron Nov 14 1963 p7). At FRADSWELL is St James the Less, **Staffordshire's earliest surviving daughter church**, dating from 1200.

3. Wolseley Hall & The Wolseleys...

The family who were given a manor because they rid the county of

wolves According to legend the Wolseley family in the C10 and King Edgar awarded them with the manor of Wolseley. Wolves then overran the county, doing great damage amongst the large folks of sheep (SA & Chron Oct 18 1956 p6). **Most bizarre case Hand, Morgan, and Owen (solicitors) have ever had to deal with** When John Hickin (d1762), claimed original founder of the firm, acted in 1753 for Mr Robins. Robins was MP for Stafford, and just had courted Ann, the young widow of John Whitby of Whitby Wood. Ann then went on to apparently deceive Sir William Wolseley, 5th bt, into marriage. This celebrated scandal is recorded in a book entitled 'The Widow of the Wood'. The house, Whitby Wood, was at Oakedge, not far from Sir William's seat, Wolseley Hall, on the edge of Cannock Chase in the parish. Hand, Morgan, and Owen, based at Stafford, celebrated their 250th anniversary in 1980 (SN Feb 29 1980 p14). **'Britain's first permanent garden on a grand scale to be created specifically for the public' in C20** Wolseley Garden Park, which opened to the public on May 1 1990, created by Sir Charles Wolseley (b1942), and his wife Imogene (E&S May 2 1999 p11). **First annual Staffordshire Garden Day** Held at Wolseley Garden Park on Bank Holiday Aug 25 1990, organised by the Rural Community Council of Staffordshire (Rugeley Mercury Aug 15 1990).

The WOLSELEY who: was **the first Wolseley to hold the office of Verderer of Cannock Forest** Robert de Wolseley, temp Henry III; **had Piers Gaverston beheaded** Robert de Wolseley, temp Edward II, last heard of fighting for the king against the Scots at Halidon Hill, 1339; was **Baron of the Exchequer in Edward IV's reign** Ralph Wolseley, became Lieutenant of Calais and was rewarded with the right to enclose a deer park at Wolseley and fortify the house; **made a baronet** Robert Wolseley (d1646), a royalist, on Nov 24 1628; was **the Parliamentarian, entertained Celia Fiennes, suspected of involvement in the Monmouth Rebellion (1685)** Sir Charles Wolseley (d1714), 2nd Bt, Celia Fiennes was his niece, and the famous C17 traveller and diarist, whose notes appeared in 'Travels on Horseback' (1697); was **Brigadier over all the horse** William Wolseley (d1690), brother of Sir Charles; Lord Justice of Ireland and a Privy Councillor; **fought at the battle of the Boyne, involved in a tragic death** William, 5th son of Sir Charles, 2nd Bt. He had widely travelled abroad over many years without mishap yet was drowned very close to home. Sir William had courteously accompanied his guest Charles Wedgwood on part of his journey and was returning to Wolseley when he was overtaken by a sudden freak storm. He and his Arabian horses were drowned at Longdon fulfilling a fortune tellers warning (SN Oct 3 1980 p8); was **accused of slander** Ralph Wolseley who made slight references to Sir John Gresley's wife, Dame Anne, whom he called 'no gentlewoman' for coming to Wolsley with an armed band, unseemly dressed in 'jack and sallet' (Staffordshire Illustrated April 1967); **67th Field Marshall of the British Army, originated the name 'Tommy Atkins'** Garnet Joseph Wolseley, 1st Viscount Wolseley of Cairo, 1894-5, a relation of the Wolseleys of Wolseley Hall. He was Field Marshall 1895-1920, and his exacting standard gave rise to the phrase 'All Sir Garnet' (A Guide to Stafford Rural District c1971 p19), meaning 'in apple-pie order'; this had practically died out by 1949 (SCP July-Aug 1949 p17); **sold off virtually all the contents of the hall** Sir Charles Michael Wolseley (1846-1931), 9th Bt, adventurer and play-boy (Rugeley & Cannock Mercury June 24 2004 p4); **became known as the American Lady Wolseley** Anna Theresa Murphy (d1937) of San Francisco, who married Sir Charles (d1931) (Wolseley: a thousand years of history. Imogene Wolseley. 2003); **last to own, live on the Wolseley estate** Sir Charles Wolseley (b1942), 11th baronet, when he and his 2nd wife, Jeannie, had to leave Wolseley Park House in 2008 to rent a barn conversion near Penkridge, having been made bankrupt in 1996 (Daily Mail Jan 3 2008 p26pc). Wolseley Park House became the seat of the Wolseleys after Wolseley Hall was demolished in 1967.

4. People...

Last sighting of Christina Collins before she was murdered By the lock-keeper and his wife at Colwich Lock, on Sunday evening, June 16 1839; the next day her body was found in the canal at Rugeley (Rugeley Mercury. July 8 1977 p26). **First provincial architect elected a fellow of the Society of Antiquaries** Thomas Trubshaw of Haywood in 1836 (SA Feb 13 1836. Feb 15 1936 p5 col 2). **James Trubshaw's severest critic** The Colwich architect was accused by Charles Masefield, author of the Little Guide to Staffordshire (1910), of 'having spoiled several Staffordshire churches' (LGS p117). **All Britain under 16s Snooker Champion 1955, Boys' Snooker Champion 1955, Boys' Midland Billiards Champion 1955, English Boys' Billiards champion 1957, English Boys' Snooker champion 1957** Peter Shelley (b1940), of Great Haywood (SA June 23 1955 p10p. Dec 12 1957 p14 cols 1-2). **2nd place in Great Britain and Northern Ireland in the Grade VI music exam 1956** Diana Thomas, aged 16, of 'The Gables', Bishton, as set by the Associated Board of the Royal Schools of Music (SA & Chron Jan 26 1956 p1p). **Shoeing Smith National Champion runner-up 1969** David Duckett, 23, of Fosters smithy, Great Haywood, beaten only by a quarter of a point by the Champion of Championships (Rugeley Times. Aug 16 1969 photo). **European Young Riders Championship gold medalist 2004** Emma Shaw of Great Haywood, horse rider (BBC Midlands Today Oct 2004). **Colwich's villain** Frederick Arthur Cross, 33, an occupant of a nissen hut on the former RAF Station at Hixon, who murdered Donald Haywood Lainton, 28, an insurance broker's agent from Stockport who was on his way to Sutton Coldfield for a business appointment on Feb 25 1955. But the roads being bad because of the weather he turned back calling in at the Coach and Horses Inn, Great Haywood, to ring to cancel his appointment and to get refreshments. The two were seen leaving the pub together. Lainton's car was discovered at Willslock, and his body - stabbed in the neck, chest and face 10 times - nearby on a farm track. With no obvious motive it was rumoured Cross had murdered so that his life might be taken. He was found guilty of murder and executed - thus making it 'one of the strangest cases of all time' (SA & Chron March 3 1955 p1 col 1. July 21 1955 p6p). **Colwich's saddest** Samuel Middleton, aged 7, son of a farm labourer at Tolldish was killed by lightning at Swansmore on Aug 12 1901, trying to shelter under a tree from it with 6-year-old Ernest Bottimer, and an infant. The flash of lightning is said to have been exceptionally vivid, and completely shattered the tree. It left a zig-zag mark on Samuel's chest, and his neck and arms were badly discoloured (SA Aug 17 1901 p4 col 7). **Colwich's poorest** In 1821 Rugeley received money from Colwich for board of its poor in Rugeley workhouse (SRO D6447/1/). From 1837 the poor could be housed at Stafford Union workhouse at Marston. **Colwich's earliest recorded will** Belongs to Margaret Wade otherwise Finney, and is dated 1613. **Fradswell's kindest** In the 1830s the poor of Fradswell who attended church on Christmas day received 6d from rental of lands bequeathed by Thomas Bradbury of Oulton, by will, dated 1734. **Fradswell's poorest** In 1785 Fradswell entered into an agreement to house its poor in Leigh workhouse (SRO D3033/4/7/2). **First person in the parish register** Margeria Hordorn of Little Haywood, widow, buried March 29 1590. **Choicest quote** Arthur Mee in The King's England series: Staffordshire. 1937, said 'It lies in beauty by the Trent, with the lofty hills of Cannock Chase splendid in the distance.'

5. Shugborough & The Ansons...

'.. welcome for more reigning monarchs than any other Staffs. village' Haywood, on account of the medieval Bishops of Lichfield having a residence on the site of what became Shugborough Hall (SA & Chron Oct 11 1956 p6). **'Among the stateliest' great houses of Staffordshire** Shugborough Hall (Staffordshire Handbook c1966 p15). **Second longest house entry in Pevsner's 'Staffordshire'** Shugborough at 116 lines (BOE pp236-239). **'Grandest portico in Staffordshire by far'** Shugborough Hall by Samuel Wyatt 1794 (BOE p31). **One of the best collections of pictures of a country house in the country** Those depicting Shugborough at Shugborough (Dianne Barre, Jack Leighton Seminar. Keele Uni. Nov 5 2008). **Earliest monument of the Greek Revival in Europe** (after Stuart's one at Hagley Hall, Worcs) The Grecian Doric Temple at Shugborough built 1758. **First in the revived post of hermit at Shugborough** Ansuman Biswas, 2002; there were 54 other candidates to be paid hermit on Great Haywood Cliffs (Wikipedia 2006). **'handsomest and the largest' pineapple 'ever cut in Britain'** The New Providence Pineapple cut on 30 September 1825 at Shugborough, measuring 2 feet in circumference, of a fine globular shape, of beautiful proportion and weighing 11 lbs and three quarters, 16 oz to the pound; it was grown by a Mr Cac Murtrie (SA Oct 8 1825 p4 col 2). **Widest yew tree in the country** Perhaps the one in the park (Discovering Britain Road Atlas & Guide. Collins. 2004. p67). The **ANSON** who was: **One of the 'Seven sons of Staffordshire,' 'one of England's most remarkable seamen', 2nd Englishman to circumnavigate the world, 10th Admiral of the Fleet, is Colwich's most famous old worthy** (30 July 1761-17 Dec 1762) Admiral George Anson (d1762), world circumnavigator, born at Shugborough 1697 (ES Dec 1 2007 Staying In p13) (Staffordshire Handbook c1966 p26). He was the famous younger brother of

Thomas Anson of Shugborough Hall. He circumnavigated the world in H.M.S. Centurion 1740-44 and was Rear-Admiral 1745; Vice-Admiral 1746; First Lord of the Admiralty 1747; Baron Anson of Soberton 1747; member of the Privy Council 1750-. He notably groomed many naval officers who went on to success; a cat who accompanied him round the world is perhaps that carved on The Cat's Monument at Shugborough, the second quote is from the Geographical Magazine April 1997 pp26-28; **first bishop of Qu'Appelle, Canada** Alan Anson (A Guide to Stafford Rural District c1971 p21); **longest serving Chief Constable of Staffordshire** Col Hon George Anson (b1857) 1888-1929, 2nd son of the Earl of Lichfield (SA April 7 1888. April 9 1938 p11 col 7); **found shot dead at Newcastle-on-Tyne with a bullet through his heart** John George Anson, aged 45, son of above. His body was found at the quayside on Sept 19 1931. He had been staying at the Station Hotel in Newcastle. In WW1 he was very badly wounded; after the war he took up poultry farming in Scotland (Lichfield Mercury Sept 25 1931 p9 col 4); **last survivor of the original 35 Gentlemen of Staffordshire Cricket side** Thomas Edward Anson (1883-1960), 4th Earl of Lichfield; the side was formed in 1903 (SA April 10 1953 p1); **niece of the Queen, 'one of the loveliest debutantes at the Silver Jubilee Court of King George V and Queen Mary in 1935'** Miss Anne Ferelith Bowes-Lyon (b1918), daughter of Hon John Bowes-Lyon, niece of Elizabeth, wife of George VI; George VI and Queen Elizabeth attended her wedding at St Margaret's church, Westminster, on April 28 1938, to Viscount Anson (SA April 30 1938 p7ps); **'One of the great photographers of his generation...pioneer and ambassador of digital photography'** Patrick Anson (Lichfield) (1939-2005) (exhibition of his photographs at Shugborough, 2006); **she used her maiden name on a school commemorative plaque when married** Lady Elizabeth Anson, really Lady Elizabeth Shakerley when she officially opened a new wing of the Anson Primary School, Great Haywood, in 1972. This was seen as more desirable because of the family's strong connections (Rugeley Times Oct 14 1972).

6. The area...

Colwich is the **county's 16th largest parish**, consisting of 9,217 acres; **16th= closest parish to the county town**, 3.6m ESE; **extremist length** 6m, making it **18th= longest parish in the county**; **extremist width** 4m. **Parish's chief settlement** Colwich, the least attractive of the pretty interconnected villages of Colwich, Little and Great Haywood. **Geology** N of the Trent - Keuper Red Marls; TRENT and Sow floors - Alluvium; TRENT banks including Haywood and Colwich villages - Keuper Sandstones; CANNOCK Chase - Bunter. **Last known surviving natural inland saltmarsh in the British Isles** At Pasturefields. It is fed by a brine spring and supports a variety of salt tolerant plants usually found in grazed saline coastal habitats (Staffs Wildlife Trust no 102 April 2008 p16). **Highest points** COLWICH - 654 feet above Sherbrook Valley. FRADSWELL - Fradswell Heath at 568 feet. **Lowest points** Colwich - 220 feet at Wolseley Bridge. Fradswell - 328 feet by Gayton Brook at raised a profit of about Doglands. Colwich was **63rd most populated**

Staffordshire parish in 1801 with 886 people; **39th in 1811** with 1,688; **41st in 1821** with 1,865; **42nd in 1831** with 1,918; **44th in 1841** with 2,024; **45th in 1851** with 2,072; **56th in 1861** with 1,828; **57th in 1871** with 1,834; **60th in 1881** with 1,740; **62nd in 1891** with 1,575; **62nd in 1901** with 1,615.

SUBJECT INDEX *En to Fi*

England and Wales, fifth county mental asylum in STAFFORD 12
England dedicated to Our Lady of Lourdes, first church in CANNOCK 5
England footballer HAUGHTON 3
England for saddle and draught horses, best fairs in PENKRIDGE 3
England in C16, one of the highest spires in STAFFORD 6
England long service medalists, Royal Agricultural Society of INGESTRE 4
England on which the red grouse breeds, most southerly point in CANNOCK 4
England over-15s, played rugby for RUGELEY 9
England to at least 1974, most prolific murderer in RUGELEY 5
England to plough with a team of horses 1946, one of the few girls in
    CHURCH EATON 3
England where the custom (of sun wheels) was observed, one of the
    last places in CHESLYN HAY 1
England's 3rd most popular church for weddings 1990 CANNOCK 5
England's first Labour M.P. STAFFORD 10
England's first 'Miss Rock 'n Roll' STAFFORD 8
England's last herd of fallow deer CANNOCK 4
England's most accomplished trainer of 'jumpers RUGELEY 9
England's most photographed highway CANNOCK 3
England's most remarkable seamen, one of COLWICH 5
England, 22nd Chief Justice of the King's Bench of SHARESHILL 3
England, Best One Day Show in BREWOOD 1
England, Disease very rare in SEIGHFORD 1
England, earliest flat-roofed house in CASTLE CHURCH 3
England, finest park and gardens that are in this part of INGESTRE 3
England, first petrol made in CANNOCK 3
England, largest natural lake in private ownership in FORTON 2
England, largest village in GNOSALL 3
England, most speed cameras in CANNOCK 3
England, most tricky road in COLWICH 1
England, oldest known glass kiln in COLWICH 1
England, one of the '50 Beautiful Villages' of GNOSALL 3
England, one of the few English families who can claim unbroken
    descent from the Kings of SEIGHFORD 3
England, one of the last brasses in NORBURY 2
England, one of the purist examples of early renaissance architecture in TIXALL 5
England, one of the ugliest houses and one of the finest parks in
    TEDDESLEY HAY 2
England, only Women's Institute of its kind in STAFFORD 1

*A Mustang
Figher
which
crashed in
Creswell
parish.*

Creswell
1. Did you know that...

Creswell's top folklore The local tradition that the village was established as the result of the establishment of a monastery (SA & Chron Feb 16 1956 p4 col 7), and that a skeleton found under stonework of ruined Creswell Chapel, when excavated in the 1870s and or 1880s, was the chapel's founder. Creswell is the **county's 145th largest parish** (extra-parochial), consisting of 828 acres; **7th closest parish to the county town**, 1.6m NW; **extremist length** 1.6m, making it **26th= shortest parish in the county**; **extremist width** 1.4m, making it **22nd= narrowest parish** in the county. **Highest point** 407 feet on the summit of a hill on the NW parish boundary. **Lowest point** 246 feet by the Sow, S of The Mount. The **name Creswell first appears** in 1203. **Parish's chief settlement** Creswell, a fairly modern roadside village. **What Creswell is famous for** The eerie ruins of the little prebendal chapel, standing lonely in a field. Its chapel is **one of only three undedicated county AP churches; 52nd= last AP county church** built dating from 1450. Creswell was **158th most-populated Staffordshire parish in 1801** with 17 people; **158th= in 1811** with 19; **163rd in 1821** with 12; **163rd in 1831** with 11; **162nd in 1841** with 16; **165th in 1851** with 7; **164th in 1861** with 12; **157th in 1871** with 26; **159th= in 1881** with 29; **154th in 1891** with 56; **156th in 1901** with 46.

2. People...

Creswell's hero Capt John Perrin (1923-44), Flying 'Ace' with United States Army Air Force who delivered a P-51D Mustang Fighter (*see above*) from workshops near Derby on July 4 1944. It caught fire over Stafford but he kept it in flight to avoid housing in First and Second Avenues, Holmcroft, dying in the ensuing crash close to Home Farm and Sleepers Spinney (forming part of Primepoint Business Park by 2005). **Creswell's most famous old worthy** Rev Thomas Whitby (d1828). He inherited Creswell manor from his grandfather, and after holding the shrievalty of Staffordshire, 1773, became ordained. His parents were interesting: As a boy his father had been tutored by Samuel Johnson, and in widowhood his mother Anne Northey 'Widow of the Wood', duped Sir William Wolseley of Colwich into marriage, while courting a local politician. **Creswell's saddest** In 1968 Shirley Keenan of 3 The Mount admitted a charge of infanticide having thrown her two and half month old daughter Sian-Marie to the floor about four times; there were also previous incidents of ill-treatment. Her plea of not guilty to murder was accepted as she was found to be suffering from postnatal depression. She was put on probation for three years on the condition she undergo medical treatment (SA & Chron May 23 1968 p5). **Bride of the Year 1985** Linda Bradley, 19, dental receptionist of Creswell, out of 900 brides at the Pronuptia and Young Bridal Spectacular at Trentham Gardens in Feb 1985; her bridegroom was Richard Eliot, a policeman from Bristol (STODAY April/ May 1985 p19p). **Creswell's poorest** From 1858 the poor could be housed at Stafford Union Poor House at Marston. **Choicest quote** Henry Thorold in the Shell Guide to Staffordshire, 1978, wrote 'The little church has been a ruin for centuries: fragments of the chancel survive in a field.'

SUBJECT INDEX *Fi to Fi*

*Ellenhall is
prime dairy
farming country.*

Ellenhall
1. Did you know that...

'Some of the finest dairy cattle in Staffordshire' 108 cattle, of which 51 were dairy Shorthorns (reds and roans), of JW Bourne of Broadheath Farm (1912-37), Ellenhall, himself 'one of the best-known farmers in the county' (SA March 6 1937 p9ps). **Ellenhall's top folklore** That a former lost Norman settlement called Frankville existed between Ranton and Ellenhall, in the vicinity of which was ploughland known locally as the 'market place', and has been found a Prehistoric quern, a Palaeolithic or Neolithic axe, and a cobbled pavement, possibly the vallum of the Roman Limes Britannicus. The **name Ellenhall first appears** in Domesday Book, 1086. **What Ellenhall is famous for** Its C19 yellow brick cottages all in the estate's approved style. **Earliest deer park in Staffordshire** Ellenhall Park created c1100 (info David Jacques, 2006). **"Best lot of (cows) from one bull I have ever seen"** WB Thompson of Harper Adams College, judge at the Staffordshire Milk Recording Society competition, 1931, when he awarded 1st prize in Section I to a herd, the progeny of a living sire Eaton Rose King of JW Wardle of Lawnhead House (SA Dec 12 1931 p5). **First Stone Rural District Council meeting outside their district** Occurred at Ellenhall parish church, 1972, at the behest of its chairman, Richard Lawrence, formerly of Grange Farm, Ellenhall (SN July 13 2006 p6).

2. Church...

At Ellenhall is St Mary the Virgin, **one of 23 such county dedications** (most common dedication in the county); **36th last AP county church built** dating from 1757. **'no more picturesquely situated church in Staffordshire'** than Ellenhall' The Staffordshire Advertiser on the reopening of St Mary's on May 19 1886 after its restoration taking nearly a year (SA May 22 1886 p9 col 1). **Staffordshire's earliest-known female freemason** On a stone in the church wall there is an inscription which reads 'Anna Cope 1683 T.H. Freemason' (WSL 323/41/80. Horne's Scrapbook. No. 1. p67 facing). **Ellenhall's longest-serving vicars** Thomas Loxdale c1717-c1737, and Edward Bate c1745-c1765.

3. People...

Ellenhall's most famous old worthy Thomas William Anson (1795-1854). He succeeded as 1st Earl of Lichfield of Shugborough Hall in 1818. His father bought Ranton Abbey estate, but he greatly expanded the property, bought more land, planted coverts and spent large sums of money making it one of the finest sporting estates in the country. It was the venue for great shooting parties throughout the 1830s as depicted in a famous painting at Shugborough 'A Shooting Party at Ranton Abbey' by Sir Francis Grant 1840; portrayed are the Earl himself, Lord Melbourne, then P.M, Lord Sefton and the Earl of Uxbridge. **Ellenhall's hero** Dr Hope William Gosse, MRCS, LRCP, who was awarded an MBE for services as medical officer at Eccleshall Military Hospital in WW1. There is a curious aside to his award, for it was announced prematurely at a whist drive at the Vicarage before it was official, and this was reported in The Staffordshire Advertiser: Dr Gosse then had to send a disclaimer to the paper (SA Feb 21 1920 p8 col 2. Feb 28 1920 p8 col 6. April 3 1920 p5 col 3). **Ellenhall's villain** Sidney Woolley (b1924), carter's labourer, said to have lodged at Ellenhall between 1944-50, pulled a six-year old girl through a hedge, kicking her in the mouth and stomach, and also handcuffed and gagged the 14-year-old daughter of his landlord, forcing her through fields, hedges and over stiles, and to have indecently assaulted her whilst she was handcuffed. Sentencing him to eight years prison for both crimes the Judge said of his attack on the six-year-old "It was about as foul a crime as a man could have committed" (SA March 25 1950 p5 cols 3-4. July 8 1950 p2 col 6).

'one of the best known and best loved of all Staffordshire agriculturalists and he is certainly one of the oldest' 1948 RS Billington of Ellenhall Manor from 1909 (before which he farmed at Chebsey), retiring in 1941; chairman of the committee of the Staffordshire Agricultural Society; farm competition judge (SLM June 1948 p129p). **Ellenhall's saddest** James Riley farmer of Seggersley Farm, committed suicide aged 84 by shooting himself two hours after assisting with the milking on March 12 1904. He was found dead in the parlour. A local doctor had been attending him for some time for 'weakness and general debility' a verdict of suicide whilst temporarily insane was returned (SA March 19 1904 p5 col 4). **Ellenhall's oldest person 1892** Mrs Mary Myatt, born Ellenhall Aug 25 1791, died Seighford July 9 1892, buried Seighford. She retained her faculties to the last and conversed within an hour or so of her death. 'Her memory of incidents occurring in her childhood was wonderful, and her sharp, racy manner of expression made a visit to her an incident never to be forgotten' (SA July 16 1892 p4 col 6). **Fancy that!** A pedigree Hereford steer in the young handlers' class at a show at Bingley Hall, Stafford, startled in the showring bringing his handler Stuart Cartmail, 16, of Lawnhead Farm, to his knees so he inadvertently bowed in front of royalty (the Duke of Gloucester, who was present) (SN Nov 27 1987 p3p). **British junior national champion in endurance riding 2008** Brett Corcoran of Ellenhall, aged 11, on 'Aristotle Bay'; Brett attends Sir Graham Balfour High School (SN Dec 11 2008 p63pc). **Ellenhall's poorest** No evidence of a workhouse at Ellenhall has been found (OPBS Pirehill p214). From 1837 the poor could be housed at Stafford Union Poor House at Marston. **Ellenhall's earliest recorded will** Belongs to Richard Simcocke, and is dated April 20 1540. **First person in the parish register** Maude Bursley buried May 29 1539. **Choicest quote** Goronwy Harnaman, who did the parish features in Six Towns Magazine, wrote for the August 1965 edition 'Modernism has had but little welcome here, and the hand of time has fallen gently, bestowing a pleasing mellowness on the stonework cottages that fit so naturally with the surroundings.'

4. The area...

Ellenhall was the **county's 125th largest parish**, consisting of 1,801 acres; **21st= closest parish to the county town**, 4m W; **extremist length** 1.3m, making it **15th= shortest parish in the county**; **extremist width** 2.5m. **Parish's chief settlement** Ellenhall, an isolated, rural scattered little village. **Geology** ALL - Keuper Red Marls. **Highest point** 482 feet on the boundary NW of Park House. **Lowest point** 312 feet on the boundary by Gamesley Brook, E of Seggersley. Ellenhall was **127th most-populated Staffordshire parish in 1801** with 256 people; **130th in 1811** with 251; **128th in 1821** with 287; **127th in 1831** with 286; **131st in 1841** with 280; **126th in 1851** with 320; **128th in 1861** with 300; **131st in 1871** with 261; **134th in 1881** with 231; **131st in 1891** with 238; **137th in 1901** with 207.

SUBJECT INDEX *Fi to Fi*

Forton's mermaid beside Aqualate Mere with the eye-catcher tower for Aqualate Hall in the distance.

Forton
1. Did you know that...

Rare piece of engineering Bridge carrying Meretown road and Shropshire Union Canal in one combined structure (COS p62p). **'the oldest oaks in the county'** Those at Aqualate Park, as noted by Pitt in the early C19 (THS) (SSE 1994 p34). **Shropshire, keep your hands off Forton!** At Gnosall Rural District council meeting on July 20 1931 the clerk reported that Newport UD had sought to apply to Staffordshire County Council to have a part of Forton parish taken out of Staffordshire and annexed to Newport. Mr RE Jones of Gnosall RD said he understood Newport had previously asked to have a certain Shropshire parish given to them, but could not get it, so now they were turning their eyes to Staffordshire. But he could tell Newport that they were not going to have it - Hear, hear! exclaimed the meeting (SA July 25 1931 p10). In 1959 Forton was 'very strongly' against Shropshire's bid for 154 acres including the Islington area. Miss V H Hargreaves, a Forton representative, and against the transfer, visited every house within the transfer area, and reported that the vast majority of people wanted to stay in Staffordshire "they are Staffordshire people and they wish to remain within the county' she said (SA & Chron March 26 1959 p7 cols 5-6). In 1965 the Islington area was annexed to Newport. **Smallest thoroughbred foal ever born** 'Thumbelina', born 1978 at National Foaling Bank, Mereton, Forton; entered into GBR, weighing 23 lbs at birth (SN Sept 11 2003 p8p). **Lowest temperature in England and Wales ever** -26.1 c (15f) was recorded close by at Newport, Shrops on Jan 10 1982 (TB Jan 25 2001 p16).

2. Aqualate Mere...

Forton's top folklore According to folklore a mermaid inhabits Aqualate Mere. She is said to have some time occupied Vivary Pool until it was destroyed by the building of the Shropshire Union Canal. "If this mere you do let dry. Newport and Meretown I will destroy." She is said to have cried from the mere when it was dredged and cleaned. The **name Forton first appears** in 1198. **What Forton is famous for** Aqualate Mere. **'great mere' in consequence of it being the largest of many meres**

scattered along the county border (SSE 1994 p27); **largest natural lake in the West Midlands** but is remarkably shallow at no more than 1m deep (Staffs Wildlife Trust no 102 April 2008 p 16-17); **finest lake in the Staffordshire** (THS p274); **'said to be the largest natural lake in private ownership in England'** According to Vivian Bird, 1974 (VB p152). **Only lake in Staffordshire where herons nest: Largest reed bed habitat in Staffordshire** (NSJFS 1966 p70) (info F Gribble).

3. Church...

At Forton is All Saints, **one of 19 such county dedications** (of AP churches); **48th= oldest AP county church** dating from 1200. **In the church note** Four stained-glass windows in memory of members of the Boughey family; the original stained-glass windows are said to have been broken by two of Cromwell's officers during the Civil War (VCH vol 4 p109). **Staffordshire's only C17 documented funerary monument** Garrat Hollemans's canopied altar tomb with the alabaster effigies of Sir Thomas Skrymsher (d1633) and his wife Anne (d1656). On the side of the tomb are small alabaster figures of their five sons and four daughters (VCH vol 4 p109) (BOE p27). **Forton's longest-serving vicar** Francis Skrymsher, who served 30 years, rector 1697-1727. **Staffordshire's longest-serving chorister in one church** Mark Whitmore (1843-1920), from 1852 to 1920 (memorial in the church) (VB p154).

4. People...

Forton's most famous old worthy, chief leader in the flight to Boscobel 1651 Richard Skrymsher (d1704) of Forton, according to his memorial in the church. It was he who procured the hiding place for the Earl of Derby at Boscobel after the battle of Worcester, and Derby in turn procured it for the king (VCH vol 4 p109). **Strange but true!** A pin was discovered under the skin of the arm of Madam Skrymsher of Aqualate in C17. It was a mystery how it got there (NHS p290). The wife of Samuel Ward of Meretown did not know she was pregnant until she was about to give birth, so much so she sent for a physician instead of a midwife (NHS p270). **Forton's villains** Thomas Shropshire, 51, of Bank House Farm, Meretown, was charged before Eccleshall magistrates in 1933 with taking a gun to his tenant Maurice Nicholson and wounding him in the arm in an attempt to eject him from his property. He was fined and bound over. There were also four previous convictions against Shropshire, including one of drunkeness on licensed premises, and one of fowl stealing, for which he had served a month's imprisonment (SA March 25 1933 p7 col 3). Another character, Arthur Frederick Robinson of the Council Houses, Shay Lane, Forton, aged 37, a paint sprayer, pleaded guilty to trying to kill his wife, Elfreda, with commercial potassium cyanide on July 28 1958; was sentenced to three years probation and forgiven by his wife (SA & Chron Aug 14 1958 p1). **Forton's saddest** Edith Mary Scott Darlington, aged 4, who rushed across the road from her home in Forton on March 29 1920 and was knocked down by a car driven by Harry James Clarke of Knighton Grange, farmer. He said he was driving very slowly and sounded his horn several times. His passenger, a nurse, also said it was a pure accident. Edith was struck by the headlamp and died in hospital (SA April 10 1926 p8 col 1). **Forton's kindest** Richard Awnsham (d1732), whose bequest of £100, for schooling poor children in the parish, became the basis of other benefactions, and a general trust for a Forton school (VCH vol 4 p110). **Forton's poorest** From at least 1836 the poor may have been housed at the old workhouse at 34-38 Vineyard Road (formerly Workhouse Lane), Newport, until the new workhouse was built 1855~6, in Audley Avenue (formerly Longmarsh Lane). This building became Audley House, an old people's home, and then private flats (the infirmary of 1908, still adjoins). **Forton's earliest recorded will** Belongs to Thomas Hewster, and is dated July 4 1532. **First persons in the parish register** Robert Pygot of Newport parish and Catherine Rosse married Nov 30 1558. **Choicest quote** John Hadfield in The Shell Book of English Villages, 1980, concisely noted 'a small village with some houses of sandstone, but most of them are Victorian brick, with a Tudor-Jacobean flavour. They were meant to resemble the style of Forton Old Hall, which stands alongside the church, E of the main road.'

5. The area...

Forton is the **county's 74th largest parish**, consisting of 3,746 acres; **38th closest parish to the county town**, 7.3m due W; **extremist length** 4.2m; extremist width 3.9m. **Parish's chief settlement** Forton and Sutton, hamlets (and townships - Warton was a third township) on the Eccleshall-Newport road. **Famed for** Aqualate Mere. **Geology** AQUALATE and Meese plain - Bunter; FORTON and Sutton villages - Keuper Sandstones; WESTON JONES village and N - Keuper Red Marls. **Highest point** 341 feet a little to W of Sutton. **Lowest point** 220 feet on the Shrops border by the Meese below Chetwynd Park. Forton was **86th most-populated Staffordshire parish in 1801** with 566 people; **85th= in 1811** with 607; **88th in 1821** with 702; **87th in 1831** with 733; **85th in 1841** with 764; **89th in 1851** with 741; **91st in 1861** with 729; **94th in 1871** with 649; **100th in 1881** with 541; **96th in 1891** with 576; **101st in 1901** with 520.

Tiles in Gayton church inspired Samuel Wright to produce encaustic tiles.

Gayton
1. Did you know that...

What Gayton is famous for Moated sites, some unexplained. The **name Gayton first appears** in Domesday Book, 1086. **'one of the most typical feudal villages in the county'** SAH Burne's description of Gayton, as demonstrated by remains of the field system (NSFCT 1976 p52). **A rare occurrence** A selenite found at Hartley Green (NHS p176). **Last barrack hut of Brocton and Rugeley WW1 Training Camps** Was Gayton Parish Room, having been taken down from Cannock Chase in 1918 and re-erected at Gayton. It was removed in May 2006, stored, and re-erected in 2007 for the Marquis Drive Visitor Centre, back on Cannock Chase (Life magazine for Staffs CC employees. April/ May 2007 p8pc). **'Some of the finest dairy cattle in the country'** A herd of 164 heads of reds and roans, belonging to Messrs W and F Sherratt of Parkside Farm, Gayton, since 1892. The herd were being sold in 1936. The farm, then covering 270 acres, lies in the heart of rich, milk-producing country, and Messrs Sherratt had 'gained a reputation for soundness which it would be hard to beat' (SA Oct 3 1936 p5ps). **Gayton Princess** Mare, foaled c1975, belonging to Eric Goodwin, named 'Queen of the Shires' when awarded the Hardy Cup at the Staffordshire County Show 1980 (SN June 6 1980 p54p). **Strange but true!** In 1987 John Burke, clerk to Weston with Gayton and Fradswell Parish Council received three identical letters from Staffordshire County Council addressed to a parish clerk of Weston, Gayton and Fradswell parish councils, respectively (SN Nov 27 1987 p16).

2. Church...

At Gayton is St Peter, **one of 15 such county dedications** (of AP churches); **23rd= oldest county church** dating from the C12 or roughly 1150. **Note in the church, Gayton's most famous old worthy** Unknown person, represented by the recumbent effigy, 6 feet 5 inches long and 1 foot 9 inches wide, c1250, to his memory in the church. It was formerly in one of the aisles, and later turned out into the churchyard, hence the fig ure is somewhat worn. It is thought to represent a member of the Ferrers family (LGS p139) (JME part 1 p19) (STM Dec 1965 p43) (CHMS p31). **Gayton's top folklore** It is believed Samuel Wright (d1849), in the early C19, conceived the idea of manufacturing encaustic tiles from the tiles on the floor of Gayton church. The tiles bear the arms of Ferrers and are believed to date from the C14. The idea was patented in 1830 and the patent later sold to Herbert Minton who made this type of tile famous and such tiles became known as 'Minton tiles'.

3. People...

All-England champion hedgelayer 1927, first person to win three Staffordshire Agricultural Society (hedgelaying) prizes in one season Fred Morris of Gayton, in 1925, born Rocester 1885, hedgelayer and later an employee of Wilts United Dairy, Weston (SN Dec 6 1958 p14p). **Staffordshire Milk recording Society's Challenge Cup for British Friesians winner 1963-64** Mr JD Sherratt of Moor Leys, Gayton, with an average for his homebred herd over 1963-64 of 36 cows, 13,294 lbs, eight heifers, 11,435 lbs, at 4.22% butter fat, the calving index being 391 days (SA & Chron Feb 13 1964 p8 col 7). **Gayton's saddest** Renee Fletcher, 10 months old, daughter of John Thomas Fletcher, a chauffeur-gardener, of Cherry Cottages, Gayton, who fell from her chair on Dec 10 1932 and possibly hit her head on a fender. She seemed to recover but developed cellutitis of the scalp four days later and died at the Staffordshire General Hospital (SA Dec 24 1932 p10 col6). **Gayton's kindest** In the 1830s poor widows were receiving 2d loaves every Sunday from the charity of John Heath, 1724. Also four poor children of the parish were being taught to read out of the charity of George Browne of Hartley Green, by will, dated 1792; as soon as a child can read it is no longer funded and the churchwardens appoints another child in its place. **Gayton's poorest** The parish sent its poor to Leigh workhouse between at least 1814-32 (SRO D705/PO/1). The tragic case of George Bond and his family remains a mystery. On May 2 1812 the family were forced by a Removal Order to leave Weston-upon-Trent and return to Gayton, their native parish. But magistrates gave them temporary respite owing to Mr Bond's health. For the next year costs occur in Gayton overseers accounts relating to Mr Bond's trial, dole paid to his wife, Elizabeth, money in 1813 for the funeral of their 9-year-old son, Samuel, and paying for the apprenticeship at Hinkley of their other son, John. He appears to be John Bond, a railway gatekeeper at Half Head, Shallowford, in 1861 (SRO D705/PO/1). From 1837 the poor were housed at Stafford Union workhouse at Marston. **Gayton's earliest recorded will** Belongs to James Aspre, and is dated Jan 26 1534/5. **First person in the parish register** The first legible entry is that of Thomas Dawson son of Roger Dawson baptised Aug 14 1597, about 6th down on the register list (thanks to Rebecca Jackson for reading this). **Choicest quote** Joan P Alcock in Discovering Staffordshire, 1973, 'Gayton is a quiet village which had the essentials of life - a church, an inn and a mill.'

4. The area...

Gayton is the **county's 128th largest parish**, consisting of 1,515 acres; **25th closest parish to the county town**, 4.2m NE; **extremist length** 1.7m, making it **29th= shortest parish in the county**; extremist width 1.7m, making it 28th narrowest parish in the county. **Parish's chief settlement** Gayton, an isolated, scattered farming village. **Geology** ALL - Keuper Red Marls. **Highest point** 423 feet at Old Gayton Gorse. **Lowest point** 266 feet by Stocking Brook at the boundary. Gayton was **124th most-populated Staffordshire parish in 1801** with 273 people; **129th in 1811** with 261; **129th in 1821** with 284; **126th in 1831** with 296; **130th in 1841** with 291; **130th in 1851** with 264; **133rd in 1861** with 249; **134th in 1871** with 237; **132nd in 1881** with 236; **136th in 1891** with 221; **139th in 1901** with 180.

SUBJECT INDEX *Fl to Go*

A man-monkey boggart haunts the canal near Gnosall.

Gnosall
1. Did you know that...

Gnosall's top folklore That a man-monkey frequents Big Bridge over the Shropshire Union Canal. It was seen by a labouring man at night in 1879, and the locals thought it to be the spirit of a man drowned in the cut nearby. Big Bridge could be a bridge at the north end of the canal cut, in Norbury parish, or at the south end, in Gnosall parish. The **name Gnosall first appears** in Domesday Book, 1086. **What Gnosall is famous for** Its parish church, a former Royal Free Chapel, that is to say no bishop had jurisdiction over it. **Staffordshire's most analysed parish poor-law records** Gnosall's by SA Cutlack, whose detailed work in 1936 on the 216 apprenticeship bonds 1691-1816 was used by WE Tate in his acclaimed 'The Parish Chest: A Study of the Records of Parochial Administration in England' (1946. 3rd ed 1969). **Silver medal for excellency in church and school furniture** Messrs, H and S Addison, Anchor Works, Gnosall, at the South Wales and Cardiff International Exhibition 1888 (SA Nov 17 1888 p4 col 7). **One of the smallest boats ever to make the east to west Atlantic crossing by the northern route** 'Nova Espero', 20 feet long, skippered by Charles Violet, explorer, author and designer of Gnosall, in 1951. His trip is the subject of the book 'Solitary Journey' re-issued in 1969. Violet returned from sea in 1957 having before this worked as a teacher in Bermuda, and sailed to the Black Sea; but bad weather made it impossible to continue so he decided to try and make the coast of Africa (Staffs Illustrated. Oct 1969 Staffs Scene). **Best Kept Station first prize** Mr Griffiths, a porter at Gnosall station from 1948, could remember in 1959 a time when Gnosall won this prize (SA & Chron Nov 19 1959 p1p). **Staffordshire Best Kept Village winner (large village category) 1956, 1988, 1989, Stafford District winner**

(large village category) **1989, 1990, 1991, 1994, 1997** Gnosall.
2. Church...
At Gnosall is St Lawrence, on S side of Sellman Street, **one of 4 such county dedications** (of AP churches); **23rd= oldest county church** dating from the C12 or roughly 1150. **'... a village with one of the most noble and splendid churches in the diocese', 'Historically, archaeologically and aesthetically it is one of the most significant churches in the county'** St Lawrence's, Gnosall (STM Feb 1966 pp24-25) (Staffordshire: Shire County Guide. Peter Heaton. 1986). **One of the county's seven Cruciform churches** St Lawrence's, Gnosall (LGS p139). **'one of the finest (churches) in the county'** (VCH vol 4 p129). **In the church note** An alabaster effigy of an armed knight of c1470 which lies on a table tomb in the south chapel. Traditionally this represents a 'Baron Brough', most probably a member of the Knightley family of Brough Hall (VCH vol 4 p131). **'Contains some of the best Norman work in Staffordshire'** The ornate west crossing arch in St Lawrence's, Gnosall (Stafford Churches Trail leaflet, Stafford Borough Council. 2006). **Only known example of the Chester Hall marks of 1692** On the paten, the gift of Mrs Ann Doody (Gnosall PR). **Gnosall's longest-serving vicar, first vicar, 'one of the oldest clergymen in England'** 1901 Rev John Till, MA, vicar of Gnosall from 1845, who was 91 and 9 months when he died July 18 1901, serving 56 years (SA July 20 1901 p4 col 6). **Earliest Neo-Norman church in Staffordshire** St Mary, MORETON, 1837-38, by Thomas Trubshaw (BOE p34). At KNIGHTLEY is Christ Church, 1840-41.
3. Gnosall itself...
Unique placename in Staffordshire, Staffordshire's placename that most baffled etymologist David Horovitz Gnosall (STM Feb 1966 pp24-25) (info from David Horovitz, who confided it even baffled the country's leading etymologist Margaret Gelling). **Largest village in England** Sometimes claimed of Gnosall; but there are also 18 other UK contenders, including Wombourne (Wikipedia 2006). **Staffordshire's longest High Street** Reputedly, that through Gnosall, stretching for just over a mile (MR2 p148). **One of the '50 Beautiful Villages' of England** Gnosall is the only Staffordshire entry in this collection of Francis Frith's photographs, 2004. **Masefield's most damning description of a village** Gnosall 'a large village of no particular interest' (LGS p139). **First Staffordshire Best Kept Village winner (Large Village category)** Gnosall, 1956.
4. People...
Gnosall's most famous old worthy Rev Adam Blakeman (1596-1665), Puritan minister. He was born at Gnosall, and studied at Christ Church, Oxford from 1617. Later he preached for some years in Leicestershire and Derbyshire. In 1638 he went to North America and the following year led the original settlers of Stratford, Connecticut, a Puritan utopian community, serving as the first minister of the church until his death. **Last to kill a wolf in Staffordshire** 'Baron Brough' aka the effigy of a member

of the Knightley family in the church - the event occurred in a pit hole near Brough Hall (Gnosall PR piv). **George Burder's first sermon** The Congregationalist preacher gave his first sermon at a farmhouse in the parish in 1776 (VCH vol 4 p133) (SSAHST 1971 p52). **London Dairy Show Milking Contest prize winners 1921** Messrs James & William Watson of The Gorse Farm (Knightley Gorse?), Knightley, who won the Gold Medal and Reserve Champion Prize, respectively (SA Oct 29 1921 p9p). **1924 General Election Forecast Prize winner** Miss Kathleen Cotton of Gnosall, 24, an employee of Messrs WH Dorman & Co Ltd, Stafford, who won the coveted £1,000 prize for being the only reader of a national newspaper to correctly predict the exact number of seats each political party would win in the House of Commons in the 1924 General Election (SA Nov 22 1924 p4p, p7 col 6). **Beit Memorial Fellow for Medical Research** Dr Maurice Stacey, chemist, B.Sc. Phd, FCS, son of Mr & Mrs J Stacey of Bromstead, matriculated from Newport Grammar School in 1924 with three distinctions. He was awarded this fellowship in 1933 (SA July 29 1933 p5p). **Oldest Oddfellow in England 1935** Joseph Thursfield, born Dec 25 1837, and initiated a member of the Jenkinson Glory Lodge, Gnosall, on Sept 26 1863, beating a Leek man into 2nd place (SA June 22 1935 p8 col 4. June 29 1935 p10 col 3).

Gnosall's first centenarian Mrs Emily Louisa Flello of High Street, Gnosall, who reached the age of 101 on Sept 3 1955; In 1954 Rev H Lowe, vicar of Gnosall, looking back at parish records believed Mrs Felello to be Gnosall's first centenarian (SA Sept 3 1954 p2p. Sept 1 1955 p7p). **'one of the best known farming personalities in Staffordshire' 1961** Alfred James Bourne (1884-1961) of Brough Hall farm. Born Knypersley Hall Farm, Biddulph. Founder member of the Gnosall Branch of the NFU, twice its chairman; member of Eccleshall district committees of the Staffordshire Agricultural Society, and the Gnosall Agricultural Society. His last years were spent at Vicarage House, Ranton (SA & Chron Jan 5 1961 p1p). **Gnosall woman who went round the world before round-the-world flights** Dorothy Deakin (b1936) of Plardwick Farm, who saved up from her job as a bookkeeper with a Stafford corn firm to pay for a year's circumnavigation of the world in 1967, visiting Yugoslavia, Turkey, India, Australia, New Zealand and the United States (SA & Chron Jan 4 1968 p1). **Staffordshire's first victim of internet chatroom bullying** Possibly Jessica Littleton of Geneshall Close, Gnosall, 17, who took her own life in May 2007 (SN Oct 25 2007 p2).

Gnosall's heroes 2nd Lieut Bernard Bocking, 11th East Yorks Regt, son of Rev JC Bocking of Gnosall, awarded the M.C. for gallantry and devotion in action; he only left school in 1917 (SA Aug 24 1918 p5p). Qmr-Sergt W. Hill, 1st North Staffs Regt, youngest son of Mr & Mrs Clarke of Barn's Bridge, Gnosall, who aged 25 was awarded the Distinguished Conduct Medal for 'devotion to duty'. He was in the army before the outbreak of WW1, and served to the end of that war, only being wounded once (SA Feb 16 1918 p4 col 6p). **Gnosall's saddest** Dr Ross Stewart Steele of Willey Croft, who had been in practice at Gnosall for 37 years when he took his own life aged 60 in April 1922 with prussic acid at bedtime. He had not been well for some time and was depressed. Dr Davies, his partner, said at the end of the shooting season Steele had said as he put his gun away in a mournful tone "I doubt if I shall ever use this again" (SA April 15 1922 p7p). **Gnosall's kindest** Edward Cartwright (d1653) who gave money for clothing for 10 poor children, and shortly before his death he made provision for the founding of Gnosall Free School for 14 poor children (VCH vol 4 p133). **Gnosall's poorest** The parish workhouse, called Grovesnor House (which belonged to the Grovesnor family), stood in the High Street. The site has since been occupied by a school and then a community centre (Staffordshire PastTrack, 2008). In 1888 there was a proposal to form a new Poor Law Union centred on Gnosall; the parish leaving Newport Union, instead of it joining Stafford union (SA Jan 28 1888 p7 col 1. March 24 1888 p5 col 5). **Gnosall's earliest recorded will** Belongs to Humphrey Ellins, and is dated March 14 1619/20. **First person in the parish register** William Swane, son of William Swane and Margerie his wife, baptised March 26 1572. **Choicest quote** Goronwy Harnaman in Six Towns Magazine, Feb 1966, writes 'As Gnosall was an ecclesiastical appendage, and not a feudal manor in the accepted sense, with a baronial lord of the manor, it has no thrilling history like some of the neighbouring villages.'

5. The area...

Gnosall is the **county's 13th largest parish**, consisting of 10,577 acres; **26th closest parish to the county town**, 4.7m WSW; **extremist length** 8.4m, making it **3rd longest parish in the county**; **extremist width** 4.8m, making it **33rd widest parish in the county**. **Parish's chief settlement** Gnosall, an expanding village by the Newport road; Gnosall Heath a large residential area has also emerged nearby. **Geology** GNOSALL, Outwoods-Cotonwood - Bunter; KNIGHTLEY-Brough Hall-Cowley-Walton Grange - Keuper Red Marls; BROMSTEAD Common-Gnosall Heath, Great Chatwell - Keuper Sandstones. **Highest point** 479 feet at Knightley. **Longest view in Staffordshire** Snowdonia from Broadhill and Knightley, 100 miles away, but it is more likely to be the Cader Idris range (Gnosall PR pix). **Lowest point** 220 feet at the boundary by Aqualate Mere. Gnosall was **28th= most-populated Staffordshire parish in 1801** with 2,246 people; **29th in 1811** with 2,372; **30th in 1821** with 2,671; **28th in 1831** with 3,161; **36th in 1841** with 2,424; **36th in 1851** with 2,673; **44th in 1861** with 2,400; **45th in 1871** with 2,431; **53rd in 1881** with 2,379; **54th in 1891** with 2,099; **58th in 1901** with 2,085.

SUBJECT INDEX *Go to Ha*

Haughton Old Hall.

Haughton
1. Did you know that...

Haughton's top folklore That the Moat House, a medieval open hall house in Haughton, on the north side of the Stafford-Newport road is haunted by the ghost of a lady's maid, who always keeps one room dust free and is known by the owners as 'Mary from the dairy'. Haughton the **name first appears** in Domesday Book, 1086. **What Haughton is famous for** The hymn composing Rev John Darwell, famous for the tune for psalm 148, 1770. **1st= parish registers transcribed and published by Staffordshire Register Society** Haughton, 1902. **Darwell's 148th** Is the famous tune for psalm 148, which begins 'Ye Holy Angels Bright' written by Rev John Darwell (1731-89), hymn composer, native of Haughton. **'Reputed to be one of the finest black and white buildings in the county'** Haughton Old Hall (SN Oct 18 1958 p14p). **Strange but true!** There used to be two tanneries in Haughton and the horns of the slaughtered cattle were, until some year prior to 1958, built into the roadside banks in the middle of the village (SN Oct 18 1958 p14p). **Staffordshire Best Kept Village winner (medium village category) 1963; Stafford District winner (large village category) 2000, 2004** Haughton. **(Staffordshire) Brasserie of the Year 2006** The Shropshire Inn, Haughton, judged by Staffordshire Good Food Awards (SLM Dec 2006 p100). **'Staffordshire's answer to Blackpool'** Bob Hockenhull on BBC Midlands Today Dec 23 2008 with reference to the extensive Christmas light show the village has put on since 1984. Bert Moore was the organiser in 2008.

2. Church...

At Haughton is St Giles, **one of 4 such county dedications** (of AP churches); **5th last AP county church built** dating from 1887. **Most interesting thing** A fresco depicting St George and the Dragon, which was revealed under plaster when stripped at the restoration of the church in 1887. The painting was not saved in whole although fragments remain in three small niches, probably intended for tapers, which train traces of red paint and which were incorporated in the fresco (VCH vol 4 p141).

William Evans, the prototype for 'Adam Bede' in the novel of that name by George Eliot, did the wood work for this church, when it was being restored (WSL D323/41/80. Horne's Scrapbook. No. 2. item 376). **Staffordshire rectory held continuously by more family members than any other** Perhaps Haughton by the Royds 1822-1947. The connection began when James Royds, a wealthy Lancashire man, purchased the advowson and presented it to his son, Rev Edward Royds, who was rector 1822-31. Then his younger brother, Charles Smith Royds (b1799), 1831-79, making him **Haughton's longest-serving vicar**, serving 48 years. Then his son, Preb Gilbert Twemlow Royds, 1879-1922; he was the well-known sportsman who rode hard to hounds before his ordination, and was largely responsible for the restoration of the church, 1887. Finally, there was his son, Preb Thomas Fletcher Royds. He left to take up the vicarage of Chebsey, incumbent there 1948-52, and was residing at Field Place, Walton, Stone in 1955 (SA Jan 31 1948 p5 col 1. SA & Chron Oct 6 1955 p4. Oct 13 1955 p5 col 5).

3. People...

Haughton's most famous old worthy Rev John Darwell (1731-89). Hymn composer. Born Haughton the eldest of four children of Rev Randle Darwell, rector of Haughton. He was curate successively at Haughton, Bushbury, Trysull, and finally St Matthew's, Walsall, from 1761, where he died. He is famous for composing 'Darwell's 148th' the tune for psalm 148 first published in 1770, which starts 'Ye Holy Angels Bright.' His wife, alias Mary Whateley (b1761), and daughter, Mary (1779-1851) were published poets. **Haughton's villain** Herbert Riley, 34, who attempted to cut the throat of Mrs Matilda Bowring, 65, in a burglary attempt on her house at Allimore Green as she lay in bed on Nov 13 1918. She struggled free and got out of the window onto the roof, where her screams alerted neighbours. Riley was apprehended in an usual way. Signalman John Kenney was counting some sacks under the railway bridge at Haughton when he uncovered a man's face. He said to the man, "You are Riley and the police want you. You had better come with me." Riley was taken and put into the custody of Special Constable Parker in the coal wharf office. Then he was driven to the police station in Mr John Smith's float. He was tried at the Assizes in Feb 1919 and found guilty of intent to murder and sentenced to 6 years (SA Nov 16 1918 p4 col 8. Nov 30 1918 p7 col 1. Feb 15 1919 p6 col 5). **Haughton's heroine** Mrs Annie Lockle, the 73-year-old village postmistress who tackled a mentally disturbed intruder as he burst into the living quarters of the sub-post office at Haughton on March 20 1962. The man scared off the assistant postmistress, then knocked down Mr Lockley, then hit Mrs Lockley twice, but she seemed to calm him when she stuck him in the face: No proceeding were taken against the man, said to be a patient at St George's Hospital, Stafford (SA & Chron March 22 1962). **Haughton's saddest** Francis Shipley, of Hagley Hall, Rugeley, aged 56, head of E Williams and Co (haulage), who was fatally shot while out on a rabbit shoot at Billington Bank, Haughton, in 1938. Passing a double-barrelled sporting gun to another member of the party he received the charge in his back, and was killed almost immediately (LiMe Oct 21 1938 p9 col 6). **Cousin of one of the world's tallest women ever** George Andrews of Flat 3, Haughton, whose first cousin was Jane Bunford (1895-1922) of Bartley Green, Birmingham; she measured 7 feet 7 inches. George remembers her from his childhood. In 1972 a skeleton - believed to be Jane's - was discovered at Birmingham University's Medical School (SN Feb 4 1972 p3p). **England footballer** John Blair (b1898) of 'Glenroy', Haughton in 1959, native of Liverpool. Gained an amateur international cap, playing for England against Wales, c1920; was at sometime fullback in an international trial; played for Northern Nomads in the final of the English Cup 1927. Retired from top class football in 1934; became Stafford Area Surveyor (SA & Chron Feb 5 1959 p14p). **Miss Staffordshire 1962** Mrs Beryl Lockley of Allimore Green, aged 19 (SA & Chron Aug 2 1962 p5p). **Haughton's kindest** As well as four pre-1900 benefactors, there were a surprising number who gave to Haughton poor in the beginning of the C20, starting in 1900 with Rev CT Royds; Caroline Edith Royds, wife of GT Royds, rector 1897-1933, who gave in memory of her daughter, Mildred (d1897), a 'Mildred's Treat' for children in 1914; Elizabeth Ann and Joseph Bettelley of Fair View House, Haughton, in 1914 and 1916, respectively; and Hannah Rosetta Howells of Ludlow, in 1923 (VCH vol 4 p142). **Haughton's poorest** From 1837 the poor could be housed at Stafford Union Poor House at Marston. **Haughton's earliest recorded will** Belongs to William Astyn, and is dated April 20 1540. **First persons in the parish register** Henry Pye (?) married Alice Stanley (?) July 31 1570. **Choicest quote** Arthur Mee writes in his The King's England series: 'It has quaint cottages, old hall with timbers that have weathered all the storms since Tudor days, and a church refashioned in the 18th and 19th centuries, but with a 14th-century doorway and windows 400 years old.'

4. The area...

Haughton is the **county's 121st largest parish**, consisting of 1,903 acres; **11th nearest parish to the county town**, 2.8m WSW; **extremist length** 3.3m; **extremist width** 3.3m. **Parish's chief settlement** Haughton, a farming village aligned along the Stafford-Newport road. **Geology** ALL - Keuper Red Marls. **Highest point** 381 feet on the boundary at Parkhead House. **Lowest point** 282 feet on the boundary by Butter Bank Brook. Haughton was **106th most-populated Staffordshire parish in 1801** with 437 people; **105th= in 1811** with 455; **106th in 1821** with 473; **109th in 1831** with 490; **109th in 1841** with 480; **109th in 1851** with 510; **105th in 1861** with 516; **109th in 1871** with 459; **106th in 1881** with 501; **109th in 1891** with 439; **111th in 1901** with 410.

SUBJECT INDEX *Ha to Hi*

*The return
of the Pewit
foretells
something
ominous.*

High Offley
1. Did you know that...

High Offley's top folklore That if the Black Headed Gull or Pewit failed to return to breed at Shebben Moss Pool this meant something ominous was about to occur. The pool, situated north of Shebdon by Shebdon Bridge, south of the Shropshire Union Canal, had been enclosed by 1817 and had completely disappeared by 1922. **A High Offley** Is defined as a 'Goosnargh three weeks later' in Douglas Adams' 'Meaning of Liff' (1993) (Wikipedia 2006). **County's 98th largest parish**, consisting of 2,761 acres; 39th **closest parish to the county town**, 7.4m WNW; **extremist length** 2.3m; **extremist width** 3.3m. Offley the **name first appears** in Domesday Book, 1086. **Parish's chief settlement** High Offley, a remote, lofty farming village. **What High Offley is famous for** Being a Lichfield Cathedral prebendal estate and traversed by the picturesque Shropshire Union Canal. **Geology** MOST - Keuper Red Marls; NW TIP - Bunter (S), Permian (N). **Highest point** 476 feet N of Woodseaves. **Lowest point** 246 feet on the boundary by Lonco Brook. High Offley was **92nd most-populated Staffordshire parish in 1801** with 523 people; **92nd= in 1811** with 548; **99th= in 1821** with 569; **95th in 1831** with 613; **94th in 1841** with 658; **86th in 1851** with 786; **80th in 1861** with 883; **82nd in 1871** with 865; **82nd in 1881** with 811; **84th in 1891** with 787; **94th in 1901** with 627.

2. People...

High Offley's most famous old worthy, 16th Master of the Rolls, 39th Keeper of the Privy Seal, 81st Bishop of London, 84th Lord High Treasurer, 51st Bishop of Salisbury Nicholas de Bubwith (alias Bubbewyth), Bishop of London 1406-07; Prebendary of Salisbury; Master of the Rolls 1402-05, Keeper of the Privy Seal 1405-06; Lord Treasurer 1407-08; Bishop of Salisbury 1407-08; former vicar of High Offley (Wikipedia 2008) (SLM Autumn 1953 p17). **The poet prebendary of High Offley** Nathaniel Williams who succeeded to the Prebend of High Offley in 1630. He wrote a poem on the death of Dr Willis, the famous physician, published 1675 (Willis Browne). **High Offley's villain** Henry Oakley of Woodseaves who did not appear before magistrates at Eccleshall, and had 11 previous convictions, was fined 10s, and 9s 6d costs for being drunk at Woodseaves on Feb 27 1888 (SA March 17 1888 p7 col 3). **High Offley's saddest** Alice Mary Ethell, aged 3, who accidentally fell into a tub of boiling ale in the brewhouse of her parents' pub Wharf Inn, Shebdon on Dec 14 1896. She was badly scolded and died the following day (SA Dec 19 1896 p7 col 4. Dec 26 1896 p4 col 7). **First female chairman of Stafford Rural District Council** Miss Grace Joules of Milcot, Woodseaves, member for High Offley, in June 1958 (SN June 7 1958 p10p). **5th winners of the Staffordshire W.I. Challenge Banner** High Offley and Knightley W.I. in 1925, with 260 points (SA Oct 10 1925 p10 col 2). **The man who was said to have known "every lock and inch of canal of Staffordshire"** Ephraim Talbot (1893-1957), author of three books on England's waterways, and lock keeper of The Lock House, Tixall; he died on the towpath near his home. Born High Offley, son of an employee of the waterways authority. Worked on the canals in Staffordshire c1918-c1943 (SA & Chron Jan 2 1958 p5 col 7). **Dairy Princess of the West Midlands 1979** Susan Cook of Woodseaves (SN Dec 27 2007 p6). **High Offley's kindest** By the 1830s there were two long-standing charities:- Sir Charles Skrymsher's, to help apprentice a child of the parish. In the C19 the minister selected a poor boy or girl every year as the apprentice: And Mrs Eleanor Baldwyn's which made provision for the poor of the parish, in the C19 distributed on St Thomas' day at the church in sums varying from 2s. to 6d. according to the number in the family. **High Offley's poorest** No evidence of a workhouse at High Offley has been found (OPBS Pirehill p214). From at least 1836 the poor may have been housed at the old workhouse at 34-38 Vineyard Road (formerly Workhouse Lane), Newport, until the new workhouse was built 1855~6, in Audley Avenue (formerly Longmarsh Lane). **High Offley's earliest recorded will** Belongs to Thomas Cherrington, and is dated Oct 21 1662. **First person in the parish register** Katherine Hill, widow, buried Jan 20 1659. **Choicest quote** Michael Raven in his Staffordshire and the Black Country, 1988, writes 'When approached from the W it has the appearance of a medieval hill town with the church a landmark for several miles around.'

3. Church...

At High Offley is St Mary, **one of 23 such county dedications** (most common dedication in the county); **48th= oldest AP county church** dating from 1200. **High Offley's only female churchwarden to 1937** Mrs Ellen Gertrude Grant Vickers (1854-1937), wife of Valentine Whitby Vickers (d1899), of Offley Grove. A 'zealous' churchwoman, she worshipped regularly for upwards of 60 years at the church; churchwarden from 1914. She was prominently associated with the restoration of the church in 1887, and known for her general kindness and benevolence throughout the district. By the inhabitants she was held in the highest esteem. For 36 years she taught in the Sunday School, making the somewhat long journey from her home to the village and back on foot (SA Sept 18 1937 p7 col 5).

SUBJECT INDEX *Hi to In*

*Wren at
work on
Ingestre
church.*

Ingestre
1. Did you know that...

Ingestre's top folklore That a sulphurous olegagenous well called St Erasmus's Well on Ingestre waste, probably at the edge of the park opposite Shirleywich, had healing powers, and became a holy well in medieval times. Such were the number of pilgrims to it a chapel had to be built close by. The well had become neglected by the later C17. The **name Ingestre first appears** in Domesday Book, 1086. **What Ingestre is famous for** Its parish church, designed by Sir Christopher Wren. **Rare verse mention** Ingestre is mentioned as a town in a rare verse example of early C16 English courtly love lyric verse kept in the manuscript MS Rawlinson C813 in the Bodleian Library, Oxford (Summary Catalogue 12653) (The Review of English Studies. Feb 1990 pp12-44). **First carriage bridge of its kind ever** A wooden 'scarfing' suspension bridge across the Trent between Ingestre and Shirleywich on an accommodation road of the Earl of Talbot's, built by JR Remington of Alabama, USA, in 1848. It was remarkable for its length of 150 feet, the small dimensions of the timber used, its inexpensive cost, about £200, and its site, one impracticable for any other kind of wooden bridge. By this time many footbridges had been built of this type in America, and one in the Surrey Zoological Gardens, but no such bridge existed for carriages (SA July 15 1848 p8 il).

2. Church...

At Ingestre is St Mary the Virgin, **one of 23 such county dedications** (most common dedication in the county); **45th last AP county church built** dating from 1676. **Staffordshire's finest classical C17 church, Staffordshire's only building by Christopher Wren, 4th longest church entry in Pevsner's 'Staffordshire'** St Mary's, Ingestre, at 59 lines (BOE pp28,155-156). **Staffordshire's longest surviving electric light fittings in a church** St Mary, Ingestre, dating from 1886, and still there in the early 1970s (BOE p156). Apparently, originally powered by generators at Ingestre Hall, but is not as Staffordshire Past Track (website, 2008) states the first church in the county lit by electricity. The first was St Anne's, Chasetown, 1883.

*Charles Henry
John Chetwynd-
Talbot (1860-
1921).*

3. Ingestre Hall & The Chetwynds...

'one of the most beautiful baronial halls in Staffordshire' Ingestre
Hall, according to text on a tissue souvenir commemorating Edward
VII's visit to Ingestre and Stafford, probably Nov 18-23 1907 (WSL
D323/41/80. Horne's Scrapbook. No. 2 item 244). **One of only two halls
in C17 Staffordshire to face south** Ingestre (NHS pp40,41 tab 26 of
Ingestre Hall). **'the finest park and gardens that are in this part of
England'** Daniel Defoe in the early C18 (SL p133). **First published
book on Staffordshire** Dr Robert Plot's Natural History of Staffordshire
1686. Plot had the patronage of Walter Chetwynd (d1701). The work -
along with ones on Oxfordshire, Surrey, and Wiltshire - was of the then
new half-credulous, half-sceptical enquiring nature in the county history
format by Royal Society fellows (The Shell County Alphabet. Geoffrey
Grigson. 1966 p108). **'the little Dukeries'** Area on the eastern side of
Cannock Chase so given for the number of estates such as Shugborough,
Blithfield, Ingestre in the vicinity (Staffordshire Illustrated April 1967).
Only property owned by the Earls of Shrewsbury by 1950 Ingestre Hall; they once owned vast estates including Alton Towers (NSFCT
1950 p101). **First opening of hall to the public** From about April 1956
on Wednesdays, Saturdays and Sundays 2-7pm, and Bank Holidays
11am-7pm in summer months to Oct 1, in an attempt to met enormous
costs of the upkeep of the house (SA & Chron April 26 1956 p5ps).
'one of the oldest and most illustrious (families) in Staffordshire' The
Chetwynds (LiMe May 22 1931 p5 col 2). **Staffordshire's longest time-
lapse between weddings of the prevailing lord in the parish church**
No Chetwynd Talbot marriage took place in Ingestre church after that of
Hon Rev Arthur (3rd son of 2nd Earl Talbot), in 1832, until Lady Victoria's in 2005 (daughter of 22nd Earl of Shrewsbury and Waterford) (The
Stone Gazette. June 2005 p5pc). However, the church has been used for

weddings of collateral kin for instance Miss Venetia Heber-Percy, niece of the Earl of Shrewsbury married David Stern at Ingestre on April 24 1953 (SA May 1 1953 p1p).

The CHETWYND who: is **Ingestre's most famous old worthy, was the originator of a certain bookdesk prevalent in the later C17** Sir Walter III Chetwynd (c1633-93), Staffordshire antiquary, lord of Ingestre and many other local estates from 1669. He held the seats of Stafford and Staffordshire, the offices of J.P., D.L and sheriff, but is remembered for asking Sir Christopher Wren to design Ingestre church (1676); a Fellow of the Royal Society (1678); encouraging Dr Robert Plot to write his 'Natural History of Staffordshire' (1686); and his own history of Pirehill hundred (published posthumously in 1909). When he died without issue of smallpox, Ingestre passed to another branch of the Chetwynds. His bookdesk was said to be carved out a single piece of wood made by John Ensor of Tamworth (NHS p383); was **granted by Royal Warrant the privilege of carrying a white wand at coronations in his capacity as Hereditary Grand Seneschal (Lord High Steward) of Ireland** 19th Earl of Shrewsbury (SA May 21 1921 p7. Oct 29 1921 p4); was **premier Earl of England 1921, drove the Windsor coach to London in his teens, 'one of the first to realise the possibilities of the motor car'** Charles Henry John Chetwynd-Talbot (1860-1921), 20th Earl of Shrewsbury (*see illustration above*) (SA May 21 1921 p7p); was **one of the last Staffordshire debutantes presented at court** Lady Rose Chetwynd-Talbot, aged 17, 2nd daughter of the Earl and Countess of Shrewsbury. Also Alicia Crofton, aged 17, daughter of Major C A Crofton and cousin to Lady Rose Chetwynd-Talbot. Both in 1958. There was also two others (see below, and Stone) (SA March 20 1958 p1ps).

4. People...

Ingestre's hero Capt (Acting Major) THB Oriel RGA, son of Rev HS Oriel of Ingestre Rectory was awarded the M.C. whilst serving in France in WW1 (SA June 8 1918 p7 col 1). **One of the last Staffordshire debutantes presented at court** Miss Stephnie Todd, daughter of Mrs H Greer and the later Major HR Todd of Little Ingestre, in 1958. There was also three others (see above, and Stone) (SA March 20 1958 p1p). **First persons in the parish register** Thomas Robinson son of Thomas Robinson baptised April 26 1676 (the register is the bishop's transcript). **Royal Agricultural Society of England long service medalists** George Greatholder, head forester, of Ivy Cottage, Tixall, and his brother William Greatholder, of Pasturefields, woodman, for 40 and 42 years respectively, both on the Ingestre estate, awarded in 1953. The Greatholder family had been in the service of the Earls of Shrewsbury for generations; George and William's father was a woodman for 50 years (SA Feb 20 1953 p6p). **Ingestre's poorest** From 1837 the poor were housed at Stafford Union workhouse at Marston. **Ingestre's earliest recorded will** Belongs to Thomas Chatwyn Esq, and is dated Nov 28 1555. **Choicest quote** The antiquarian Chetwynd, Walter Chetwynd in his History of Pirehill Hundred, 1679, looked back on the earlier holders of his lordship 'Near to Hopton, on the same side of Trent, lyeth Ingestre, which

Hugo held of Rob. de Stafford, 20 Conq., but whether he were paternall ancester to ye Muttons, who not long after possest it, is hard to be determined.'

5. The area...

Ingestre is the **county's 141st largest parish**, consisting of 879 acres; **13th closest parish to the county town**, 3.25m E; **extremist length** 1.8m; **extremist width** 1.6m, making it **27th= narrowest parish** in the county. **Parish's chief settlement** Ingestre, a moanful Carolinian estate hamlet centred on Ingestre Hall. **Geology** W - Keuper Red Marls; TRENT valley - Alluvium. **Highest point** 426 feet by the boundary at The Ley. **Lowest point** 243 feet by the Trent at Hoo Mill. Ingestre was **139th most-populated Staffordshire parish in 1801** with 115 people; **140th in 1811** with 122; **141st in 1821** with 125; **141st= in 1831** with 116; **143rd in 1841** with 118; **141st in 1851** with 174; **142nd in 1861** with 151; **141st in 1871** with 163; **143rd in 1881** with 138; **140th in 1891** with 192; **144th in 1901** with 120.

SUBJECT INDEX *In to Je*

It was tradition for Wheaton Aston folk to pick Snake's head-fritillaries at Motty Meadows, in Blymhill parish, on the first Sunday in May, late 1940s.

Lapley
1. Did you know that...

What Lapley is famous for Lapley Priory and the most northerly habitat in the British Isles of the Snake's head-fritillary. **Lapley's top folklore** That Earl Alfgar (or Ælfgar), Earl of Mercia, gave the land at Lapley on which was built Lapley Priory in order to fulfil the dying wish of his son, Burchard. The son had accompanied Aldred, Archbishop of York, on a mission to Rome. Returning home he died at St Remigius Abbey at Rheims in 1061, and he is supposed to have promised the monks land on his father's estates. The **name Lapley first appears** in Domesday Book, 1086. **Rare parliamentarian garrisoned house** Lapley Hall. **Last use of Wheaton Aston village lock up** c1910 (VCH vol 4 p143). **Staffordshire's longest-running inter-parish feud** Perhaps that between Lapley and Wheaton Aston dating back to the Civil War with the Royal garrison at Lapley opposing Cromwell's men at Wheaton Aston. When the latter took the garrison they gave Lapley 'what for'. Lapley had never forgotten, not even three centuries later when Robert Murty, the Staffordshire Advertiser staff reporter visited Wheaton Aston in 1949 (SA June 11 1949 p7). **'Quietest oasis on the fringe of industrial England'** Lapley and Wheaton Aston according to the vicar of Lapley in 1959, Rev G Mathers (SN April 25 1959 p14). **Three Counties' Show 1937 Champion female Shire** White Gate Marina belonging to Mr RJ Cambridge of White Gate, Wheaton Aston, held at Hereford, and winning the 3 or 4-year-old class for Shire fillies (SA June 12 1937 p11p). **Staffordshire Best Kept Village South Staffordshire District winner (small village category) 1990, 1996, 2001, 2002, 2003** Lapley.

2. Church...

At LAPLEY is All Saints, **one of 19 such county dedications** (of AP churches); **23rd= oldest county church** dating from the C12 or roughly 1150. **'probably one of the oldest bells in the country'** The sanctus bell is believed to be C14 (SN April 24 1959 p14). **Most interesting things** The weeping chancel, like most French large churches, providing perfect acoustic properties, built in 1887 by Squire Hartley (SN April 25 1959 p14). An incised effigy of a priest of c1500 (GNHS p138) (CHMS p38) (STM Jan 1967 p26p). **In the churchyard** Grave of George Plant (d1901), who shot a police officer in the shoulder at Rugeley, fled, and then took his own life (TB Feb 1 2001 p5). Grave of William Bickford of Paradise (d1896); Vivian Bird wonders where Paradise was in the parish (VB p145). At WHEATON ASTON is St Mary's, built 1857. **First to be married in the church** Miss Moira Joan Mellor of Brook House, Wheaton Aston, to Capt Robert Michael Hutton, RE, of Bardsey, East Keswick, near Leeds, on March 6 1954 (SA March 12 1954 p1).

3. People...

Lapley's most famous old worthy Burchard (d1061), son of Alfgar (or Ælfgar), Earl of Mercia. He died returning from having accompanied Aldred, Archbishop of York, on a mission to Rome and was buried by the monks of Rheims. In fulfilment of his son's dying promise Alfgar gave the monks land at Lapley and elsewhere in Staffordshire. They founded Lapley Priory 1061-86. **Strange but true!** The Sawyers families who lived at Lapley Court, Wheston Aston, in the C17 were about 12 persons resulting from interchangeable marriages (NHS p313). **Royalist scout who found a lucky horseshoe** John Dawe, who was a soldier in the garrison at Lapley in the Civil War. Commanded to go out as a scout he found a horse shoe by the wayside and put it in his girdle. When he was shot in a skirmish the bullet hit the horseshoe and saved his life (NHS pp305-306). **Personal friend of Pugenie, wife of Emperor Napoleon III** Miss Vaughan of Lapley House and Park House, Lapley. When the Emperor lived at Chislehurst after his abdication in 1870 (SN April 25 1959 p14). **Lapley's hero** Capt Frederick Hay Swinfen of the 5th Dragoon Guards, lord of Lapley manor on the death of his father, Francis Swinfen in 1838. He distinguished himself in the Charge of the Heavy Brigade at Balaclava in the Crimea War, Oct 25 1854. For two weeks in late March and early April 1856 there was great rejoicing at Lapley and Wheaton Aston when he successfully gained possession as heir-at-law to the Swinfen estates after the famous Swinfen v Swinfen case; Lapley church bells rang a merry peal for several days, a flag flew from the church tower, and there was much feasting (SA April 5 1856 p8 col 6) (VCH vol 4 p147). **She had a cheese accepted by Queen Victoria** Margaret Ann Cambridge (1859-1937), wife of Alderman G Cambridge, JP, of Old Hall, Wheaton Aston, daughter of Richard Mullock of Poulton Hall, Chester, a well-known and highly respected family of Cheshire cheesemakers, who had a cheese accepted by Queen Victoria. Mrs Cambridge continued the cheesemaking tradition at High Hall Farm, on the Earl of Bradford's estate. She played a prominent part in the rebuilding (1910) of the Zion Church, founded 1814. She was 'revered by all who knew her.' Her funeral procession to Lapley, where her interment took place, was nearly a mile long, and there were many beautiful wreaths and floral tributes (SA March 20 1937 p2 col 7). **Stretton Hall Fete Beauty Contest winner 1920** Miss Beamond of Lapley, with a clear majority of votes, out of 37 contestants (SA Sept 25 1920 p9p). **Wheaton Aston villains** Howard Smith of Hawthorn Villas, and William Smith of

Sowdlies, who so 'frightened other people in the village to such an extent that nobody would give evidence against them'. A case of their audacity to intimidate a witness with violence even in the presence of two police constables was bought before Penkridge Police Court in late Aug 1939. During it the defendants claimed they were being 'framed' and even alluded to the fact no other witnesses could be found to testify against them. PC Stokes said: "People in the village are afraid to come forward and speak against you two." Hon WH Littleton, chairman, said Wheaton Aston was getting a bad name through various people, and it had to be stopped once and for all. There was trouble over two years earlier, with Edgar Smith, William Arnold Smith, and Arthur Bryan, all of Wheaton Aston, refusing to leave the Hartley Arms, threatening the publican, and assaulting the police: The Smiths had previous convictions against them, and it was alleged they had been terrorising Wheaton Aston for some time (SA May 1 1937 p5 col 2. Sept 2 1939 p5). **Champion horse ploughman of the British Isles 1952** Walter Carrington of Lapley. This was despite he did not work on the land, but at the Midland Tar Distillery at Four Ashes. He borrowed a horse from Lapley House Farm, and another from Fred Swift at Wheaton Aston in order to plough 50 furrows in five hours, only losing 3 marks, at the competition at Cruckton, Shrops (SA Oct 17 1952 p3 col 7). **National Association of Boys' Clubs Boxing champion 1954, first Midland Heavyweight Champion** Tony Smith of Wheaton Aston when he beat Ken Brady of Retford at Leicester in 1960. In 1959 Smith beat Alex Barrow of Ghana in heavyweight boxing at Reading Town Hall, weighing 13 stone 3 and a three quarter pounds, whilst Barrow - a favourite to win Jack Solomon's £500 heavyweight competition at Wembley later in 1959 - weighed more at 13 stone 7 pounds. Also in 1958 Smith beat Terry Girlestone of Rotherham at Leicester, and then Stan Davis of Kettering at Smethwick Baths, to 'keep his unbeaten professional record'. His brother Max, returned to the Middleweight ring in 1958 after a two-year lapse, and by May 1960 was still unbeaten after nine contests (SA & Chron March 3 1955 p10 col 1. Jan 1 1959 p8 col 6. May 26 1960 p7. Nov 19 1959 p16 col 3. Nov 3 1960 p16p). **Air Training Corps' national 100m sprint winner 1978** Gregory Day, air cadet with Cosford ATC squadron, of Wheaton Aston in 12 seconds (SN Aug 21 2008 p74). **Man whose coffin was carried on a narrowboat** Jack Waldron (1919-2003), of Wheaton Aston, who ran a boar repair business. On the day of his funeral in July 2003 his coffin was taken from West Midlands Co-op Funeral Home, Penkridge, to the Tavern bridge in Wheaton Aston, and then travelled for 40 minutes on his daughter's narrowboat, Cepheus, along the Shropshire Union Canal to Lapley Wood Farm Bridge, where it was taken over land to All Saints, Lapley (E&S July 12 2003 p17p). **Lapley's kindest** Thomas Scutt, by his will dated 1702, provided a salary for a school teacher at Wheaton Aston to teach 'all poor children and scholars' in the parish of Lapley, and for the poor, clothing and a money dole on Easter Monday and Christmas Day, respectively (VCH vol 4 p154). **Wheaton Aston's poorest** In 1756 £0.0.6 is paid for mending 'ye Parish house' which may be a poorhouse; in 1779 rent was paid for the 'Poors house'. In 1763 £0.16.6 is paid towards the workhouse charge. In 1771 £0.5.0 is paid for 'the lady's Entrance at ye workhouse'. By 1781 Wheaton Aston were badging the poor (SRO D3082/6/1). **Lapley's poorest** In 1791 a public meeting was held at Church Eaton workhouse at which it was agreed to take the poor of Lapley (SRO D3377/48). Between 1818-21 there are frequent references to the 'Poor House' in the Lapley 'Town Book' (SRO D3082/6/2). From 1836 Lapley parish was in Penkridge Union, renamed Cannock Union from 1870s. From 1872 the poor were housed at the new Union workhouse on Wolverhampton road, Cannock. **Lapley's earliest recorded will** Belongs to Thomas Sawer, and is dated Oct 26 1532. **First persons in the parish register** Laurence Pickstoke and Isabell Frekley married Jan 19 1538. **Choicest quote** Vivian Bird in his Staffordshire, 1973, wrote 'Across fields I tramped among the stubble of recently-stooked barley, through bracken neck high, over green pastures with lengthening shadows to the crunching of cows as they cropped the grass. Once a whirring covey of partridges erupted from the corn, and I came at last to winding lanes which took me through the village to the church.....From the porch I looked over much of Staffordshire and all Shropshire, stretched towards the sunset with the Wrekin dark and prominent. The even upland skyline of Cannock Chase closed the east behind the church.'

4. The area...

Lapley is the **county's 78th largest parish**, consisting of 3,542 acres; **32nd closest parish to the county town**, 5.9m SSW; **extremist length** 3m; **extremist width** 4m. **Parish's chief settlement** The parish church is in the quiet village of Lapley. But the bigger settlement and other township is Wheaton Aston. **Geology** ALL - Keuper Red Marls. **Highest point** 454 feet on the boundary at Ivetsey Bank. **Lowest point** 293 feet on the boundary by Whiston Brook. **Rare plant** Wood reed or Arundo Epigeios in a hedge between Stinking Lake and Ivetsey Bank, in the late C18 (SHOS vol 1 part 1 p99). Lapley was **68th most-populated Staffordshire parish in 1801** with 759 people; **76th in 1811** with 746; **71st in 1821** with 916; **73rd in 1831** with 912; **72nd in 1841** with 952; **74th in 1851** with 962; **85th in 1861** with 828; **88th in 1871** with 779; **90th in 1881** with 744; **86th in 1891** with 767; **85th in 1901** with 742.

*Old main
gateway
to Stafford
Gaol.
Courtesy of
Joan Anslow.*

Marston
1. Did you know that...

Marston's top folklore According to Gavin Gibbons in his 'The Coming of the Spaceships' (1956) a vidya was seen by Mr and Mrs Botham over Marston on Sept 4 1954. **Parish's chief settlement** Foregate liberty, a suburb of northern Stafford, which had a priory, the County Industrial Home and Stafford's workhouse, gaol and infirmary. **Marston is famous for** Stafford Common. **World's smallest racehorse 1935, world's largest pig 1935** 'Wee Jimmy' of Buenos Aires, aged 5 and half, standing at 23 inches high, weighing 37 pounds, and the pig was 'Billy', 2 years old, and weighing more than half a ton. Both were exhibited at Pat Collins' fair on Stafford Common on June 28-30 1935 (SA June 29 1935 p6, col 7, p7p). **Lorry which carried the mill motor armature forming part of 'one of the largest reversing mill equipments in the country' 1935** A 14-wheel lorry of Marston Road Transport Ltd, which carried the 73-ton, 12-foot diameter armature from its place of manufacture, English Electric Company, Stafford, to the British Iron & Steel Co. Ltd works in Cardiff. The journey, via Wolverhampton, Kidderminster and Gloucester, was expected to take week (SA Nov 30 1935 p11p). **'The worst slums in country' 1962** Conditions in the Common Ward, Stafford, north of Bellasis Street, near Stone Flats. At Stafford Town Council Meeting on Oct 30 1962 Cllr HH Coghlan said: 'You will see the worst slums of England there. Because of subsidence, to get into some of the houses you have to go in sideways.' Speaking of Field Place in particular Cllr JS Kelly said "It is being used as a doss-house by gentlemen of the road, who also use it as a calling point" (SA & Chron Nov 1 1962 p13 col 4).

2. Churches...

At Marston is St Leonard, **one of 5 such county dedications** (of AP churches); **29th= last AP county church built** dating from 1794. In Marston Road, Stafford, is St Alban, 1896 (VCH vol 6 p250).

3. People...

Marston's most famous old worthy Edwin Bostock (d1883), who moved his father's boot and shoe business from Stafford town centre to Foregate Street, Foregate. There in 1855 he began the mechanisation of Stafford's footwear industry with the closing-machine. In 1871 he secured control of his brother's shoe factory at Stone. The company, later Edwin Bostock & Co. Ltd (1898), and later Lotus Ltd (1919), at a new factory in Sandon Road, Foregate, from 1903, expanded throughout the C20, to dominate Stafford's shoe and boot industry (VCH vol 6 p218). **First physician of the Staffordshire General Infirmary, discoverer of digitalis** William Withering (1741-99), born Wellington, Shrops, 1766-75, buried Edgbaston. When he was slowly dying of tuberculosis at the end of the C18, the punning comment was made that 'the flower of physicians is withering' (SLM Sept 1951 pp14-15il). **Marston's WW1 hero** Sergt WT Plant of 153 Marston Road, of A Battery 160th Brigade RFA, was awarded the Croix de Guerre for conspicuous bravery in Oct 1918 whilst serving in the 34th Division in France. In Spring 1918 his gallant conduct at Fieurbaix was noted in a report by Major-Gen RW Barnes, commanding the 57th Division (SA Jan 4 1919 p3 col 7p). **Marston's WW2 heroes** Bomber Pilot Eric Johnson, born Enson 1922, but moved with his parents to a farm on the Harrowby estate at Marston in 1923. Joined 419 Squadron, Royal Canadian Air Force, in 1942. He was personally presented by George VI with the Distinguished Flying Cross in 1943 for completing many sorties over Germany; the Air Force Cross in 1947 for gallantry as a pilot instructor; the BEM in 1986 for a lifetime service to the Crown. Trevor Myatt, born at No. 98 Marston Road, Foregate in 1924, was awarded the Distinguished Flying Medal for gallantry in March 1945 when, with another during a flight, he relieved a wounded and trapped rear gunner in his gun turret (Stafford At War. an SN publication. 1995 pp13,14p, 16il). **3rd in Miss England (Personality Girl) 1934, Miss Staffordshire 1936** Miss Nellie Hooper (b1915) of Tillington Street, Foregate, Miss English Electric 1935, Miss Stafford 1936; she was the 4th Miss Staffordshire ever (SA Dec 8 1934 p7p) (Stafford Pageant: The Exciting Innovative Years 1901-1952. Gordon Henry Loach. 2007). **Miss Staffordshire 1946** Miss Betty Hill, a 19 year old policewoman of 220 Stone Road, Stafford. The national press dubbed her 'the woman cop who 'copped' a beauty competition prize'; Miss Stafford 1946; she was the 9th Miss Staffordshire ever (SA May 25 1946 p8p) (Stafford Pageant: The Exciting Innovative Years 1901-1952. Gordon Henry Loach. 2007). **British Crown Green Individual Merit bowling champion 1953, All-England bowls champion 1954** Bill Slater (1905-1984), of 226 Sandon Road. He played in the Stafford League, playing for Lotus and Amasal (SA Aug 7 1953 p2 col 6, p5 cols 8-9. Feb 9 1956 p1 col 2) (CAd Jan 27 1984 p25). **One of the eight guardsmen who carried Winston Churchill's coffin** Lance-Sergeant Lincoln Perkins, aged 24, of 23 Lovatt Street, Foregate. He had attended Kingston Secondary Modern School; awarded the BEM in 1965 (SA & Chron Feb 18 1965 p13p). **Miss Staffordshire 1980** Angela Brown of Stone Road, Stafford, aged 18, a machine operator at Lotus, Miss Lotus Queen of Clubs 1980. She was perhaps the first black holder of the Miss Staffordshire title (SN June 6 1980 p1p). **'Miracle baby from nowhere'** Alfie Siviter born Dec 7 2007, according to his mother, Trudi Siviter, 39. She was told she would never have children after treatment to remove cancer cells which were found in her cervix, two ectopic pregnancies, several attempts at IVF fertility treatment and the removal of one-and-a-half ovaries. The Siviter family were then of Walden Ave near Stone Flats (ES Jan 14 2008 p15pc). **Marston's poor** From 1837 the poor could be housed at Stafford Union Poor House, built 1837/8, Marston Road, Foregate. The building became an old people's home and hospital, Fernleigh, in 1948, and was demolished in 1971 (VCH vol 6 p231). **Last person born in Stafford workhouse** Mrs Doris Bourne (b1915) of Hyde Lea, believed she was; her father, Bill Dix, was the workhouse master 1904-35 (SN Jan 28 1972 p5). **Marston's earliest recorded will** Belongs to William Tumkynson, and is dated June 18 1552. **Choicest quote** Staffordshire General and Commercial Directory (1818) says 'Marston is a village and liberty in the parish of St Mary Stafford about three miles to the north of that town, upon a good loamy soil, excellent both for corn and pasture.'

4. Stafford Gaol...

Largest county prison in the country Stafford Gaol. In 1886 it was capable of housing 842 prisoners. In 1914 there were 762 cells (89 for females) (SA Sept 15 1939 p9 cols 1,2). **First turnkey of the new gaol at Stafford** John Harvey who took up post from 1 Sept 1794. **Last hung on the flat roof of the original Lodge Gate** Anne Statham for the murder of her daughter, 1817, during which execution the scaffold collapsed, after which the new portable drop was used (Around Stafford. Roy Lewis. 1999. p65p of original gate-lodge, in demolition 1952). **First hung on the new portable drop erected in front of the original Lodge Gate** Samuel F Campbell, for forgery, 1817, this would be using a scaffold on wheels pushed out through the main gateway (SN Jan 25 1980 p8) (Around Stafford. Roy Lewis. 1999. p65). **First hung not dissected** See Ranton and Wolverhampton. LAST HUNG AT THE PRISON: **for forgery** John Highfield, 1828 (SN Jan 25 1980 p8); **for highway robbery** John Reynolds in 1833 for highway robbery with intent to murder (SN Jan 25 1980 p8); **who was female** Sarah Westwood, aged 42, for poisoning her husband, 1844 (SN Jan 25 1980 p8); **publicly** William Collier, on Aug 7 1866 for the murder of Thomas Smith at Black Planting Wood, Kingsley parish; apparently hung twice, the first time the rope slipped when the trap door swung down; so that thereafter executions were held in private (Staffordshire Chronicle May 23 1942); **ever** Josiah Davies, 1914 for murder of his landlady (SN Jan 25 1980 p8). **'One of the last Staffordians to remember executions in the town'** Mrs Eva Starley (d1979), who recalled "During the last few days of the old century I remember passing the gaol every day on may way to school, and on certain occasions, we ran hurriedly past because the 'Black Flag' had been hoisted over the prison to signify that an execution had taken place' (Stafford: A History & Celebration. Roger Butters & Nick Thomas 2005 p63).

5. The area...

Marston is the **county's 130th largest parish**, consisting of 1,487 acres; **2nd closest parish to the county town**, 0.15m N; **extremist length** 2.1m; **extremist width** 1.9m. The **name Marston first appears** in 1081. **Geology** Keuper Marls. **Highest point** 400 feet S of Yarlet. **Lowest point** 272 feet by the Trent. Marston was **143rd= most-populated Staffordshire parish in 1801** with 99 people; **144th in 1811** with 100; **144th in 1821** with 96; **140th in 1831** with 119; **139th in 1841** with 178; **137th in 1851** with 206; **124th in 1861** with 345; **106th in 1871** with 490; **93rd in 1881** with 664; **93rd in 1891** with 623; **82nd= in 1901** with 779.

SUBJECT INDEX *La to Le*

Norbury
1. Did you know that...

When the largest motor transport vehicle in the world got stuck in Norbury A lorry capable of carrying 100 tons proceeding along Newport Road at Woodseaves got ditched at Norbury Lane-end on March 8 1934. It was carrying a 51 ton dead whale, popularly known as 'Eric the Whale', from Southend to Morecambe. The driver had failed to give notice of its presence in the district to the police under the Act of Motor Vehicles Authorisation of Special Types Order, No. 1, of 1933 (SA April 21 1934 p7 col 4). **Norbury's top folklore** Norbury Old Manor house, the ancient seat of the le Botiler or Butler family, three-quarters of a mile east of Norbury, was demolished in the earlier C19 apparently because it was so haunted. Its stones were reused to built Norbury Manor house, to the south in the mid C19, and some believe the ghosts 'flitted' with the stones. There are stories of a phantom horse in the stables and disturbances in the house. **'The Village that has Time on its Side'** Norbury, according to Miss MMB Higham in Staffordshire Life magazine, being a village which is 'no place for change' (SLM April 1948 p103). **Best echo of its kind in Staffordshire** According to Dr Plot that which rebounded off Norbury Old Manor house (NHS p29 tab 19 of the hall) (SD p61). **Britain's biggest litter of pigs ever** Perhaps the litter of 22 pigs in late Jan 1960 belonging to Mr SJ Stubbs of Blakemore View, Norbury; by Feb 18 1960, three had died (SA & Chron Feb 18 1960 p1). **First nature reserve bought by Staffordshire Wildlife Trust** 35 acres of Loynton Moss in 1970. The Trust was at that time called Staffordshire Nature Conservation Trust (Staffs Wildlife No. 76. May 1999 p15). **What Norbury is famous for** The enormous cuttings of the Shropshire Union Canal, an engineering nightmare. The **name Norbury first appears** in Domesday Book, 1086.

2. Church...

At Norbury is St Peter, **one of 15 such county dedications** (of AP churches); **88th= oldest AP county church** dating from the C14 or roughly 1350. **In the church note** In the founder's arch a fine painted stone effigy of a cross-legged Ralph le Botiler, the elder, or his son, who succeeded to the manor in c1307 (VCH vol 4 p161). The east chancel window was designed by Miss Charlotte S Burne, folklorist, in 1873.

Earliest brass in Staffordshire That to Lady Hawys de Botiler, wife of Ralph (the younger), who died in 1359, in Norbury church (SPJD p43). **2nd earliest alabaster effigy in Staffordshire** A mutilated knight (?Sir Edward Botiler, d1412, grandson of the younger Ralph), and ladies (?Sir Edward's wife and mother), at western end of the N side of the nave, both of c1360-80 (BAST vol 69-71 p2). **One of the last brasses in England** That to John Skrymsher (d1667); Masefield says there are only about a dozen later brasses in England (LGS p194). **The Easter altar frontal that took 42 years to make** That for Norbury church designed and made by the Burne family (SLM Autumn 1953 p21). **Norbury's longest-serving vicar** Sambrooke Higgins, who served 64 years, 1759-1823. **Norbury's saddest** Rev Thomas Bury, vicar of Norbury, who inveigled against the Long Parliament and called its members usurpers for which he was cast into prison. He later died at Norbury, four months after the execution of Charles I in 1649 (SLM Autumn 1953 p21). **Bishop Hackett's villain** Rev Christopher Comyn, Rev Thomas Bury's successor, who was suspected of Presbyterian tendencies. An anecdote is preserved in a manuscript at Lichfield which records "when this man first waited upon Bishop Hackett his Lordship attacked him with this tart expression, 'I hear you have often said that Hell is paved with Bishop's skulls; I desire you tread light on mine when you come there.'" However, Comyn eventually became a Prebendary of Lichfield and in his will made in 1692 he describes himself as a Priest "according to the Order of our Holy Mother the Church of England, the most sincere part of the Catholick Church." (SLM Autumn 1953 p21).

3. People...

Norbury's most famous old worthy, 'the first adequate English laureate with no one to take his place until Keats' Richard Barnfield (1574-1627), poet. Born and baptised at Norbury, the seat of his mother's family. He could also be claimed a Shropshire worthy because the Barnfields were of Edgmond, or a Stone one, where his grave and the site of his residence (Darlaston old hall) are. It is almost certain that he was in close touch with Shakespeare and some of his poems such as his sonnet "If music and sweet poetry agree," and the ode beginning "As it fell upon a day, In the merry month of May," were always included in "the Passionate Pilgrim" and wrongly ascribed to Shakespeare. He published no more works after the age of 24. The quote about him is from Swinbourne (SLM Autumn 1953 p21) (SA April 16 1954 p6. SA & Chron Sept 13 1955 p6 cols 3-4). **Norbury's villain** Possibly Ralph de Botiller who was probably behind the murder of William de Cliderhowe, vicar of Norbury. Cliderhowe was accused in 1302 of poaching fish by night out of the squire's pools, but was acquitted. According to Assize Rolls in 1305 he was murdered by William the Woodward, a servant of Ralph le Botiler (LGS p194). **Norbury's bravest** On Aug 14 1959 John Barry Hughes, aged 22, of Gnosall, who whilst drinking with a friend at Norbury Junction Inn, saved a six year old boy of Cannock from drowning in deep water in the canal basin, despite being a non-swimmer. After struggling to the bank, with the aid of his friend, he gave the boy artificial respiration and he was saved (SA & Chron Aug 20 1959 p1p). **'one of Staffordshire's most distinguished contemporary writers' 1955** Lieut Col Alfred H Burne, military historian, author of 'Lee, Grant and Sherman' (1938), 'The Art of War on Land' (1944), 'The Battlefields of England' (1950), 'More Battlefields of England' (1952), and 'The Crecy War' (1955), son of Col AH Burne of Loynton Hall, and brother of SAH Burne, deputy chairman of the Staffordshire Quarter Sessions, Staffordshire antiquarian (SA & Chron March 24 1955 p4 col 8. April 28 1955 p6 col 7). **Weston Jones' poorest** According to Weston Jones township accounts the township was renting a poorhouse between at least 1789 and 1796 (SRO D1718/11). **The parish's poorest** From at least 1836 the poor may have been housed at the old workhouse at 34-38 Vineyard Road (formerly Workhouse Lane), Newport, until the new workhouse was built 1855~6, in Audley Avenue (formerly Longmarsh Lane). **Norbury's earliest recorded will** Belongs to Robert Rabon, and is dated 1527 (but this could relate to Norbury, Derbys). **First person in the parish register** Johes son of Wilelm et Katherine Hawkins baptised Jan 2 1538. **Choicest quote** John Hillaby in his Journey through Britain (published by Paladin), 1968, was taken by boating paraphernalia found at Norbury canal junction 'Some miles beyond Newport the canal runs into Staffordshire and suddenly becomes busy with boats. That morning proud owners were busy letting them out; launches and long narrow barges, beautifully done up like merry-go-rounds in sky-blue and scarlet. The bottoms of women in jeans bulged from the open cockpits as they bent down to wash up; their menfolk tinkered with engines and hauled up triangular flags on bits of string... In the jolly waterside pub at Norbury they call each other skipper and drink not too much.'

4. The area...

Norbury is the **county's 81st largest parish**, consisting of 3,361 acres; **37th closest parish to the county town**, 6.9m W; **extremist length** 2.6m; **extremist width** 3.7m. **Parish's chief settlement** Norbury, a small village; there are the hamlets Weston Jones, Loynton and Oulton. **Geology** NORBURY - Keuper Sandstones (Norbury Manor, Park, village, Oulton), Keuper Red Marls (Doley Brook), Bunter (Radmore Lane, Shelmore); WESTON JONES - Keuper Sandstones (Loynton village), Keuper Red Marls (Weston Jones village, Weston Wood). **Highest point** The Roundabout at 430 feet. **Lowest point** 243 feet at Whitleyford Bridge. Norbury was **115th most-populated Staffordshire parish in 1801** with 371 people; **120th in 1811** with 357; **124th in 1821** with 349; **115th in 1831** with 438; **122nd in 1841** with 353; **123rd in 1851** with 358; **121st in 1861** with 364; **123rd in 1871** with 344; **125th in 1881** with 318; **116th in 1891** with 368; **115th in 1901** with 383.

SUBJECT INDEX *Le to Lo*

Elizabeth I is supposed to have stayed at the White Hart Inn, Penkridge.

Penkridge
1. Did you know that...

Penkridge's top folklore There is a tradition Elizabeth I, who is said to have passed through Penkridge in 1575, stayed at the White Hart Inn, on the main road at Stone Cross. Or that she only dined there, perhaps as the guest of her master of horse, Ambrose Dudley, Earl of Warwick, brother of Robert Dudley, Earl of Lancaster (the white hart is a Lancastrian symbol). Mary Queen of Scots is said to have been refreshed there on two occasions during her captivity in Staffordshire. **Staffordshire's oldest known bridge** Boulderstone Bridge which crossed the Penk N of Penkridge and was made up of Ice Age boulders. The **name Penkridge first appears** in 858. **'the famous place which is called Pencric'** Description of Penkridge in a charter of 958. **One of only two places in Staffordshire with a Roman name** Penkridge (the other is Lichfield) (PNSZ p17). **Smallest and quaintest cruck-framed cottage in Staffordshire** Perhaps Doxey Wood Cottage opposite Doxeywood Farm on the Bradley Penkridge border (MR p46p). **Oldest habitable house in Staffordshire** How the Old Deanery in Pinfold Lane, Penkridge, has been described. The central bay of stone was originally the residence of the Dean of Penkridge Collegiate Church. The wings were added c1552 (Penkridge Parish: A selection of walks with historical notes. Penkridge PC & Lt Cdr RC Wilkes. 2nd ed. by 1978. p8). However, another source says the Old Deanery contains no medieval work, has no link with the college, and was built after the dissolution (VCH vol 5 p111). **Penkridge's oldest inn 1951** The Blacksmith's Arms, or 'Two Steps', a black and white building in Market Street, which was faced with closure at the end of 1951 (SA June 22 1951 p5 col 7). **Most unintelligible place** According to Henry Parslow in a letter to Brook Bridges on enclosure of open field strips, dated 1698, 'Penkridge is the most unintelligible place that ever I saw, for, besides my Lord's Manor, there are in it manors of my Lord Willoughby, Sir Edward Littleton, Mr Congreve and, I think, two or three more, none of which are separated by known bounds, but are confusedly intermixed...' (LHSB G15 p11). **Staffordshire's 2nd and 7th earliest commutation of tithes when they were dealt with under a parliamentary enclosure act** Gailey Common 1773, and Water Eaton

1799, by allotments of land, respectively. **'one of the best places to embark on a canal tour'** Penkridge (Staffordshire Handbook c1966 p15). **Only six-sail mill in Staffordshire** Butterhill Mill, in use by 1820 (VCH vol 5 p141) (SVB p62p,63). **Most important engineering work on the GJR line in Staffordshire** Penkridge Viaduct by Thomas Brassey (d1870), according to Robert Sherlock (IAS p185). **'prettiest rural station in Staffordshire' 1877** May be considered Penkridge railway station, on account of either side of the railway, bordering the platform, are rows of the mountain ash (- 'one of the prettiest trees of the wood'), which are delightful when in fruit in Sept (SA Sept 15 1877 p5 col 1). **Produced some of 'the finest saddlery in this part of the country'** Pearsons of Penkridge, c1920 (SN Feb 21 1959 p14). **One of the last most-sizeable places in Staffordshire to get gas** Penkridge, still without a gas supply by late July 1869 (SA July 31 1869 p7 col 4). **Largest room in Penkridge 1869** On the site of or adjoining the George and Fox Inn, measuring 44 feet by 23 feet, belonging to The Teddesley Lodge of Odd Fellows, built by Robert Gilbert and designed by his son EC Gilbert (SA July 31 1869 p7 col 4). **First visit to Penkridge by the Archbishop of Dublin since the Reformation** Possibly when Dr Gregg, Archbishop of Dublin, came to preach in St Michael's on July 1 1934; the archbishops of Dublin were deans of the collegiate church of Penkridge in the Middle Ages from their combined royal grant in 1216, and a condition of the original gift was that the Archbishop and his successors should not be Irishmen (SA July 7 1934 p9p). **First meet of the Staffordshire Beagles** They met at Dunston Post Office on Oct 16 1929 (LTM March April 1972 p58).
Fancy that! Herr Artur Jacobi, captain in the German air force, chief inspector of road accidents under General Goring and a leading Nazi travelled all the way from Berlin to attend Penkridge Police Court on Oct 24 1938 to give evidence on behalf of Wilberforce Noel Jordan of Solihull involved in a road accident at the junction of Watling Street and Engleton Lane, Gailey, in July 1937 at the six-day international motor-cycle trial organised by the Auto-Cycle Union; his motorcycle had collided with a motorcar. The Chairman (the Hon WH Littleton) said the Bench were much obliged to him for coming such a long way to give evidence, and the car driver was fined (SA Oct 29 1938 p10 col 6). **'One of the chief centres for training the Land Army'** The Staffordshire Farm Institute at Robaston in WW2 (SA Sept 23 1939 p6p). **'one of the first in the county to go in for'** the yard and parlour system of milking Drayton Manor Farm, Dunston. The owner Mr W Snelson, was giving demonstrations in the use of the system in late 1956. The system kept an automating tab on the quota of cows allowed from the yard to the parlour (SA & Chron Nov 8 1956 p5ps). **When the Archers came to Coppenhall** When Miss Gwen Berryman (Doris Archer) and Miss Joy Davies (Helen Fairbrother) of the BBC radio soap opera were star guests at Coppenhall Village Fete on June 12 1954 (SA June 18 1954 p3p). **Penkridge Parish Council's first 'social' meeting** Was a dinner at the Spread Eagle Hotel, Gailey, on Feb 9 1955 to celebrate the

60th anniversary of the council, formed Jan 2 1895 (SA & Chron Feb 17 1955 p5 cols 1-3). **Staffordshire's first stretch of motorway** Opened to the public by Ernest Maples, Transport Minister, on Aug 2 1962 at Dunston, and was the 5.5 mile stretch first known as the Stafford by-pass (CAd Aug 9 1962). **First one of its kind in Britain** A sleek, white 100mph ambulance, which started patrolling the Stafford by-pass (first section of M6 in Staffordshire) in early Oct 1962 (SA & Chron Oct 11 1962 p15 col 6-7). **First crash of note on first stretch of motorway in Staffordshire** Was in week 14-21 Sept 1962 involving Anthony John Tripp, aged 24, of 11 Ladbrook Road, Solihull, after his car overturned at Dunston. About two months earlier there had been an accident before the motorway opened on the link road at Tillington (SA & Chron Sept 27 1962 p10 col 7). **Staffordshire Best Kept Village winner (large village category) 1962**; **South Staffordshire District winner (large village category) 2002** Penkridge. **Staffordshire Best Kept Village winner (small village category) 1962** Stretton.

2. Churches...

At PENKRIDGE is St Michael, **one of 12 such county dedications** (of AP churches); **55th= oldest AP county church** dating from 1220. **'now one of the most beautiful village churches in the kingdom'** St Michael's after the restoration of 1881, which was funded by Lord Hatherton (SA April 7 1888 p5 col 5). **Longest bell ropes in Staffordshire** Believed to be those at Penkridge at 75 feet (SN Feb 21 1959 p14). **First peel or part of a peel to be rung by a local band of ringers** When the Penkridge local band of ringers (treble L Morris, 2nd S Hill, 1st F Morris, 2nd E Turner, 3rd H Clarke, 4th B Cheadle, 5th CJ Bastone, tenor, J Davis) rang a quarter peel of grandsire doubles on the back six bells, treble and second in front, for the morning service on Sunday Nov 13 1938, in 43 minutes, with the bells half muffled, conducted by CJ Bastone, deputy head ringer (SA Nov 19 1938 p4 col 8). **Noted for the large number of memorials** (SA Sept 9 1939 p7p). **Earliest dated gravestone in the churchyard** Henry Pickstock (d1500), it lies by the chancel door (HOP p17note). **The 'Lonsdale Oak'** was planted on Dec 16 1867 in the churchyard in honour of the late Bishop of Lichfield (SA Dec 21 1867 p4 col 5). **Penkridge's longest-serving dean** Alexander de Bicknor who served 32 years, 1317-49. **Penkridge's longest-serving vicar** Richard Slaney, who served 22 years, 1808-30. At COPPENHALL is Saint Lawrence, **county's 2nd earliest surviving daughter church**, dating from C13. **'Best specimen of Early English architecture in Staffordshire'** St Lawrence (SA & Chron Dec 1 1955 p4). Pevsner called it 'A perfect C13 village church' (BOE p108). At DUNSTON is St Leonard (1876-78). At GAILEY is St John (1849-50). At PILLATON is St Modwen (1488). At STRETTON is St John (C12 (but then Stretton was separate parish), 1860).

3. Horses, fairs, sport...

What Penkridge is famous for Its former horse fairs. **Earliest record-ed horse racing in Staffordshire** At Penkridge 1680, held after the Midsummer Fair (HOS p64). **Best fairs in England for saddle and draught**

horses The early C19 Penkridge fairs in April and October (THS p256) (OWEN) (SOP p172) (HOP p67-71). **'greatest horse-fair in the world'** Daniel Defoe on the late Sept or early Oct fair of 1278 at Penkridge. **First Penkridge Carnival** 1947 (SA Supplement July 25 1952). **Young Bird (pigeon) Race winner 1953** Mr B Heath from Dunston with a blue chequer cock, winning by a margin of 14 yards per minute with a velocity of 1,114 yards per minute (SA Aug 7 1953 p5 col 4). **Southport 24 Hour Race winners 2008, and 3rd 2008** South Staffordshire Sailing Club, based at Gailey, using a Lark class boat called South Staffs Lark, and coming third in the same year in a GP14 class dinghy. This is the UK's premier endurance, and only, race for single, classic sailing dinghies. South Staffordshire SC have competed ever since the race began 1967; and on winning it were the first Staffordshire team to do so. It is run by West Lancashire Yacht Club (Southport 24 Hour Race website) (SN Oct 2 2008 p76).

Bishop Hurd.

4. People...

Penkridge's most famous old worthy, 'the Beauty of Holiness' Allusion to Richard Hurd (1720-1808), bishop of Lichfield (1774-1781), born at Congreve, son of a Staffordshire yeoman. He was know as 'the Beauty of Holiness' for his moderate and orthodox beliefs and being suspicious of religious enthusiasm. Preceptor to the Prince of Wales and Duke of York. The inscription on his memorial in Penkridge church reads "Through ability and merit he became Bishop of Lichfield and Coventry (1774-81)", adding "from modesty he was unwilling to accept the Archbishopric of Canterbury (1783)" - a decision he took while bishop of Worcester (1781-1808). **'one of the earliest local correspondents of the Staffordshire Advertiser'** Mr Bennet, attorney-at-law, of Penkridge; his wife died 1804 aged 35 (SA March 19 1904 p3 col 3). **'the Staffordshire 'Healer''** Bridget Bostock of Coppenhall, a healer of the most miraculous sort. Achieved regional notoriety in the summer of 1748, with near 600 diseased and disordered people coming to her to be cured, when she was aged about 70. As a churchgoer, she also enjoyed the support of Rev William Harding, vicar of Coppenhall (GM 1748?) (TB Aug 1994 p7il).

Staffordshire's longest-serving ecclesiastical parish clerk Perhaps John Bolton clerk for Coppenhall from May 1851 to May 1901, during which time he served four vicars, four churchwardens, and saw the entire population change, with not one person nor even the descendant of any person residing in the parish who lived there when he became Parish Clerk (SA May 18 1901 p4 col 7). **Strange but true!** Thomas Robson of the Littleton Arms Inn, Penkridge, went to catch a train to Stafford, to attend the market, on May 8 1886. He reached Penkridge Station late while the 2.37 train was at the platform. In the excitement of the moment he tried to cross over the buffers of one of the carriages and while doing so the train started, being unable to reach the platform, he retained his standing position upon the buffers, holding on by the bar, and in this position reached Stafford safely. The incident created a good deal of excitement at Stafford (SA May 15 1886. May 16 1936 p5 col 1). **Penkridge's villain** Ewan Mathieson, aged 61, who battered to death with a heavy hammer his landlady and suspected lover Mrs Gladys Applebee, on Oct 8 1958. The 55-year-old widow kept a general store in Cannock Road, Penkridge. Mathieson then committed suicide by putting his head in a gas oven (SA & Chron Oct 16 1958 p1). **Penkridge's villainess** Thurza Elizabeth Wright, under-housemaid at Stretton Hall, indicted for arson at the hall on Feb 26-27 1919, aged 17. She started 20 fires, lighting curtains and upholstery. At her trial she was found to be mentally unstable, suggested by the fact she brought other's attention to the fires. Having no previous convictions she was bound over to her mother (SA July 5 1919 p5 col 3). **Penkridge's heroes** Corp E Till of the Tank Corps and Pte C Morris of the North Midland Division Royal Army Medical Corps, both of Penkridge awarded the M.M. for bravery in the field in 1918. Till was formerly of the Hanley Police Force; Morris played for Penkridge FC and worked at the Littleton Collieries (SA Sept 7 1918 p5 col 6p). Corp TH Haycock of Francis Green Lane, King's Own Yorkshire Light Infantry, former gardener at King's Bromley Manor, and his brother Pte JH Haycock, Coldstream Guards, former butcher's assistant, were both awarded the M.M., for gallant work on the French front, the later had previously been awarded a certificate for gallantry at Gouzeaucourt (SA Oct 5 1918 p5p col 6). **Penkridge's bravest** James Bellington a porter at Penkridge railway station who lifted a confused old lady from Dudley Port crossing the railway line to safety within a 100 yards of an express train from Stafford hitting her in early Aug 1900 (SA Aug 4 1900 p4 col 6). **Penkridge's saddest** Miss Sylvia Wilcox, aged 14, of Yew Tree Cottage, Penkridge, who was shot dead with a double barrel sporting gun at Yew Tree Farm, whilst fetching milk on Aug 19 1936. Whilst waiting for it with some younger children they saw the weapon leaning against a shed. A seven year old boy picked it up, and proceeded to play with it, putting it on his shoulder and saying "Hands up". To their consternation the gun went off. Sylvia was wounded in the abdomen and wrist and died before she could get to hospital (SA Aug 22 1936 p7p).
The 1st Miss Staffordshire, Miss Staffordshire 1933 Miss Mabel Thurstone of Penkridge, Miss Penkridge 1933, winning the Stafford

Pageant Queen contest, which from 1933 was styled Miss Staffordshire, at the Borough Hall on April 17 that year, with the crowning ceremony on June 23 (Stafford Pageant: The Exciting Innovative Years 1901-1952. Gordon Henry Loach. 2007) (SAWW2 p16). **First Penkridge Festival Queen** Sally Edmunds, aged 15, of Boscomoor Close, Penkridge, in 1980 (SN Aug 15 1980 p5p). **Nurse probationer** Miss Evelyn T Monckton, daughter of Francis Monckton of Stretton Hall who was awarded this title in recognition of meritorious work for nursing service in English and French hospitals from 1915 (London Gazette) (SA Jan 18 1918 p5 col 2). **One of the last Staffordshire men to die in action in WW1** Perhaps Sidney Arthur Plant of Mill End, Penkridge, aged 21, of B Company 10th Essex Regt (formerly in 4th South Staffs Regt) killed on Nov 4 1918; two other men from Stafford also died on this day (SA Dec 14 1918 p6 col 3). **One of the finest vets in the country** Eddie Straiton (1917-2004), writer and broadcaster, who had a surgery in Cannock Rd (MR2 p246). He married at Waterfall (see); gave advice to pet owners on the Jimmy Young show on BBC R2; was the technical advisor for the BBC TV series 'All Creatures Great and Small'; OBE c1997; retired to near Stone. His son, Ed (b1990) of Stone, was one of four British 'heroes' chosen to take part in the Beijing Olympics torch relay 2008 (BBC news Nov 2004) (E&S July 19 2008 p13p). **'one of the country's leading experts on agriculture' 1951** Dr Geoffrey Hearne Bates (1899-1951) of Leacroft, Robaston, principal of the Staffordshire Farm Institute 1935-51. Fellow of the Royal Society; Senior Agricultural Adviser to Norfolk CC 1930-35; author of several books on grassland problems, weed problems, potato cultivation, and plant ecology (SA Aug 31 1951 p4p). **Strange but true!** A 16 year old apprentice to a joiner near Spread Eagle (Gailey), after some altercation with his master about cleaning a pair of boots to his master's exacting satisfaction and fed up with cleaning boots on Sundays in revenge cut off his own fingers of his left hand (SA April 14 1838 p3 col 2). **Penkridge's kindest** The Littleton family of Pillaton Hall (later Hatherton and Teddesley Halls) have endowed educational and welfare provision in Penkridge, as one would expect of the parish squires. Of the many Penkridge benefactors the earliest known is Thomas Stevens, who by will dated 1730, left land to endow the village school, and to the poor of the parish (VCH vol 5 p137). **Penkridge's poorest** There was a parish workhouse on the N side of Cannock Road, formerly Husbandman Street, opposite Reynolds Cottage. In the later C19 it was used as cottages, but had been demolished by 1959. From 1836 Penkridge was in Penkridge Union (renamed Cannock Union from 1870s), but the Union workhouse was at Brewood. From 1872 it was on Wolverhampton road, Cannock (VCH vol 5 pp52,105). **Penkridge's earliest recorded will** Belongs to Richard Mownfort, and is dated about Sept 15 1550. **First person in the parish register** Johannes Warde buried Jan 13 1572. **Choicest quote** Lord Hatherton of not-far-off Teddesley Hall wrote in his diary for March 21 1841 'Rose at 7. Church at Penkridge, which I delight in. Church so full, such a respectable congregation of farmers, tradesmen and their families, and of poor people, and such an array of school children, and 200 people, and such good old fashioned Parish singing, unspoilt by wind instruments, and a Clergyman with a good voice, and excellent character, and a common sense service.'

5. The area...

Penkridge is the **county's 6th largest parish**, consisting of 14,753 acres; **10th closest parish to the county town**, 2.5m S; **extremist length** 8m, making it **4th longest parish in the county**; **extremist width** 7m, making it **9th= widest parish in the county**. **Parish's chief settlement** Penkridge, a small market town, which would be far prettier if it hadn't had its heart ripped out by the Stafford road dual carriageway. **Geology** W of the Penk - Keuper Red Marls; E of the Penk - Keuper Sandstones. **Highest point** Butter Hill at 503 feet. **Lowest point** 255 feet by the Penk near Actonmill. Penkridge was **26th= most-populated Staffordshire parish in 1801** with 2,275 people; **27th in 1811** with 2,486; **26th in 1821** with 2,896; **29th in 1831** with 2,995; **30th in 1841** with 3,129; **31st in 1851** with 3,316; **36th in 1861** with 3,146; **38th in 1871** with 3,058; **37th in 1881** with 3,134; **39th in 1891** with 2,973; **42nd in 1901** with 2,944.

SUBJECT INDEX *Lo to Mo*

Dutch troops at Ranton Abbey in World War Two.

Ranton & Ranton Abbey
1. Did you know that...

Ranton Abbey's top folklore In c1940 Ranton Abbey House, situated alongside the abbey ruins, was requisitioned by the War Office and occupied by Dutch Army Officers to a certain night in 1942 when the house accidentally burnt down. The officers are supposed to haunt the property, or one room is reputedly haunted and that room remained, strangely, undamaged by the fire of 1942. **Ranton's top folklore** There is a tradition that during the outbreak of cholera at Stafford a small market was held at Ranton and all coins were passed through water in a shallow stone basin, now lost. The **name Ranton first appears** in Domesday Book, 1086. The **name Ranton Abbey first appears** in 1166 as St Mary's (abbey) of the Assarts. **What Ranton is famous for** In Ranton it is the C19 murder case (see Ranton's Villain below). In Ranton Abbey it is the abbey, a house of Augustinian canons founded from Haughmond, c1150, of which some of the W tower, dating from C15, survives. **'One of the finest sporting estates in the country'** Ranton Abbey estate in the 1830s (SNTG p47). **Staffordshire's most extraordinary alien sighting** Two men with high foreheads, white skin and long hair, and wore blue clothes and transparent helmets who came out of a space craft at Vicarage Farm, as seen by Mrs Jessie Roestenberg and her two sons, Oct 21 1954 (The Coming of the Space Ships. Gavin Gibbons. 1956. pp64-75) (MMSE p130). **Ranton Forest King, Ranton Ironmaster, Ranton Harold, Ranton Combination** Were all stallions in the Ranton Stud of JW Wardle advertised in Staffordshire Advertiser to pregnate local mares (SA April 20 1918 p4).

2. Church...

At Ranton is All Saints, **one of 19 such county dedications** (of AP churches); **61st= oldest AP county church** dating from the C13 or roughly 1250.

3. The area...

RANTON Ranton is the **county's 123rd largest parish**, consisting of 1,843 acres; **12th closest parish to the county town**, 3.2m W; **extremist**

length 2.1m; **extremist width** 2.1m. **Parish's chief settlement** Ranton, a winding linear village. **Geology** ALL - Keuper Red Marls. **Highest point** 430 feet at Ranton Green. **Lowest point** 262 feet by Clanford Brook, E of Coton House Farm. Ranton was **122nd most-populated Staffordshire parish in 1801** with 285 people; **125th in 1811** with 278; **125th in 1821** with 334; **129th in 1831** with 273; **129th in 1841** with 292; **127th in 1851** with 312; **130th in 1861** with 283; **130th in 1871** with 267; **130th in 1881** with 265; **130th in 1891** with 249; **128th in 1901** with 265.

RANTON ABBEY Ranton Abbey is the **county's 150th largest parish**, consisting of 748 acres; **27th closest parish to the county town**, 4.8m W; **extremist length** 1.4m, making it **20th= shortest parish in the county**; **extremist width** 1.3m, making it **14th= narrowest parish in the county**. **Parish's chief settlement** None but the estate office/ farm by the ruins of the Abbey. **Geology** ALL - Keuper Red Marls. **Highest point** 564 feet near Lawnhead. **Lowest point** 314 feet by Hextall Brook. Ranton Abbey was **160th= most-populated Staffordshire parish in 1801** with 14 people; **161st= in 1811** with 14; **164th= in 1821** with 11; **160th= in 1831** with 17; **157th in 1841** with 28; **160th in 1851** with 18; **162nd in 1861** with 13; **166th in 1871** with 2; **162nd in 1881** with 12; **165th in 1891** with 6; **163rd in 1901** with 13.

4. People...

Ranton's villain, 1st= murderer hung at Stafford Gaol not sent for dissection Richard Tomlinson, 22, who took a stone to the head of his lover Mary Evans, 20, and suffocated her on Dec 16 1833 in Stocking Lane as the couple (both of Ranton), were returning from staying with relations at Knightley, because she would not retract a taunt. Found guilty of murder and hung on March 19 1834, he was buried in the precincts of Stafford Gaol; hitherto murderers were sent for dissection at the County Infirmary. He must have been of rotten stock because his mother Elizabeth Tomlinson poisoned her husband, John. Both were of Ranton. He was buried on Nov 1 1822. She died of jaundice later in Nov 1822. **58th worst Briton** Ozzy Osbourne, rock musician with Black Sabbath, as polled in a Channel 4 TV poll 2003; he resided at Bullrush Cottage 1971 to at least 1976 (SN Sept 25 2003 p80). **'Mr Ranton'** W Douglas James (1916-2007). Moved to Ranton from Gnosall, aged 14. Ranton parish councillor 1947-85; mayor of Stafford 1988. His father, Frank (1872-1956) of The Villa, Ranton, was also highly respected locally (SA & Chron July 5 1956 p11 col 4) (SN March 8 2007 p7pc). **Ranton's saddest** Sarah Jinks of Ranton, widow, aged about 70, found dead in her house on Sept 16 1904, having complained to a neighbour the day before of a nasty fall. A post-mortem reveealled her heart surrounded by an unusual large clot of blood, with a ruptured vein of the heart varicose. The doctor, Dr Steele, had never seen a similar heart before, and she had died a very rare form of death (SA Sept 24 1904 p4 col 7). **Ranton's kindest** In 1628 Richard Chamberlain of Doxey, made some provision for the poor of Ranton, as well as the poor in Seighford and Haughton parishes. His charity was being distributed to Ranton poor by the churchwarden on the Sunday after Christmas by the 1830s. **Ranton's poorest** In 1840 Ranton vestry voted to sell its parish workhouse; it was bought at auction at The Gate Public House by John Worthington, Boo(uc)klemaker of Seighford for £73 (SRO D4305/1/1). Stafford Union Poor House at Marston was the destination for the poor of Ranton from 1837, for the poor of Ranton Abbey from 1858. **Ranton's earliest recorded will** Belongs to Thomas Baylie, and is dated Oct 27 1533. **First person in the parish register (Ranton)** Ralph Shelly of Ranton and Elizabeth Warde of Wotton married before the JP Thomas Whitgreave April 28 1655. **Choicest quotes (Ranton)** Henry Thorold in Staffordshire: A Shell Guide, 1978, summed up Ranton succinctly 'Rustic little Ranton'. **(Ranton Abbey)** William White in his Directory of Staffordshire, 1834, says 'considerable remains of this abbey are still standing. They consist principally of a lofty well built tower; and the outer walls of the church, which are extremely low; together with a small portion of the cloisters.'

SUBJECT INDEX *Mo to My*

Christina Collins assaulted prior to her murder near Rugeley.

Rugeley
1. Did you know that...

Rugeley's top folklore The murder of Christina Collins on the canal a mile from Rugeley has much folklore connected to it (*see above*). Her body was found lying upside-down in the canal by Rugeley viaduct at 5.00am on June 17 1839, the day after she was murdered. It has become a legend her body was carried up Brindley Bank to the Talbot Inn, blood dripping and permanently staining sandstone steps there. Stains of unmistakable red marks were seen before WW2, and the steps became known as 'The Bloody Steps'. A new set made of concrete, close by, and down the narrow path outside the waterworks railings at Wolseley Road, had replaced these by 1973. The area is believed to be haunted by her ghost (Rugeley Times Aug 18 1973. Jan 27 1983) (Rugeley Post Jan 14 1976) (Rugeley Mercury. July 8 1977 p26). 'The Wench Is Dead, a novel by Colin Dexter, was dramatisation for the Inspector Morse TV series in May 1998. The **name Rugeley first appears** in Domesday Book, 1086. **'the largest and handsomest market town in the Cuttlestone hundred' 1834** Rugeley (W) (VCH vol 5 p149). **'one of Rugeley's oldest buildings' 2005** The Vine Inn, on land between Sheepfair and Lion Street, Rugeley, dating from the C17 (SN Jan 20 2005). **'one of the prettiest places in Europe'** Rugeley according to an inhabitant interviewed for the Illustrated Times Feb 2 1856. The inhabitant goes on to say the country around is most beautiful for miles.. "There are nothing else but noblemen's mansions and grounds; and do you think they would come down and live here if it wasn't a pretty spot?" (Illustrated Life and Career of William Palmer of Rugeley. Ward and Lock 1856 p35). **Last Rugeley Horse Fair** 1932. **Rugeley's first radio broadcast** The second case of the 'Rugeley Flitch (of bacon) Trial' re-enactment based on the Dunmow Flitch custom, part of Rugeley Hospital Carnival, staged at the Town Hall on the evening of July 16 1935, broadcast by the BBC. William and Emma Cope of Park View Terrace were awarded the 40lb flitch (SA July 20 1935 p4 col 6). **Dog who guarded his mistress' clothes after she had committed suicide** Miss Adeline Simpson, a shop assistant, employed at a fish and chip shop in Market Street, resident of Green Lane, took her own life in the river Trent, leaving her coat and handbag on the Trent and Mersey Canal towpath, near the aqueduct at Bellamour crossing, over the river Trent. On May 6 1935 men found her coat and handbag lying near the edge of the water, with her dog resenting all attempts to remove them. In her handbag was a suicide note; her body was found the next day in the river Trent (SA May 11 1935 p7 col 5). **Rugeley's first Civic Sunday** May 3 1936 (LiMe May 8 1936 p5 col1-2). **Rugeley's first-ever blood donation session** A mobile unit from Birmingham on Tuesday Oct 2 1951, organised by the WVS, catering for 93 volunteers (SA Oct 5 1951 p5p). **'The largest ox in the world'** It was apparently on show as an attraction at the Rugeley Horse Show on Aug 14 1954 at Hagley Hall grounds (LiMe Aug 13 1954 p3 col 1). **Rugeley's first show house** Opened at Old Eaton in 1960 (Rugeley Times Jan 3 1970). **The first telephone call via the satellite, Telstar, made on the ordinary telephone network in this country** From Rugeley Council Chamber between Cllr Leslie J Madden, chairman of the Town Council and Mr JP Ward, chairman of Rugeley International Friendship Society, and Howard G Knowlton, a former president of the Western Springs community and the chairman Mr Robert Lavidge, at Weston Springs, Illinois, between 9.00-9.50pm on Thursday July 26 1962. The call was one of 23 linking American towns and cities to their twin communities in 16 Western Europe countries. The US Embassy in London arranged the call; Western Springs was apparently chosen because it had a link with the Bell Telephone company. Rugeley, its twin town, was the only UK place chosen for the 'People to People' telephone experiment with US. Telstar was launched on July 10 1962 (SA & Chron July 12 1962 p1 col 6. July 26 1962 p15. Aug 2 1962 p5p) (Rugeley Times Jan 3 1970) (Looking Back On Rugeley. Alec Neal. 1993. p17). **Rugeley's first pre-school play group** Opened at Etching Hill in 1963 (Rugeley Times Jan 3 1970). **One of the 100 best inns in the nation for accommodation 1970** Eaton Lodge Hotel, Rugeley, as listed in the 1970 Egon Ronay Guide, chosen out of nearly 4,000 hotels, restaurants, pubs etc in Britain. In Feb 1989 it became Banks Brewery's second Milestone restaurant to open (Rugeley Times Nov 15 1969) (Rugeley newspaper Feb 2 1989). **Birmingham Garden Show Gold Medal 1973** Elmore Park Garden Centre, Rugeley, in the Shrubs and Conifers class (Lichfield & Tamworth Magazine Oct 1972 p35). **Rugeley's first winebar** Bojolly's, Albion Street, opened July 1980 (Rugeley Times Nov 22 1980 p8).

2. Politics and civic life...

First meeting of the Rugeley Local Board of Health Oct 17 1865; William Salisbury was elected first chairman (Rugeley Times Dec 18 1971). **'Rugeley's oldest councillor' 1918** Charles Lees (1840-1918), of Horse Fair, born Rugeley, and was one of the town's 'oldest and most respected inhabitants' by 1918. He was sometime farmer of Moreton Grange Farm, Colwich, and later of Birches Farm, Rugeley; member of the old Local Board from 1878; of the old Burial Board; chairman of Rugeley UD in 1899; director of the Rugeley Gas Company; trustee of the Landor Charity (SA June 8 1918 p4 col 7p). **Rugeley Urban District Council's 500th house** Built for the Coal Board, along with 42 other houses, on the St Michael's estate officially opened in the last week of Nov 1957 by Julian Snow, MP. The first was to be tenanted by William McGinnis and his family, a miner at West Cannock Colliery No. 5 pit (SA & Chron Nov 28 1957 p9p). **First woman chairman of Rugeley UDC** Mrs LM Sutton, wife of a member of the council, in 1959; she was also the first woman elected to the council (Rugeley newspaper May 23 1959) (SA & Chron May 28 1959 p7 col 6. June 4 1959 p6p). **First man to be chairman of Rugeley UDC thrice, 1st chairman of the Staffordshire Police Authority (1968), 'Mr Staffordshire'** George Newman (1906-80), born Rochdale, miner at Littleton and Brereton Collieries. Firebrand Socialist leader who thrived on controversy, came to Rugeley from Stafford in 1929 and became the town's first Labour councillor, 1934. He served as chairman of Rugeley UDC 1940-41, 1946-47, 1963-64. He served on Staffordshire CC 1937-77, Chairman 1964-66 and 1973-77; George Newman Cottage, Staffordshire's short-stay hostel for aged people (and the country's first), was named after him, 1948. Striped of his CBE and jailed for 15 months in Feb 1977 after being convicted of 16 charges of corruptly receiving a total of £2,000 in connection with planning applications. Peter Atkins in his 'As I see It' in Stafford Newsletter Sept 12 1980 p8 described him as 'outrageous, outspoken and unforgetable' (SA & Chron March 28 1963 p5p) (Rugeley Times Jan 18 1966?) (E&S Sept 8 1980 photo). **Youngest chairman of an Urban Authority in the country 1962** Les Madden of Rugeley UDC, aged 28, claimed by Cllr George Newman (SA & Chron May 31 1962 p8 col 4). **Rugeley Urban District Council's First Social Welfare Officer** Miss Madeline Wilton, a child care officer with Staffordshire County Council, of Baswich Lane, Stafford, appointed 1968 (SA & Chron May 2 1968 p11). **One of two local authorities in Staffordshire allowed to keep its own safety committee under reorganisation in 1972** Rugeley (Lichfield & Tamworth Magazine Oct 1972 p36). **First election contested by Screaming Lord Sutch after he changed his name by deed-poll** The 1990 Mid Staffordshire by-election, covering Rugeley. The Official Monster Raving Loony Party, led by David Sutch (d1999) alias Lord Sutch, received 336 votes, and for the first time beat the National Front. The by-election was called because the sitting member John Heddle had committed suicide (Wikipedia, 2008). **'Mr Rugeley'** Councillor Albert Rowley (1927-1991), engineer at GEC Stafford, of Armitage Road, Rugeley; served on Rugeley UDC from 1954; Cannock Chase DC from 1973. He was known affectionately as 'Mr Rugeley'; a suite in Rugeley Leisure and Arts Centre, and bench in Elmore Park are named after him (newspaper cuttings, Rugeley Library).

3. Churches...

At RUGELEY is St Augustine of Canterbury, **the only such county dedication** (for AP churches); **41st= oldest county church** dating from 1190 (However, according to Mr EC Toye the original church was built c1150, with numerous later additions and alterations. The remains of this church are known as the Old Chancel). **Staffordshire's most interesting funerary monument of between 1660-80** Thomas Landor (d1670) in the Old Chancel (BOE p33 - misprints name Lauder). The present church, also dedicated to St Augustine, was consecrated Jan 21 1823. **In the church-yard of the present church** Grave of John Parsons Cook (1824-55), who was murdered by the poisoner William Palmer. It lies just inside the gate of the new churchyard. Both Cook and Palmer attended a cockfighting at Cross Keys, Hednesford, and Cook's ghost is reputed to haunt Ghost Row, Cross Keys. In the County Museum, Shugborough, is a copy of his funeral card (LGS p206) (CCBO pp85-86) (STMSM March 1974 p28). **Oldest living Etonian 1936** Rev Henry Frederick Howard born 1845, son of Rev Henry Edward John Howard, Dean of Lichfield 1833-68, former curate of Rugeley. He left Eton in 1862. With a Christ Church College, Oxford, contemporary, Charles Berners, he rowed a 1000 miles from Oxford to London, and by inland waterways, across the Continent, at a time when such a venture was unknown (SA Sept 12 1936 p10 col 1). St Mary's Mission church, Horse Fair and Sandy Lane, existed 1874-c1916 (Rugeley Times June 18 1966 p7). At BRERETON is St Michael, 1837. **Notable thing** A framed map of Southern Africa. It was presented to Redbrook Lane School by Dr David Livingstone who came to lecture to the school in 1846, at the invitation of the then vicar Rev JE Wetherall. On it he marked his discoveries. At first the map hung in the Girls' school (known in 1957 as Brereton C of E Primary School). In 1891 at the rebuilding of the school it was sent away to be cleaned, and that which did not relate to Livingstone was cut away. By 1957, when a bid by the British Museum for the map was turned down, it was still hanging at Brereton C of E Primary School (SA & Chron Feb 21 1957 p6 cols 4-5). **In the churchyard** William Saunders d1887 (see People, below). Some of the victims of a coach accident which claimed the lives of 12 returning from a holiday in Blackpool, killed less than a mile from arriving back in Rugeley on Aug 6 1940. At ETCHINGHILL A mission chapel in Church Lane, was built 1881 (VCH vol 5 p166). The new church, built 1964, was dedicated to the Holy Spirit. It was rebuilt in Mount Road in 1991 (info MK Neal and D Bradbury). On the PEAR TREE ESTATE is The Good Shepherd, Hislop Road, built 1959. At SLITTING MILL is St John the Baptist, Church Close, built 1871 VCH vol 5 p166).

NON-CONFORMIST **First dissenters' meeting in Rugeley** A Congregationalist meeting c1794 at a cottage in Brereton Road, near the entrance to Newman Grove, belonging to Samuel Sleigh, hatter (100 Years of Congregationalism in Rugeley. G Keys. pp5,7 il of cottage) (Rugeley Times Jan 24 1976 pp10-11). **Rugeley's oldest annual meeting 1963** Probably the annual meeting of the Heron Court Congregational Church; the 165th was held in 1963 (SA & Chron Feb 28 1963 p8 col 4). From 1813 the Congregationalists had a chapel in Elmore Lane. In 1874 they moved to a new church attached to Heron Court mansion. By 1974 it was planned to demolish it because of mining subsidence. Heron Court United Reformed and St Paul's Methodist churches united as St Paul's in 1976. The Wesleyan chapel, Lichfield Street, Rugeley, built 1839, enlarged 1870, was rebuilt in 1966 and renamed St Paul's in 1967; it united with Heron Court United Reformed Church in 1976 (Rugeley Times June 17 1967. Jan 24 1976 pp10-11). Rugeley Evangelical Free Church,

Green Lane, was due to open on Sunday March 6 1983 (Rugeley Post June 7 1982). ROMAN CATHOLIC SS Joseph and Ethelfreda, Heron and Talbot Streets, Rugeley, opened Aug 31 1851, built by Charles Hansom, brother of the cab inventor. The spire was added in 1868. The old school, erected 1847, was demolished 1931. **First ever non-catholic to address a congregation at the church** Rev Preb CJA Payton, vicar of Abbots Bromley, Anglican Rural Dean, at a unity mass on Sunday evening Jan 23 1972 (Rugeley Times Jan 29 1972. May 6 1972 p. Oct 12 1974 p5).

4. People...

Fancy that! William Creswell, an apprentice to Anthony Bannister of Rugeley, in the C17, could whistle so artfully that scarce anybody out of sight could distinguish his notes from those of a flageolet (NHS p284). **Needle worker for royalty, 'the ingenious Quaker lady'** Mary Knowles, born Rugeley 1733. The quote is from James Boswell. She was the lady whose intellect tormented Dr Johnson. In 1790 she published 'A dialogue between Dr. Johnson and Mary Knowles' (SA May 20 1933 p9 col 1); she undoubtedly started the fashion of producing needlework pictures, which attracted the attention of George III's wife, Charlotte, commissioning her to do royal portraits (Rugeley Times Jan 30 1982 p4). However, it could be said needlework pictures were popular from at least the mid-C17. In addition, she was a poet and prominent in the anti-slavery movement (DNB) (info MK Neal, D Bradbury). **'Old Cheese'** Thomas Cheshire (d1840), assistant executioner at the Old Bailey from 1808. He accompanied William Calcraft to Stafford in 1840 to hang Owen, Thomas and Ellis, condemned in the Christine Collins case. Spurned by relations in Rugeley Cheshire got drunk in The Shoulder of Mutton Inn, failed to get to Stafford for the execution, and was discharged without a pension. He died in disgrace in the workhouse (TB June 1989 pp16-17. March 1993 pp18-19). **Rugeley's villain** William Palmer (see below). **'Rugeley's most distinguished son'** Thomas George Bonney (1833-1923), born Rugeley, son of the headmaster of Rugeley Grammar School, and curate of St James, Pipe Ridware. Attended his father's school, and then Uppingham School, where his interest in geology was awakened by a teacher who was keen on fossil collecting. During convalescence in the Alps he took up the geology of the region. President of the Geological Society 1884-86; chairman of the British Association 1910. Author of 'The Story of a Planet' (1893), 'Building of the Alps' (1912), and 'The Present Relations of Science and Religion' (1913). His grave in Rugeley Cemetery is a granite tomb (SA Dec 31 1910 p6 col 3) (Rugeley Post Dec 1 1976).

Claimed he had seen every motor car in England, 1895, 'pioneer of the modern style of local history writing', Rugeley's historian Walter Noble Landor (1864-1955), of Chadscroft, Church Street, Rugeley; Rugeley UDC 1898-1915; Staffs CC 1910-18; member of the Self-Propelled Traffic Association (forerunner of the Royal Automobile Club) as early as 1896. His own 1895 claim was made before it was legal to drive motor cars on public roads, and only five or six were in existence, these being shown at the Crystal Palace. He was the first president of Rugeley's local history society, The Landor Society, named after him, founded in 1953. The second claim was made to the Landor Society in 1968 by then County Archivist Frederick B Stitt. He said he was one of the first to use local evidence, instead of merely lists and documents, for his history of Rugeley, compiled c1904-c1947, and remained unpublished. Xerox copies of the original typescript are in WSL and Rugeley Library (info Margaret Neal) (Rugeley Mercury Aug 28 1953. July 1 1955) (Rugeley Times Sept 28 1968). **Rugeley's hero** Pte Walter Henry Shepherd of Lichfield Street, Rugeley, awarded the M.M. on Sept 12 1918 for gallantry and devotion to duty, whilst on active service in the Holy Land; he only joined up aged 18 in 1917 (SA Sept 28 1918 p5 col 4p). **Rugeley's bravest (boy)** Matthew Gould, a muscular dystrophy sufferer, presented with the Child Of Achievement Award in Feb 1990, when aged 10 (Rugeley newspaper Feb 7 1990 photo). **Rugeley's bravest (woman)** Miss Hackett, daughter of Percy Hackett, Rugeley's registrar, who entered a cage with a lion shown at the town fair, 1913 (TB July 1994 p19p). **Rugeley's bravest (men)** Robert Brooke, solicitor aged 30 of Upper Brook Street, Rugeley, received the Royal Humane Society Award, for saving a boy who fell through ice on Jan 15 1881. Brian Blake, a manufacturer's agent from Slitting Mill, aged 44, also received the Royal Humane Society Award for saving the life of Stephen Griffiths of Chaseley Road, aged 9, from drowning in Horns Pool in June 1973 (Rugeley Mercury Oct 12 1973) (Rugeley Times Oct 13 1973).

Staffordshire Police Force's first fatal shooting of one of its own Perhaps the accidental shooting of William Saunders, 40, an Additional Constable, by PC Jerimiah Daniel O' Leary at Brereton, July 8 1887 (TB June 8 2000 p5). **Rugeley's first Carnival Princess** Evelyn Hill of Lion Street, Rugeley, aged 9, chosen 1936 (LiMe June 26 1936 p5 col 4). There was a Carnival Queen and a Carnival King of Mirth for a number of years previous to 1936 (MK Neal, D Bradbury). **Miss Staffordshire 1935** Miss Ruby Brown, Miss Rugeley 1935; she was the 3rd Miss Staffordshire ever (Stafford Pageant: The Exciting Innovative Years 1901-1952. Gordon Henry Loach. 2007). **Staffordshire's largest family 1938** Perhaps that of George Bushnell, Cannock and Rugeley Colliery miner, and his wife, of Birch Lane, Brereton, with 18 children:- Maggie, 32, Doris (Mrs Hall), 31, George 29, Algernon 28, Dora, 27, Lucie 25, Bertha 24, Frederick 23, Clifford 21, Claude 19, Dennis 16, Ronald 14, Donald 13, Eileen 12, Gwennie 11, twins Leslie and Lilian 10, and Geoffrey 8; nor had any of them incurred a doctor's bill (SA Dec 10 1938 p5p). **6th Bishop of Auckland** Rev William John Simkin, born Rugeley, served 1940-60; curate of Christ Church, Stafford; vicar of Wairoa 1911-; later Bishop of Waikato (SA May 8 1948 p5 col 2). **Rugeley boy who**

RUGELEY PEOPLE - Tom Coulthwaite, William Palmer, George Newman. Second row - Walter Noble Landor (d1955), Don Halden 'the Rugeley Bomber'. Bottom row - man in Donkey Jacket, Pte Shephard, Cllr Leslie J Madden making that famous call.

won prize on A.T.V.'s 'Double Your Money' Edward Orme, aged 15, apprentice mechanic of 80 Hardy Ave, Rugeley, winning £32 on this T.V. programme on May 22 1958 (SA & Chron May 29 1958 p6p). **'the second Ruby Murray'** Verlyn Jackson (Mrs Verlyn Dobbins) (b c1940), singer, of Ashleigh Road, Pear Tree Estate; was performing at the Hammersmith Palais in 1962 (SA & Chron Jan 11 1962 p6p). **Interflora Florist of the Year 1987 runner-up** Jane Crompton of Jane's Floral Studio, Upper Brook Street, Rugeley (Rugeley Chronicle Oct 9 1987). **Gerry Hinks' stage debut** A production of Robin Hood at Aelfar School 1951 aged 12, for this former sales manager with Kuwait Airlines of Rugeley who, on redundancy, became a radio/TV actor and latterly as playwright. His first TV role was in 'The Bill' (SN Nov 22 2007 p4pc). **Rugeley's kindest (male)** William Chetwynd of Rugeley (d1691), whose benevolence made possible various doles to the same 20 poorest parishioners for life - a bread dole every Sunday, 2d. on St Thomas's Day (Dec 21), and 2d. on Good Friday; as well as money to the vicar to preach to these poor on St Thomas' Day and Good Friday, the surplus to apprentice the children of poor parishioners. The money was duly laid out by his sister Mary Chetwynd, who added a further £100 of her own, and the charity carried on into the C20, when transferred to general assistance for the local poor (VCH vol 5 pp170-171). **(female)** Miss Sarah Hopkins (d1844), sister of the Slitting Mill ironmaster, of Stone House, Slitting Mill. She left £1000 for charitable purposes in Rugeley, which were still running in 1981 (Rugeley Post Dec? 1981 (cutting in Rugeley Library)). **Rugeley's poorest** A workhouse appears to have been built on Etchinghill field in 1778. Early inmates included the Slater family in Oct 1780. In 1805 the vestry resolved to have the governor, John Atkins, removed because he was inadequate (SRO D6447/1/1. D3243/4/1). From 1836 the poor could be housed at Lichfield Union Poor House. From 1840 this was in Trent Valley Road, Lichfield. It became part of St Michael's hospital. **Rugeley's earliest recorded will** Alice Reeve, and is dated 1627. **Brereton's earliest recorded will** George Fautless, and is dated Oct 17 1618. **First person in the parish register (Rugeley)** George Abbotte buried Feb 19 1570. **(Brereton)** Anne Green daughter of Richard, miner, and Sarah baptised Nov 19 1843 (and two others on the same day).

5. William Palmer...

THE CRIME AND TRIAL **Palmer's last or 14th victim, the crime for which he stood trial** John/ Joseph Parsons Cook (VB p118) (CCF p196) (SPN p100) poisoned at the Talbot Arms, Market Street, Rugeley (later the Shrewsbury Arms, now (2008) Shrew Kafe Bar), 1855. **First ever trial in Britain where someone was accused of murder using strychnine** Palmer (A Biography - looking back at The Rugeley Poisoner. Dave Lewis. 2003 p102). **'the greatest villain that ever stood in the Old Bailey dock'** Palmer, according to Charles Dickens in 'Household Words' June 14 1856. **'Never was a crime more cruel, treacherous and cold-blooded; never was it brought home by proof more cogent and irresistable'** Palmer according to The Times at the time. **First ever tried under the an Act to empower the Court of Queen's Bench to order certain offenders to be**

tried at the Central Criminal Court Palmer, as an application for him to be tried in London necessitated the passing, on April 11 1856, of the Special Act, 19th Vic Cal 16 (SA April 19 1856 p6 col 5). The Observer said of the trial which lasted 12 days in May 1856 'The circumstances attending the judicial proceedings in the case of the Queen v. William Palmer are without precedent in the records of criminal trials in this country. Although the prisoner was only tried on one indictment, there were upwards of a hundred witnesses subpœnaed, and the total number of persons connected immediately or remotely with the proceedings exceeded two hundred'. **'one of the most interesting criminal trials which have taken place for many years..'** (The Manchester Guardian May 15 1856 p3). **'the longest, greatest, gravest and most important criminal trial of the nineteenth century'**(the Law Times). AFTERMATH **Effigy on show in Madame Tussaud's Chamber of Horrors for some 127 years** Palmer. **Palmer's last home** A large timber framed house in Market Street, Rugeley, rented from the Ansons of Shugborough from 1847 until his arrest. By 1981 the property was the shop Blagg, ironmonger. His death mask is at the William Salt Library in Stafford. **'last (survivor) of those who had anything to do with the racing affairs of William Palmer'** John Faulkner, who died aged 102 in 1933, then the 'world's oldest jockey'. Faulkner said one of the mounts he best remembered was Rip Van Winkle, one of Palmer's racehorses (SA Feb 4 1933 p11 col 2). **2nd last Rugeley inhabitant that remembered him** Charles Wood (b1844) of 5 Crossley Stone Terrace, who could recall Palmer in 1939; in particular the sensation which the murder of Cook in Nov 1855, created (Rugeley Mercury Sept 29 1939 p123). **His last surviving patient, last to remember him** Mrs Emma Price (1844-1945) of 37 Wolseley Road, Rugeley, born at Slitting Mill. When aged 98 she remembered going to visit the Doctor with her mother to have a gathered finger attended to. She also remembered him sitting in the stocks in front of the Town Hall. By 1942 she was believed to be the last living link with Palmer (LiMe Jan 23 1942 p7 col 6. Jan 14 1944 p5 col 3). **'Last link with Palmer' returned to Rugeley** When Rugeley Urban Council was presented with the prescription in the doctor's own handwriting which led him to the scaffold. The exhibit was in the collection of Dr Edwin Smith, former coroner for south-west London, and was used by him for lecturing on forensic medicine at St Thomas's Hospital, and presented in 1946 by his widow. It is signed "Wm. P." and is for opium. On the opposite side is the chemist's bill for 10d. for opium and strychnine (SA May 25 1946 p5 col 1). HIS LASTING REPUTATION **Staffordshire's most infamous son, Staffordshire's coldest killer! most prolific murderer in England to at least 1974, what Rugeley is famous for** William Palmer, the serial poisoner, a native of Rugeley (TB May 1996 p1) (GBR 1974 p196), **'The Rugeley Poisoner', 'The Prince of Poisoners', 'the epitome of the 'modern' Victorian poisoner'** The poisoner references refer to Palmer as dubbed in newspapers at the time of his trial, the last claim was made by Ian Burney, Senior Lecturer at the Centre for the History of Science, Technology and Medicine, Manchester University, in History Today, March 2008 pp35-41. **Dramatised on TV** By Keith Allen in Yorkshire Television's drama series 'The Life and Crimes' of William Palmer, on Tuesdays March 3, 10 1998. The village of Helperby, Yorks, was used as the set (Rugeley Post Oct 30 1997 p4ps).

6. WW2...

Royal family's Rugeley bolthole An April Fool's Day hoax by Rugeley Mercury (April 1 1999) claimed State papers released under a 60 year embargo revealled the Royal family could have been evacuated to Hagley Hall, Rugeley, in the event of a German invasion of England. Rather it was Hagley Hall near Stourbridge. **First whole-time evacuation centre in Staffordshire** Opened at the old Studio in Anson Street, Rugeley, on Feb 2 1942. It was a sort of day centre for evacuees from Margate in the town with washing and ironing facilities, as well as cooking and a reading room (LiMe Jan 30 1942 p7 col 6) (info MK Neal, D Bradbury). **Rugeley's survivor of the ill-fated destroyer, Hardy** Able Seaman Leonard Hall of Spring Hill Terrace, Rugeley, presented on his return to Rugeley by the townspeople with a gold wristlet watch. The Hardy sunk during the first epic sea battle of Narvik, April 1940 (LiMe May 10 1940 p7p). **Rugeley Able Seaman on HMS Prince of Wales** Kenneth Harding (b1919) of 'Seven Oaks' Brereton Road, Rugeley, in Aug 1941: It was the 'Prince of Wales' which took Churchill to meet Roosevelt in WW2 (LiMe Sept 5 1941 p3). **Rugeley's Amethyst hero** O.S. Kenneth Peter Williscroft (b1930), of Cross Roads, Rugeley, a member of the crew of the Amethyst, since March 1948. The consort ship was attacked in the Yangtse whilst Williscroft was on the Bofors guns. After the commander had been mortally wounded, he was ordered with another seaman to carry him from the bridge. The other man was killed and later he was wounded in the back and both legs (SA Oct 29 1949 p6p. Nov 19 1949 p7p). **Freedom of Bletchley Park recipient** John Godwin (1922-2003), born Hednesford, attended Rugeley Grammar School. Rejected from the arm forces in WW2 on medical grounds, so he volunteered for the Radio Security Service, involving the interception of enemy coded radio messages, work carried out at Bletchley Park. After WW2 he became a school teacher, and wrote many books on Staffordshire and Rugeley (for which Rugeley Town Council presented him with a certificate in 1999). By 1986 he was residing at Church Lane, Rugeley, later he retired to Stoney Stanton, Leics, where he died (Lichfield & Rugeley Chronicle Nov 7 1986 p3p) (Rugeley Post April 29 1999 p5. Oct 23 2003). **Best VE Day celebrations in Staffordshire** Claimed to be Rugeley's, by Cllr L Watson, chairman of Rugeley UDC when interviewed by the Rugeley Times and South Staffordshire Advertiser May 12 1945. On VE Day (May 8) the Prime Minister's speech was relayed through loudspeakers to over 1,500 people in Market Square. Special services were held at all the churches. Dancing took place in the Town Hall, and in the open-air from Market Square to the end of Anson Street until 2.00am. The next day one of the largest tea parties ever staged in the town catered for over 1,000 children. There was more dancing and an impromptu fireworks display towards Slitting Mill, culminating in the singing of Auld Lang Syne in the Market Square at midnight (Rugeley

Mercury May 11 1945).

7. Work...

First blast furnace in the Midlands to use the Indirect Process One of Lord Paget's early charcoal fired iron smelting works to SW of Furnace Coppice (CCM), early 1560s (HOS 1998 p96). **Earliest recorded iron slitting mill in the Midlands** That which gave its name to Slitting Mill, started by Thomas Chetwynd, 1623 (VCH vol 2 p111) (Iron and Steel Industry. Schubert p306) (SVB p152) (HOS 1998 p96). **Made the green leather seats for the House of Commons** After WW2 the Phoenix Tannery, once based in Rugeley (Looking back on Rugeley. AW Neal). **Part of the first Atlantic cable** It was made in Queen Street, Rugeley (LiMe Aug 20 1954 p2 col 7). **British Road Services' top award winners 1954** Stafford Group based in Wolseley Road, Rugeley, judged by .BR.S. for its general standard of cleanliness, appearence and maintenance and operation efficiency in competition with 160 groups throughout the country (LiMe Aug 20 1954 p2 col 7). **Invented the 'Donkey Jacket', pioneered the mail order business** George Key (d1921), who set up in business on the second floor of a building in Lower Brook Street, Rugeley, in 1888, where his father had a tailor business. The garment was developed later that year in recognition of the need for stronger warmer clothing for navvies maintaining the donkey pumping engines in the construction of the Manchester Ship Canal. A firm to produced a double ridge cord cloth for him, and the coat became known as the Donkey Jacket. Through his catalogue, The Keystone, he pioneered the mail order business: Ladies' clothes were sold by mail order after WW1. The firm lasted to 1984 (Rugeley Times March 27 1971. May 8 1971. Sept 4 1971. Oct 25 1980 p4) (Looking Back on Rugeley. p16). **World/national? service record with one firm** Misses Ida Ellsmore and Amy Shaw, both aged 76 in 1973, who had worked side by side at George Key (Rugeley) Ltd, Keystone Road, since Feb 1912 to Nov 1973, a total of nearly 62 years. On retirement they were presented with Swiss 17 jewel gold wrist watches - but Ida still worked for the firm in April 1974, when she was thought to be 'the longest-serving employee still working in the whole country' (Rugeley Times Nov 3 1973 photo) (Rugeley Mercury April 5 1974). **Rugeley's last horse and milk float** Chris Brown of 34 Cross Road, Rugeley, milkman from 1948, and his pony, 'Kit', still working in Nov 1962 (SA & Chron Nov 29 1962 p10 col 5).

8. Mining...

Smallest pit operating in Rugeley area 1953, last coal pit in the Brereton area to close Brick Kiln Pit alias Brereton Colliery, closed 1960. In 1953 it was consistently producing the highest proportion of the daily average output turned on a Saturday of any colliery on the Chase (due to its voluntary Saturday shift) (LiMe March 27 1953 p4 col 2) (info Harry Thornton). **New drilling machine patentee** Thomas H Lund (b1875), of Ivy Villa, Brereton, former engineer at Brereton Colliery, 1953 (LiMe Aug 21 1953 p8p). **First completely new mine opened by the National Coal Board after nationalisation, National**

Coal Board's first colliery, 'most modern in country' Lea Hall, first shafts sunk 1954, officially opened July 19 1960, first coal produced 1960 (Lichfield Mercury July 22 1960 p1p) (SL p264) (SP-t). The last quote is from West Midland Division of the NCB at the early planning stage 1956 (Lichfield Mercury Oct 19 1956 p4 il of model of how the colliery will look). **First British colliery to mine a million tons of coal in 1965** Lea Hall (Staffordshire Handbook c1966 p73). **First British colliery to have direct access to a computer through a terminal link connected to the Coal Board's computer centre at Cannock** Lea Hall in 1968. The link provided the colliery management with information very quickly, to aid the control of the pit's operations (LTM Jan Feb 1972 p22).

9. Sport...

ATHLETES **European Championship Marathon 2nd 1938 (1st time Britain represented), AAA Marathon Championship winner 1946** Squire Yarrow, born Hackney 1905, of Burton Manor Road, Stafford, former Camp manager at Shooting Butts School 1947-, then helping to form Rugeley Athletes Club; welfare officer at Stafford BRC Engineering Co Ltd 1958- (SA & Chron June 16 1960 p15p). **First Staffordshire Youth Sports Day winners** Rugeley area, at English Electric ground, Stafford, in 1948 with the most points. The first event of this kind was a rally of 27 clubs for Mid Staffordshire Youth Clubs only at Riverside Girls School, Stafford, in 1947, when the additional physical recreation activities appear to have not been competitive. The event continued until at least 1953. The County Youth Athletic Trophy Competition Shield for most number of points was won by Cannock and Rugeley Cheadle area team in 1952, and by Cheadle area team in 1953 (SA June 14 1947 p8 col 4. July 10 1948 p6 col 6. July 24 1953 p5). **All-England Schools Cross Country Championship (junior section, girls) winner 1972, 1973, 1974** Helen Hill (b1961), of Somerset Avenue, Rugeley. Her 1972 win made her the youngest girl ever to win the junior section. In 1973 she was admitted onto Rugeley UDc's Scroll of Honour (Rugeley Times March 24 1973 photo) (Rugeley Mercury May 25 1973 photo. March 1 1974). **First Cannock Chase People's Marathon** 1983, the first winner was Jack Greatholder of Great Haywood, 41 year old builder, in 2 hours, 35 mins, 54 seconds. The route was Market Square, Rugeley to Ravenhill Park (Rugeley Times Sept 1 1983 p10p). **Set new record for running the Pennine Way** Mike Hartley, a MEB meter reader of Church Street, Rugeley, in 2 days, 17 hours and 20 minutes in 1989, aged 37; this knocked 3 hours 34 mins off the previous record set in 1984 (Rugeley newspaper Aug 17 1989 photo).

BOXING **National Coal Board light-heavyweight champion 1954-55** Douglas George Bradbury, aged 25, of 122 Queen Street, Rugeley, miner (SA & Chron March 3 1955 p6 cols 8-9). **'Rugeley's 'Mr. Boxing''** Major RS Clarke, boxing trainer - training: Ernie Ball, NCB heavyweight champion and TA finalist 1960; Jackie Wood of Burnthill Lane, light-middleweight, NCB champion 1962 and England representative, TA champion 1962; Billy Williams, Lea Hall Colliery employee, NCB bantam champion 1960, 1961 and Mid-Counties representative (see below); Tony Beardmore, NCB area flyweight champion, TA finalist 1960, represented TA and Army 1960; Brian Halsali Mid-Counties finalist 1960, TA quarter-finalist 1960. Clarke, born Peterborough, came to Rugeley in 1958 as Company Sergeant Major, a Permanent Staff Instructor of 'B' Company, 6th North Staffordshire TA (SA & Chron April 7 1955 p10p of Jackie Wood. Feb 16 1961 p9p. May 4 1961 p18 col 9. May 24 1962 p20 col 2). **First time two members of any TA (Territorial Army) clubs in the country had reached Wembley at the same championships** When Billy Williams of Rugeley, bantamweight, of 'B' Company, 6th North Staffordshire TA fought against Jack Bodell, member of 6th North Staffordshire TA Boxing Club at Empire Pool, Wembley, in the final of the ABA Championships on April 28 1961; Bodell won (SA & Chron April 20 1961 p14p). **'The Rugeley Bomber', 'one of Rugeley's best loved sportsmen'** Don Halden (1948-2003), boxer (closely associated with Bartley Gorman of Uttoxeter) and miner at Lea Hall Colliery (TB May 1995 p31p. Oct 23 2003 p31p).

FOOTBALL **Fancy that!** In 1978 Nigel Towle, aged 19, goalkeeper with Brereton Town played against Kidderminster Harriers in the West Midlands League just three hours after his marriage to Margaret Cockayne, aged 16. When he let in the only goal of the match Margaret said "Never mind, there's always next week" (E&S Oct 18 2008 p8). HORSE RACING **Last Rugeley Horse Fair** 1932. **'Wizard of the Turf', 'England's most accomplished trainer of 'jumpers", first man to train three Grand National winners** Tom Coulthwaite (1861-1948), born Pendleton, Manchester, horse trainer, came to Hazel Slade in 1899. Coulthwaite Way in Rugeley is named after him. The first quote is from local historian John Godwin in his 1993 biography of Coulthwaite, the second is again Godwin in the Rugeley Times March 1 1975 pp14-15. **Grand National Winners 1907, 1910, 1931** Eremon, Jenkinstown, and Grakle were trained by Tom Coulthwaite at Flaxley Green and Hazelslade (SSE 1990 pp87-100). RUGBY **Played rugby for England over-15s** Ronald Heath, aged 19, of Bower Lane, Etching Hill, when he played for the national side against Wales on Easter Saturday 1958 (Rugeley Times March 22 1958 photo). TENNIS **Staffordshire Champion winner 1962, Midland's Women's champion 1962** Angela Higgott, of Nethermoor, Chaseley Rd, Etching Hill, aged 21 (SA & Chron Sept 13 1962 p18 col 1p)

10. The area...

Rugeley is the **county's 23rd largest parish**, consisting of 8,449 acres; **28th closest parish to the county town**, 5.3m ESE; **extremist length** 4.4m; **extremist width** 5.5m, making it **21st= widest parish in the county**. **Parish chief settlement** Rugeley, a market town. **Geology** BRERETON village, Trent banks - Keuper Sandstones; CANNOCK Chase - Bunter; CANNOCK Chase SE fringe - Middle Coal Measures; TRENT basin - Alluvium. **Highest point** Rifle Range Corner at 674 feet. **Lowest point** 223 feet by the Trent. Rugeley was **31st most-populated Staffordshire parish in 1801** with 2,030 people; **31st in 1811** with 2,213; **29th in 1821** with 2,677; **27th in 1831** with 3,165; **26th in 1841** with 3,774; **26th in 1851** with 4,188; **28th in 1861** with 4,362; **30th in 1871** with 4,630; **25th in 1881** with 7,048; **26th in 1891** with 6,942; **26th in 1901** with 7,327.

11. Transport...

Only garage (for motor cars) between Birmingham and Manchester c1895-1905 Degg's garage, Rugeley (info Julie Shires). A William Degg, blacksmith, at 14 Market Street, occurs in trade directories 1884-1904. **Rugeley's worst road accident** When 12 people (9 were from Rugeley) lost their lives trapped in a blazing motor-coach on the Wolseley Road, Rugeley, at 2.00am on Aug 6 1940. Three coaches owned by Whieldon were returning to Rugeley after an outing to Blackpool and crashed when they had to swerve to avoid a stationary vehicle on the road (LiMe March 21 1941 p7 cols 6-7). **'Murder Mile'** Stretch of A51 road from the bridges at Rugeley to the Red Lion Inn, Brereton, so dubbed by Cllr GW Newman in 1963, because of its width and great number of side road junctions causing traffic dangers (SA & Chron March 14 1963 p19 col 3). **'cheapest petrol in UK'** An independent petrol station in Wolseley Road, Rugeley, in Jan 1996, owned by Don and Roy Richardson, owners of the Merry Hill shopping centre, when they cut the cost of unleaded fuel by 50% (motorists got one litre free with every litre purchased) for one day until the storage tanks ran dry. 800 customers bought 50,000 litres in half a day. Overall the offer had cost the Richardsons' between £50,000 and £100,000. The sale was a protest against Esso, who had promised to match any price offered by a rival filling station within a one-mile radius (ES June 7 2008 p32).

12. Rugeley Power Station...

'world's biggest cooling tower' (LiMe Dec 5 1958 p7), **'world's largest cooling tower'** (SA & Chron July 23 1959 p6p), **tallest cooling tower in Britain, one of the largest dry cooling towers in the world** (GBR 1967 p139) (Burton Observer & Chronicle. Aug 15 1974 p7), **world's first big dry cooling tower, largest vertical wind tunnel in the UK** (MK Neal, D Bradbury) Rugeley 'A' Power Station cooling tower, at 350 feet tall, 326 feet in diameter, containing 2,750,000 feet of tubing and carry 1,700 tons of water, and Lichfield Cathedral could fit inside it (LiMe Dec 5 1958 p7). **Power station with first fully centralised control room** Rugeley 'A' Power Station (pamphlet 'Rugeley 'A' 1961-95'). **Has more aluminium work than any other building in the country** Perhaps Rugeley Power Station, with its 'M.J.' precast roofs, used on the continent, but never previously used in Britain (LiMe Dec 5 1958 p7). **Power station with most improved safety record in the Midlands 1963** Rugeley Power Station, awarded by Central Electricty Generating Board Midlands Region, beating 13 other stations (SA & Chron Aug 8 1963 p7).

The 'gentle governess' ghost haunts Seighford Hall.

Seighford
1. Did you know that...

Seighford's top folklore A ghost called the 'gentle governess,' a former deceased governess, is said to have checked on new governess', shortly after their appointment at Seighford Hall. The ghost of the same or another governess is said to have appeared at the hall to avenge the wife of a past owner, who allegedly murdered her after discovering she had had an affair with her husband, and deposited the body in a pool in the grounds. Another, or the same, was the figure of a lady carrying a basket who was seen disappearing into a wall of the hall by campers in the grounds. **What Seighford is famous for** Seighford airfield, a prominent WW2 Midlands airfield. **Staffordshire's most town-like timber-framed country house** Clanford Hall Farm, of 1648. It was built four square (which is rare) like a town house (info the owner Mr Bill Brown). The **name Seighford first appears** in Domesday Book, 1086. **First convictions for trespass on a railway line in Staffordshire** Thomas Tonkinson, Thomas Holmes, John Lowndes, and William Dawson at Stafford petty sessions for wilful trespass over and upon the Grand Junction Railway line at Bridgeford on Oct 18 1837; each fined 2s. 6d. and costs (SA Nov 11 1837 p3 col 1). **First railway sabotage in Staffordshire** When large stones were deliberately placed on the GJR line 3 miles north of Stafford on Nov 4 1837 bringing the last train that day, the southbound from Liverpool, to a halt. There were no injuries (SA Nov 11 1837 p3 col 1). **Disease 'very rare in England'** In 1911 William Alfred Boult, an emery wheel maker, aged 26, of Hawthorn Terrace, Doxey, died of elephantiasis, which the doctor at the inquest, Dr L Gray, declared "was very rare in England". His right leg was three times the size of a normal leg (SA Oct 7 1911 p7 col 1). **First Staffordshire parish to discuss a WW1 memorial for its village green** Seighford parish council, according to the Staffordshire Advertiser. Their meeting on Nov 28 1918 was mainly in favour of a memorial for the Green. A further meeting on Jan 7 1919 decided in favour of a granite cross to be erected for the Green (SA Dec 7 1918 p7. Jan 11 1919 p5 col 1). **The mill that ground coffee for overseas troops in WW1** The mill by the Meece at Great Bridgeford. In

WW2 its wheels were dismantled so that they could be used for making of munitions (SA & Chron Aug 2 1956 p6 col 7). **Seighford and District Horticultural Society's first show** Seighford Hall on Aug 27 1955 (SA & Chron Sept 1 1955 p8). **First UK manufacturer of white aluminous abrasive, Europe's largest manufacturer of grinding wheels 1970s** Universal Grinding Wheel Co. Ltd, Doxey Road, Doxey, in 1942 (Stafford Borough Official Guide. 1976. p47) (VCH vol 6 p220). **Largest factory of its kind in Europe** Universal Grinding Wheel Co. Ltd, in late 1950s, covering a 44 acre site (VCH vol 6 p220). **Largest manufacturer of abrasive and grinding wheels in Europe** Universal Grinding Wheel Co., 1970s (SN May 18 2006 p13). **'Derrington Dreadnought'** Was a stallion at Hill Farm, Stafford, advertised in Staffordshire Advertiser in 1934 to pregnate local mares, foaled in 1929 (SA April 14 1934 p12).

2. Churches...

At SEIGHFORD is St Chad, **one of 4 such county dedications** (of AP churches); **8th= oldest county church** dating from 1100. **In the church note** Table top tomb to **Seighford's most famous old worthy** Sir William Bowyer (1491-1593), squire of Heathhouse Grange, in the Grange Farm area, grandson of William Bowyer of Knypersley. His "splendid tomb is one of the treasures of the church" and gives his age at death as 102. It is **one of the last alabaster monuments of the Royleys' workshop of Burton upon Trent before Dutch sculptors took over** and is an exact replica of another monument at Wolverhampton except it has a linen collar instead of a ruff. His wife, Mercy (nee Stone of London), is in a long gown and ruff. On the sides of the tomb are their six children, one in swaddling clothes (LGS p209) (JME part II pp32-33 pl. 15 (a)). **Most unusual memorial** Is a portrait of the Rev EC Perry in stone and originally formed part of the decoration on the huge vicarage he had built at Seighford in 1880. His bust used to peer from a corner by the vicarage front door, but Perry's predecessor disliked the figure and had it removed to where it now stands (SN Nov 15 1958 p14). **Dr Johnson's first tutor** Rev William Jordan, vicar of Seighford 1731-9 (OSST 1935 p46). **Seighford's longest-serving vicar** Edward Bate, who may have served 27 years, 1738 (?) to 1765. At DERRINGTON is St Matthew, built 1847, corner of St Matthew's Drive and Church Lane. **'one of only two thatched Methodist Chapels in the country'** That at Derrington in 1959, built c1859 by the Earl of Lichfield (SN April 18 1959 p14), 50 feet long, with one half being a dwelling called the Old Church House (SA & Chron March 1 1956 p10p). At DOXEY is St Thomas and St Andrew, Doxey Road, next to the black and white house, built 1875, rebuilt 1975.

3. People...

'one of the few English families who can claim unbroken descent from the Kings of England' The Elds of Seighford Hall. According to Burke the descent is from Edward I, through his son, Edmund Plantagenent, surnamed of Woodstock, thence by intermarriage from the earls of Kent, Arundel, and Somerset. It was in the C17 that the marriage of Richard Elde, Treasurer and Paymaster of the Forces in Ulster, occurred with Margaret, daughter of John Wrottesley, who was 9th in descent from Edward I; Col Frederick Eld of Seighford Hall is 8th in descent from Richard Elde; by 1917 there were comparatively few English families who could claim unbroken descent from the Sovereigns of England (SA Oct 13 1917 p3 col 3. Jan 19 1926 p7 col 4). The quote is from SA June 12 1953 p4 col 8. **Last Eld to live at Seighford Hall** Charles Edward Eld, second son of Col Frances Eld who succeeded to the estate on the death of his elder brother Francis E Eld. He moved to Templestowe, Leamington in c1896 (SA Jan 19 1926 p7 col 4). **Last Master of Ceremonies at the 'Old Ship' in Brighton** John Eld, 3rd son of Francis Eld of Seighford Hall, he was also the 3rd Master; the final ball was held on Nov 20 1854 (BS p155). **Staffordshire's 6th oldest man ever** A Seighford man who lived to the age of 124, becoming a father again aged 100.

Seighford's war hero L-Corp Samuel Bullbrook (1892-1920) of the King's Royal Rifle Corps, of 267 Ventnor Terrace, Doxey. Before WW1 he was employed at Bostock & Co's factor. During the War in one of the German attacks on the British line, he was proceeding with his company to the relief of comrades who were hard pressed, when a shell burst among them, and he was badly wounded on the right arm, his leg was also wounded. He subsequently became a patient in different military hospitals, and underwent several operations. Never rallying he eventually died of his wounds at Kinver Sanatorium of laryngitis, following an attack of influenza. He had been awarded the Mons Medal and Service Medal (SA April 3 1920 p3p). **Doxey's war hero** Flight Sergeant Joe Willshaw, born Doxey 1921. Fighter pilot who flew Hawker Hurricanes with No. 80 Squadron in North Africa. He was awarded the Distinguished Flying Cross for gallantry and devotion to duty in June 1945 after flying 60 reconnaissance missions with No. 16 Squadron Photo-Reconnaissance in the Liberation of Europe 1944-45. He spent the rest of his working life at Universal Grinding (Stafford At War. an SN publication. 1995 p15p). **Doxey's bravest** Bill James (b1943), who saved a neighbour, Mr Till, in a dramatic rescue from his house on fire in Aug 1978. In mid May 1980 Mr James' pre-fab in Greensome Close was gutted in a mysterious fire, fortunately he was out at work at Universal Grinding, and the rest of his family were out (SN May 23 1980 p11). **Great Bridgeford's heroines** The ladies of the village who attended the wounded of the Great Bridgeford train disaster, 7.55pm June 17 1932, when the Rhyl to Birmingham train jumped the points and derailed. The women tore off parts of their dresses and commandeered men's shirts and handkerchiefs to bind up the injured's wounds; they kept their heads wonderfully, despite the cries of pain from the injured (Daily Mail 1932 cutting which proclaimed in a heading 'Village heroines of train smash' in Wilks scrapbook, WSL D1863, vol 2 p122). **Miss Staffordshire 1951** Miss Elizabeth Venables, a Universal Grinding employee, and reigning Miss Universal; she was the 13th ever Miss Staffordshire. **Christopher James Trophy winner 1979** PC Alan Merrick of Derrington for doing most to improve police and public relations (SN Oct 25 2007 p6). **Seighford's kindest** Dame Dorothy Bridgman of Castle Bromwich, Warws, bequeathed lands at As ton Yard, the rental from which went to teaching poor children to read; Francis Eld of Seighford Hall left a bread dole, according ot a benefactions board in the church; Sir Edwin Cooper Perry (d1938), GCVO, MA, MD, son of Rev EC Perry, principal officer of the University of London 1920-26, and vice-chancellor 1917-19, knighted 1903. He was in the habit at Christmas time of sending money to the Vicar of Seighford to be distributed to old people who knew his mother, and tradition carried on by his daughter (SA Dec 24 1938 p9 col 6). **First British woman to conquer Everest (1993)** Rebecca Stephens visited Cooper Perry primary school in March 2003 (SN March 20 2003 p17p). **Seighford's poorest** The parish overseers' accounts Easter 1805-1806 mention 'Paid for mending the stairs at Poor house...£0.2.6'; and 200 bricks costing £0.6.0 for the floor were needed between 1817-18. The property, which was sold c1836 for £87, may be identifiable with the 'new house' mentioned in 1801? (SRO D731/12) (SIAS. No. 2 p59). From 1837 the poor were housed at Stafford Union workhouse at Marston. **Seighford's earliest recorded will** Belongs to George Aston, and is dated 1526. **First person in the parish register** George Harvie buried March 30? 1561. **Choicest quote** Staffordshire General and Commercial Directory, 1818, says 'The village of Seighford consists of a few scattered houses well thatched. The general face of the country is level, and in a high state of cultivation.'

4. Seighford airfield...

'a rare animal in the world of existing rural airstrips' Seighford Airfield, because it has a runway in excess of 6,000 feet - for a few years a jet airliner was based there, and it also hosted the test flying of several Canberra jet bombers and Lightning supersonic fighters (TB Jan 15 2004 p12). **Strange but true!** John Aubrey Pothecary of Salisbury, a 24-year-old flying instructor, flew in an Auster aircraft to pay a social call to his uncle at Great Bridgeford but lost his way. So, allegedly, he came down to 100 feet to ask villagers the way to Seighford aerodrome. Stafford County Magistrates' Court on Oct 26 1954 fined him £10 for flying dangerously low, with £5. 7s. costs, and £5 for landing on Seighford Aerodrome without permission (SA Oct 29 1954 p1 cols 4-5). **The Seighford hermit** Bill Weaver (b1896), watchman and guard of the Ministry of Food food depot on the edge of Seighford airfield from 1940 to May 1955. Thereafter he continued his routine unpaid, despite having nothing to guard because he loved his job too much. His devotion earned him the title of the 'friendly hermit' in the locality. He was kept company by five stray cats, and fed by kind-hearted housewives at the nearby Polish camp. This was one of the **'Little Poland'** communities, a resettlement camp for Polish refugees, the others being those at Little Onn, and Stafford (SA & Chron Feb 2 1956 p4 col 5p. Oct 26 1961 p1 cols 2-3). **Longest runway in the Midlands region 1965** Seighford at 2,010 yards, as claimed by Benn Gunn, Chief Test Pilot for Boulton Paul Aircraft Co. to Stafford Chamber of Trade AGM 1965, pointing out its potential for commercial development. Castle Donnington Airport's runway was then 1,900 yards long; Birmingham Airport's 1,800 yards; Halfpenny Green's 1,300 yards (SA & Chron March 4 1965 p1). **First**

Seighford Circuit cycle race Seighford Airfield, summer 2008. The winner was Paul Belfield of Stone Wheelers (The Stone & Eccleshall Gazette. Sept 2008 p43).

5. The area...

Seighford is the **county's 55th largest parish**, consisting of 4,741 acres; **5th closest parish to the county town**, 0.6m WNW; **extremist length** 4.1m; **extremist width** 3.3m. **Parish's chief settlement** Doxey has become a fair-sized residential suburb of Stafford; Derrington is a satellite dormitory village of Stafford; Seighford remains a rural village. **Geology** MOST - Keuper Red Marls; SOW valley - Alluvium. **Highest point** 407 feet on Creswell boundary, NNE of Great Bridgeford. **Lowest point** 246 feet by the Sow, near Doxey. **Second largest stretch of water in Staffordshire in C17** Ladford Pool (NHS p43). **Largest concentration in the West Midlands of water rail** 13 pairs at Doxey Marshes (Staffs Wildlife No. 79 May 2000 p 30). Seighford was **65th most-populated Staffordshire parish in 1801** with 841 people; **67th in 1811** with 866; **76th in 1821** with 851; **74th in 1831** with 898; **76th in 1841** with 903; **83rd in 1851** with 851; **89th in 1861** with 808; **87th in 1871** with 781; **89th in 1881** with 756; **83rd in 1891** with 793; **77th in 1901** with 947.

SUBJECT INDEX *Pe to Po*

Shareshill church bells were said to have the sweetest peal in the Midlands.

Shareshill
1. Did you know that...

What Shareshill is famous for Its associations with Rev William Henry Havergal, composer of sacred music, vicar of Shareshill 1860-70, although he lived elsewhere for much of this time because of blindness and infirmity. However, his youngest child, Frances Ridley Havergal (1836-79), essayist and hymn writer, remembered for her best-known and loved hymn 'Take my Life, and let it be Consecrated, Lord to Thee,' was resident at Shareshill during her father's incumbency, and gained a local reputation as a wonderful person (CAd Oct 22 1982 p12 il). **Shareshill's top folklore** There is a traditional St Mary and St Luke's church, originally stood on Saredon Hill but 'as fast as the workmen put it up by day, the pixies took it down by night and rebuilt it in Shareshill' (Spotlight. Nov/ Dec 1999 p3). The **name Shareshill first appears** in Domesday Book, 1086. **'The Shareshill affair'** Concerned allegations of corruption and theft on the parish council 1995-2003 made by councillor Robert Poole (b1931). He accused chairman, Patricia Williams, of corruption, and parish clerk, Jack Greenaway, of stealing from parish funds to buy items like a £7 classical music CD and a mobile phone. Despite two police investigations and an in-depth analysis of the council's accounts by auditors which cleared the clerk, Mr Poole refused to back down, driven on by moral duty, believing the council to be hiding matters from him. He intimidated the clerk and chairman so much they resigned or lost their seats. Police officers had to eject Mr Poole from some meetings, which had descended into uproar. The case went to the High Court in early July 2003 (E&S July 10 2003 p9ps).

2. Church...

At Shareshill is St Mary and St Luke, **only such duel dedication in the county** (for AP churches); **40th= last AP county church built** dating from 1743. **Most interesting thing** Two effigies off a table-tomb by the sills of the E windows on N and S aisles, c1562, of Sir Humphrey Swynnerton and his wife Cassandra (nee Giffard) (d1562), from the old church; their daughter Margaret married Henry Vernon of Sudbury and so founded the modern line which took possession of the Hilton estate

(LGS p211) (JME part II pp23-24). **'the sweetest peal in the Midlands'** The bells of Shareshill, first heard in 1624, and a note in the church records says they are the sweetest peal in the Midlands. A sixth bell was added in 1899 (CAd Nov 6 1975 p9p). **Shareshill's most famous old worthies** Rev William Henry Havergal (1793-1870), composer of sacred music and writer on the subject. He was born High Wycombe, Buckinghamshire. Vicar of Shareshill 1860-70, although he was absent for much of his incumbency owing to blindness and infirmity. He died at Leamington. However, his youngest child, Frances Ridley Havergal (1836-79), essayist and hymn writer, remembered for her hymn 'Take my Life, and let it be Consecrated, Lord to Thee,' was resident at Shareshill during her father's incumbency, and much loved by parishioners. She was born at Astley, near Stourport and is buried there.

Frances Ridley Havergal (d1879).

3. People...

22nd Chief Justice of the King's Bench of England Sir William de Shareshull (1289/1290-1370), English lawyer, Chief Justice of the King's Bench from Oct 26 1350 to July 5 1361. **Chaplain of the Savoy Chapel, The Strand, London** Rev Cyril L Cresswell by 1936, son of the vicar of Shareshill (SA April 18 1936 p5 col 2. May 9 1936 p10 col 8). **'one of the oldest parish clerks in the country' 1950** John Buck (1865-1953) of St John's Road, Cannock, having been parish clerk of Saredon, Shareshill and Hatherton parish councils for 50 years, retiring in 1950; he was also clerk to parish meetings at Huntington and Hilton before parish councils were constituted there in 1937 and 1949 (SA Aug 7 1953 p7 col 8). **National Kata Karate under-16s runner-up 2008, Central England Regional Champion 2008** Amy Worrall, 10, of Stable Lane, Calf Heath (Brewood/ Hatherton), attends Havergal Primary School, Shareshill (E&S May 23 2008 p30p). **Shareshill's villain** John Haynes (b 1819 in Shareshill), labourer; he appeared before Stafford magistrates in 1850 for stealing 12 garden hoes on Dec 4 1849. He was a prisoner in Stafford Gaol in 1851, and in 1855 found guilty of theft at Willenhall and transported to Australia for 14 years. He obtained his ticket of leave in 1858 and was occupied as a carpenter, marrying bigamously a widow Rachel Blayney at Tibradden, Western Australia in 1875. He died 1898 at Moonyoonooka and is buried in Geraldton cemetery, near Perth, Western Australia (TB Sept 28 2006 p6p). **Shareshill's saddest** Nicola Jevons (b1977) of Church Road, Shareshill, kidney disease sufferer, for whom all 718 Shareshill villagers raised £100 per head to buy a £10,000 dialysis unit in 1982, in addition there were many other fund-raising ventures beyond the parish. But suffering renal failure in early June 1982 she was rushed to hospital and suffered a cardiac arrest and brain damage during an operation (CAd Feb 26 1982 p1p. April 16 1982 p19. May 27 1982 p20. July 16 1982 p3. July 8 1983 p11) (E&S March 4 1982 p12p) (Chase Post March 11 1982 p1p. June 17 1982 p1. July 22 1982 p3. Oct 4 1982 p1).

Sharehill's kindest Sarah Knight of Cannock, by will of 1847, gave an annual income of £5 to the Minister of Shareshill for the distribution to the poor of the parish. **Saredon's kindest** A person called Southwell or Southall devised land for poor widows of Saredon township, which was producing a rent of 12 shillings by 1786 (VCH vol 5 pp181-192). **Saredon's poorest** Saredon township accounts for 1761 record Martha Mincha (Minshaw?) was taken to Cannock workhouse; she was a burden on the township in 1763, and 1765; and in 1762 a payment made for 'ye woman at ye workhouse'. In 1764 Saredon was badging the poor (SRO D3144/6/1). **The parish's poor** From 1836 Shareshill was in Penkridge Union, renamed Cannock Union from 1870s. From 1836 the poor were housed at Brewood's workhouse; from 1872 at the new Union workhouse on Wolverhampton road, Cannock. **Shareshill's earliest recorded will** Belongs to John and Alice Harrison, and is dated May 7 1564. **First person in the parish register** _____ & Mary Dickenson married Jan 21 1564. **Choicest quote** In Memorials of Frances Ridley Havergal by her sister MVGH, 1880, she is quoted - in a quote that evokes the parish - 'Yet I hope dear papa will find comparative rest and strength in consequence, by going to the little country parish of Shareshill. Papa is so very much to me, so much more than all besides!"

4. Motorways...

Britain's first toll-motorway M6 Toll Road which joins the M6 SW of Saredon Hall Farm, opened Dec 9 2003, and is 27 miles long. **Most busy thoroughfare in Europe** M6 - 27 miles of it runs through Staffordshire. The first section opened was the Stafford by-pass by Transport Minister, Ernest Maples, on Aug 2 1962 (BBC R4. You and Yours. Oct 25 2006). **Most haunted British motorway** M6; bottomless Roman soldiers have been sighted in the South Staffordshire area (BBC R4. Today programme. Oct 31 2006).

5. The area...

Shareshill is the **county's 96th largest parish**, consisting of 2,827 acres; **50th closest parish to the county town**, 9m due S; **extremist length** 2.5m; **extremist width** 3.3m. **Parish's chief settlement** Shareshill, a village, which surpasses in size the tiny villages of Great and Little Saredon in the adjoining township of Saredon. **South Staffordshire Dis** trict's smallest parish 1978 Saredon with a population of 300 (CAd Dec 22 1978 p10). Geology SAREDON - Bunter (most), Permian intrusions (Great Saredon, Little Saredon), Keuper Sandstones (extreme W); SHARESHILL - Permian (Shareshill village), Bunter (Laney Green), Bunter (W), Middle Coal Measures (Warstone). Highest point 508 feet near Warstone. Lowest point 328 feet at Goldie Brook Bridge. Shareshill was 103rd= most-populated Staffordshire parish in 1801 with 441 people; 99th in 1811 with 493; 97th in 1821 with 583; 105th in 1831 with 520; 98th in 1841 with 594; 103rd in 1851 with 540; 104th in 1861 with 531; 103rd in 1871 with 511; 96th in 1881 with 612; 94th in 1891 with 619; 91st in 1901 with 667.

SUBJECT INDEX *Po to Pr*

Sheriff Hales
1. Did you know that...

Sheriff Hales is the **county's 94th largest parish**, consisting of 2,907 acres; **54th= closest parish to Stafford**, 9.3m WSW; **extremist length** 2.7m; **extremist width** 3.3m. The **name Hales first appears** in Domesday Book, 1086; Sheriff Hales in 1271-72. **Parish's chief settlement** Sheriff Hales, a small village with most of the housing away from the church by the main road, transferred to Shropshire in 1895. **What Sheriff Hales is famous for** John Wesley's visits. **Sheriff Hales's earliest recorded will** Belongs to Thomas Myllis, and is dated Jan 15 1522/23. **Sheriff Hales' most famous old worthy** Rev John Woodhouse, active Parliamentarian, who took Holy Orders but became a Presbyterian. He established a famous Academy at The Manor House in Charles II's reign and relinquished it c1696. It was a kind of little provincial university for nonconformists, to which came some of the young men whom the Test Acts barred from the great universities. Alumni - Henry St John (Lord Bolingbroke), and Robert Harley (Lord Oxford). **Choicest quote** John Piper and John Betjamin in the Shell Guide to Shropshire (1962) sum the village up with that breathtaking brevity/ clarity for which Shell Guides are renowned 'Half-timbered houses in a winding hollow. Church scraped. Open-work brick barns.' **Geology** ALL - Bunter. **Highest point** Woodcote Hill at 551 feet. **Lowest point** 275 feet by Bolam's Brook by the county boundary. Sheriff Hales was **107th most-populated Staffordshire parish in 1801** with 416 people; **88th in 1811** with 594; **91st in 1821** with 656; **90th in 1831** with 688; **91st in 1841** with 688; **91st in 1851** with 698; **92nd in 1861** with 650; **93rd in 1871** with 656; **95th in 1881** with 621; **102nd in 1891** with 522; **103rd in 1901** with 485. At Sheriff Hales is St Mary, **one of 23 such county dedications** (most common dedication in the county); **61st= oldest AP county church** dating from 1250.

SUBJECT INDEX *Pr to Ra*

Stafford St Chad
1. Did you know that...

Staffordshire's 169th largest parish, smallest parish, consisting of 9 acres. **Closest parish to the county town**, 0.12m SE; **extremist length** 0.225m, making it the **shortest parish in the county**; **extremist width** 0.2m, making it **equal narrowest parish in the county**. The **name Stafford first appears** in 913. **Parish's chief settlement** It has always been a part of central Stafford. **What St Chad's is famous for** Perhaps being Izaak Walton's birthplace. On the E side of Greengate is St Chad, **one of 4 such county dedications** (of AP churches); **13th= oldest county church** dating from 1120. **Longest-serving vicar** Richard Jackson, who served 52 years, 1745-97. **First time William A Marson played music in a church** St Chad's, playing the harmonium on Sunday Oct 7 1860, continuing to play until June 11 1861 when the instrument was removed by the Rev E Horley to whom it belonged. WA Marson (1840-1912), grocer, lay reader, and general Stafford character, kept a scrapbook and set up a shop of curiosities in Stafford (WSL M530. William Marson's Scrapbook vol 1. p83). **First person in the parish register** Margeria, daughter of Johannis and Margeriae Phillips baptised Jan 19 1636. **Choicest quote** Samuel Gilson, Perpetual Curate in his report for Census Sunday, 1851, wrote 'The parishioners I should think about 500 people, but it is in the midst of a thickly populated and destitute district.'

SUBJECT INDEX *Ra to Ro*

Stafford is a propre littel Towne walled abut standing in the middst of the shire, uppon the River of Sow, which falleth into the Trent. 3 myled est from the toune. The castron standith almost a myle from the Towne.

Stafford St Mary
1. Did you know that...

Earliest known picture of Stafford Dates from 1588 (*see above*). The inscription runs 'Stafford is a proper little town walled about standing in the myddst of the shire upon the River of Sow which falleth into the Trent three miles east from thence. The castle standeth almost a myle from the Towne' (Stafford Survey prepared for the Borough Council by JH Higson. 1948. p13). **Stafford's top folklore** That the Saxon hermit and Mercian prince, Bertram had a hermitage on the island of Betheney in c705; that St Bertram's Chapel, was built on the site in c1000, by his cross, and to contain his shrine. It is believed the chapel stood at the W end of St Mary's church. **Coton's top folklore** The ghost known as the Little Grey Lady is said to have flitted from the old Coton Hill mental asylum to the new Stafford District General Hospital, which replaced it in 1984. **Hopton's top folklore** There have been sightings of ghosts of some of the dead of the Battle of Hopton Heath (1643), including a man on horseback in Civil War costume seen riding up Salt Lane, and battle sounds heard by some of the inhabitants of Salt. **St Thomas' Priory's top folklore** The priory is supposed to be haunted by the ghost of a damsel who was murdered by soldiers in the precincts. She returns to haunt at various times of the year such as Halloween and Candlemas. **Salt's top folklore** Weston Hall south east of Salt village is haunted by several ghosts - a lady in green, a nurse, a woman in white, and a lady in grey. During WW2 land army girls billeted there are said to have found it so haunted they preferred to camp in the grounds. **Whitgreave's top folklore** It is said a Whitgreave maid could know the identity of her future husband if she take a 'lock of an ash' (an ash leaf without the final leaflet), to her house and hang it above the door and notice the name of the man who first came in; his name would be the same as the one she would marry. **First skulls of their type found in Britain** Armenoid/ Giza type skulls, of the people who ruled Egypt during the second dynasty, found on the site of the Grapes Hotel, Stafford, close to the river Sow, in May 1929. No scull had yet been found in Britain with a cephalic index range of 85 to 90.28, having a greater breadth than English sculls of any date, due to the very prominent parietals; raising the question whether ancient immigrants passed through Central Europe without be-coming mixed with Nordics (WSL 323/41/80, Horne's Scrapbook, No. 1, p82) (NSFCT 1929-30 pp174-5). The **name Stafford first appears** in 913. **What Stafford is famous for** Being the county town of Staf-fordshire, a corporate borough, with a foreign (the parish beyond the borough), shoes, electrical engineering and timber-framed town houses. **'the dullest and vilest town in England'** How the future Lord Campbell then barrister on the Oxford Circuit described Stafford, 1819 (VCH vol 6 p201). **Unique derivation for a surname** Stafford will be from Staf-ford in this parish (PDS). **First room for Stafford borough archives** Mayor's office, under the Shire Hall, built 1617 (HOS 1998 p133). **The man who made a model of the battle of Hopton Heath** John Sutton of New Garden Street, Stafford, in 1965, aged 20, when studying history at college (SA & Chron Aug 5 1965 p8c). John became an authority on this Civil War battle, fought on March 19 1643, which resulted in a royalist victory. He is accredited with proving the true site of the battle. **One of the earliest first-hand accounts of conditions in the colony of Geor-gia** Probably that by Capt George Burrish, RN, stationed there in 1729 to guard the colony from threat of invasion by the Spaniards in Florida. He had a mural tablet in St Mary's, Stafford (OP pp16-17). **Staffordshire's 9th earliest commutation of tithes when they were dealt with under a parliamentary enclosure act** The great and small tithes of the lord of the manor of Stafford and Corporation of Stafford in St Mary's, Stafford, by allotments of land and money payments, 1799-1800. **First meeting of the Stafford Rifle Volunteers** Took place on Jan 9 1860 (SA Jan 14 1860 p5 col 4). **'Hopton Prince'** A shire stallion of Barnfields Shire Horses, foaled in 1901 toured in 1904 to impregnate local mares (SA April 30 1904 p8 col 7).

The dog that ran away to WW1 Prince, an Irish terrier, pet of Pte James Brown of Stafford. On Pte Brown's mobilization in Aug 1914 - he had been stationed with the 1st Batt North Staffs Regt in Buttevant, County Cork, from 1912 - Prince moped his master's loss. In an extraordinary turn of affairs the dog left Brown's wife's care in London, eloped with the Queen's Westminster's and was taken to France where he was spot-ted by his master in the town of Erquinghem. Prince remained on the Western Front faithfully tending his master until the end of the war. His repatriation and quarantine fees were paid for by the Soldiers Dog Fund. In 1921 Prince ate a piece of poisoned meat in the street and died. His story was verified by the RSPCA (TB Jan 1994 p18). **Unique medical case** Perhaps that of two men who died of natural causes in so short a time as was never known before and led to their dying on the same bed. Sgt Benjamin Rees, 33 of the Military Provost Staff Corps at the local Detention Barracks, and his acquaintance William Vann, 46, an 'enor-mously fat' boot and shoe press-cutter of Newport Rd, returned late to Rees' lodging in George St, Stafford, after visiting a fried fish shop on Jan 11 1919. The next day the landlady discovered the two men dead in bed together. Prof Leigh of Birmingham, invited to pronounce, said he did not know of any similar instance in medical literature. He knew of a case in which a single person died from suffocation during a post-epileptic sleep, but he had never known of two people dying together from natural causes in so short a period of time as in the present case. Rees may have bitten his tongue during an epileptic fit and subsequently suffocated. Vann might have died in his sleep from heart failure - his liver and kidneys were seriously diseased - through pressure of a distended stomach (SA Jan 18 1919 p5. Feb 22 1919 p3 col 3). **Unique W.I. branch** The Stafford branch in 1955 was thought be the only one of its kind in England, being situated right in the middle of a borough. It was founded in 1919 to help the other branches round Stafford, but by 1955 was very much its own Institute. The Women's Institute is usually regarded as a rural organisation (SA & Chron March 17 1955 p4 col 7). **First radio broadcast about Stafford's history** Perhaps that for the Midland Regional programme series 'the microphone at large' relayed from the Swan Hotel to London on Jan 24 1935. The broadcast commenced with a peal of bells from St Mary's church (SA Jan 26 1935 p7 col 1). **One of the country's oldest surviving Royal British Legion branches** Stafford, formed July 1921, only weeks after the Royal Charter was given to the national organisation (SLM June 2006 p43). **Britain's first mobile playhouse** The Century Theatre, founded 1952, came on tour to Stafford in Dec 1957, but got virtually 'stranded' and consequently was threatened with never taking to the road again (SA & Chron Dec 26 1957 p4 col 6). **Strange but true!** In 1956 a female chimpanzee called Babu, became the patient of the doctor of Mr and Mrs Frederick Mountford of Pitcher Bank, Stafford, to whom Babu belonged, to cure it of its cold. The animal had been rescued from the wild (SA & Chron Feb 2 1956 p4 col 5p). **First expeditionary force landing site on earth for aliens from outer space** Stafford area, according to a theory expounded by science fiction writer Gavin Gibbons in his book 'The Coming of the Space Ships' (1956), after he saw his first space ship near Shrewsbury on Dec 27 1953, there followed sightings of UFOs all in 1954 at Seighford; Stone and Weston Roads, Stafford; Stone; Weston Bank; Milford Common; and Ranton. Gibbons believed the aliens had Hixon and Seighford airfields in their sights (SA & Chron Dec 13 1956 p6. March 10 1960 p10). **First Staffordshire County Show on its current permanent showground** Began Wednesday May 28 1958, on the Uttoxeter Road, Hopton Heath site (SA & Chron May 29 1958 p1ps). **UK's largest ever search for oil** When Eric Varley, Energy Minster, issued a licence to Shell UK explore an area of 1,289 square miles centred on Stafford, in 1975, with gravity checks allowed in every square kilometre; drilling for oil began in 1980 at Woodside Farm, Ranton (SN Jan 15 2009 p6). **Staffordshire Best Kept Village winner (medium village category) 1985, 1986; winner (small village category) 1989, 1992; Stafford District winner (small village category) 1989, 1991, 1992** Hopton; **Stafford District winner (small village category) 1997, 2000** Salt. **'forefront of Northern Soul music'** 1980s Stafford (Stafford: A History & Celebration. Roger Butters & Nick Thomas 2005 p112). **British Youth Band 2007** Stafford Lancers in the British Youth Band Association National championship (SN Oct 18 2007 p19). **National home of Chief Archivists in Local Government (1980)** Staffordshire Record Office, Eastgate Street, in 2002. **First Staffordshire place history for children** Possibly 'Stafford A Little Book' by Joan Anslow, 1996, in that it is a publication specifically aimed at children, unusually topographical rather than educational.

2. Banking...

Fifth oldest surviving provincial bank, Staffordshire's earliest bank John Stevenson's Bank 1737, later part of Lloyd's (WSHL p1) (SLM Spring 1955 p14). **First person to forge Bank of England notes** Richard William Vaughan, a Stafford linen draper, 1758 and he engaged different artists to make and engrave a copper plate from which he printed notes, it is said, to the extent of £5,000, depositing them in the hands of a young lady as a proof of his wealth, and in order to further his cause as a suitor. Someone, however, acquainted the authorities, and eventually Vaughan was hanged for a crime which had greatly alarmed the Bank of England (SIOT p43) (Wilks' Scrapbook, WSL D1863, newspaper cutting vol 2 p20).

3. Transport...

AIRCRAFT **Stafford's first balloon ascent** At 3.35pm on Oct 26 1830 by Mr C Green jnr from the Gas Works, Chell Road, near Broadeye, accompanied by Mr Dickenson, grocer of Stafford. The pair passed over Radford, Weeping Cross, Teddesley, near Penkridge, Cannock Heath, Shoal Hill, Cannock, Churchbridge, before landing at Landywood (SA Oct 30 1830 p4 col 2). The feat is unrecorded in Godwin's 'Early Aeronautics in Staffordshire'(1986). **First aeroplane flight over Stafford** That flown in by Louis Paulhan, a French aviator, in the Daily Mail race for the prize £10,000, at 4.40am on Thursday April 28 1910 at a height of 300-400 feet. It was over Stafford he deviated from following the railway line to fly straight over the town (SA April 30 1910 p5 cols 3-4). **First British airman to 'loop the loop' and fly upside down** BC Hucks, who visited on the Whitsuntide holiday in Stafford, 1914 (SA & Chron May 21 1964 p8). **'Staffordian'** A Mark V B Spitfire paid for with funds raised in Stafford. It was delivered to the famous 452 Australian Squadron at RAF Kenley on Aug 5 1941; their ace Pilot Officer Keith W Truscott scored six kills with the plane, but was brought down in it returning over the Channel on Nov 13 1941, Truscott just managed to bale out, but the plane was lost in the sea (Stafford At War. an SN publication. 1995. p5il). **Wife of the first pilot who appeared in air displays in England and Canada on the same day** Miss Elizabeth Hooper of 334 Eccleshall Road, Stafford, a former first demonstrator at the electricity showrooms at Stafford, who married Squadron Leader DT Skeen in 1946. In Sept 1958 he captained the four jet delta wing Vulcan which took off from Farnborough Air Display landing six hours 40 minutes later at the Canadian National Exhibition, Toronto (SN Oct 18 1958 p4p).

RAIL **Staffordshire's first railway fatality** William Dearn, an oil mechanic at Stafford Station on the Grand Junction Railway, struck on the line by the Basilisk engine bound for Liverpool on Sunday Nov 11 1838.

It had unexpectedly returned to Stafford on the down line. The engine crushed his right arm and side and literally severed his head from his body (SA Nov 17 1838 p3 col 5. Nov 19 1938 p3 col 3). **Drove the engine of the first express train between London and Birmingham, the first train across the desert from Cairo to Suez 1858, brought Livingstone across the desert** Thomas Melling (d1896) of Stafford. On a special occasion he did the Cairo to Suez journey (131 miles) in 2 hours 20 minutes without stopping, for which he was presented by the mother of Mohammed Said Pasha, Viceroy of Egypt, with a gold watch. He was also the first engine driver employed on the Stafford and Uttoxeter Railway (SA Dec 19 1896 p4 col 7). **First motor cab service from Stafford Station** Two cabs replaced horse-drawn cabs from Sept 23 1911 (SA Sept 23 1911 p7 col 2). **Stafford's first Diesel train service** A two-coach train which ran from Stafford to Birmingham on March 5 1956 (SA & Chron March 8 1956 p1p). **Fancy that!** Three signalmen from the same signalbox at Stafford (No. 5 signalbox) have all served as Mayor of Stafford - Thomas H Tunnicliffe 1930-32, Charlie Jones 1953-55, Rees Llewellyn Tyler 1963-63 (SA Nov 14 1952 p4 col 5). **Stafford's oldest small coffee house 1960** Coffee Tavern, a wooden shed by Stafford Station. In 1960 it was demolished when the present station building was erected. It started as a cafe for railway employees c1905 (SA & Chron June 2 1960 p6p). **Record for visiting the northernmost (Thurso), southernmost (Penzance), westernmost (Arisaig), and easternmost (Lowestoft) stations in Great Britain** Tony Davies of Stafford in 37 hours 34 minutes on April 14-15 1993 (GBR 1995 p124). **UK's first train television service** Central Trains, running between Birmingham and Stafford, and Lichfield, with on board TVs (BBC Midlands Today July 27 2004).

ROAD **First motor mail service in the North Wales Postal District** (Stafford was in this District) Ran between Stafford (Station Post Office) and Rocester via Uttoxeter and Weston-upon-Trent (22 miles) from Sept 14 1911 at 3.30am. The contractor was the Gaol Square Motor Company. The van was specially built by Bagnall, coachbuilders, the chassis was of the Delaunay-Belleville type (SA Sept 16 1911 p6 col 7). **First zebra crossing fine at Stafford** On Jan 21 1952 when motorist, Edward George Pettit, aged 50 of Second Ave, was fined £2 for failing to stop for a pedestrian (SA Jan 25 1952 p6 col 4). **First man to exceed 100 mph with a 750 c.c. engine** Capt GET Eyston in M.G. 'Magic Midget' at Bonneville Salt Flats, Utah, who came to speak to the Stafford and District Car Club at the Swan Hotel in Feb 1956 (SA & Chron Feb 2 1956 p4 col 4). **World record price for a 1954 Vincent Series-C 'White Shadow'** £81,800 at Bonhams' £1-million Sale at The Classic Motor Cycle Show, Bingley Hall? Stafford, April 29 2007; only a relative handful of these motor bikes are known to survive. It sold to a private UK collector (website, 2008).

WATERCRAFT **'HM Submarine Perseus'** Adopted by the people of Stafford as a result of the town's fund-raising efforts during Warship Week in Nov 1941. The craft was built in 1930. The only known

Staffordian who served on it was Chief Petty Officer Frank Douglas Plant. Perseus' last patrol ended in tragedy on Dec 1 1941, when she sank having hit a mine with the loss of all her crew somewhere off the Isle of Zante, West Greece (Stafford At War. an SN publication. 1995. p8). **'City of Stafford' merchant vessel** Built in the U.S.A., launched 1943; length 442 feet; beam 58 feet, gross tonnage 7,210, and capable of carrying a dead-weight cargo of 11,000 tons. The vessel was first named Samtorch, and was granted to Ellerman Associated Lines under the Lendlease programme, who renamed it 'City of Stafford' (SA April 15 1950 p7p).

Stafford's arms and corporation mace.

4. The Shire and Borough...

One of the oldest offices in the municipal history of the borough The office of High Steward, the first was Humphrey, Duke of Buckingham in 1455 (SA Feb 11 1933 p8 col 4): **First commoner to attain the Stewardship** WT Richardson in 1955, aged 70, succeeding the Earl of Lichfield, who retired on health grounds (SA & Chron Sept 15 1955 p1 cols 3-4. Jan 7 1960 p1p). **First known freeman of Stafford** Walter de Stafford, mentioned as Provost 1164 (The Freeman of Stafford Borough 1100-1997 Jack Kemp 1998). **Last parade of the Staffordshire Yeomanry Regiment of the Queen's Own Mercian Yeomanry in Stafford** On Saturday May 31 1980, exercising their right to the freedom of the borough (granted 1946), and were carrying their regimental guidon standard for the final time. Elizabeth II presented a new guidon to the Queen's Own Mercian Yeomanry (formed 1971), in June 1980. The route was from Kitchener House, Lammascote Road, to the town centre (SN June 6 1980 p11ps). **Unique method of displaying corporation mace** By royal decree Stafford and City of London alone are forbidden from resting their maces in horizontal positions (FSP p53). **Stafford's first mayor** Mathew Cradock (1583-1636), born Stafford, 1614-15 (SN Jan 14 1939). **Thrice Mayor of Stafford, 1st R.C. chief magistrate of Stafford since the passing of the Municipal Corporations Act** Dr Ebenezer William Taylor (1851-1925), mayor 1907-08, 1908-09, and 1911-12 (SA Dec 12 1925 p9 col 5). **1st Stafford mayor to die during his Mayoralty since the passing of the Municipal Corporations Act** James C Marson in 1876; the 2nd was FW Pitt in 1935 (SA Aug 24 1935 p7 col 1). **1st woman Mayor of Stafford** Mrs EM South of Leecroft, Rowley Park, widow of CF South, head of the firm of Messrs South & Stubbs, for 1933 (SA Nov 12 1932 p11p). **1st single woman Mayor of Stafford** Miss Iris Moseley (the 350th Mayor), in 1964 aged 43. For her Mayoress she chose her mother, Mrs Ada Moseley, aged 64, with whom she lived in Mynors Street, Stafford (SA & Chron May 28 1964 p11p). **1st chairman of Stafford RDC to wear his own badge of office** Mr AJ Jones on May 26 1962 (SA & Chron May 31 1962 p10p). **1st women appointed to the bench for Stafford borough** Miss GJ McCrea (headmistress of Stafford Girls' High School), Mrs A Dix, and Mrs EM South, in May 1921 (SA Oct 27 1934 p9p of Miss McCrea). **Last assizes in Shire Hall** The last session ran between Oct 19 to Nov 12 1971 (SN Aug 31 2006 p6). **First distinctively religious gathering held in the (new) Borough Hall** Was held by the Stafford Young Men's Christian Association on the evening of Sept 25 1877 (SA Sept 29 1877 p4 col 5, p6 col 4). **First televisation of Stafford burgess enrolment ceremony** Feb 10 1950, for BBC Television Newsreel; 20 new burgesses were admitted (SA Feb 11 1950 p5p).

5. Buildings...

Oldest secular stone building in Stafford 2002 The Surgery Bar and Restaurant, Crabbery Street; formerly the Noah's Ark Inn, (Stafford: A History & Celebration. Roger Butters & Nick Thomas 2005 p61). **Tallest timber-framed house in England** (Staffordshire Breaks 2006. Staffordshire Tourism), **largest remaining timber-framed town house in England** High House, Greengate Street (Staffordshire County Guide 2006/7 p39). **Stafford's most interesting street** Greengate Street, according to The Birmingham Weekly Post June 2 1923 p9. **Most ambitious Georgian town house in Staffordshire** Chetwynd House (BOE p30). **Shire Hall clock first illuminated with gas** Oct 18 1850 (SA Dec 28 1850 p6 col 7). **'one of Stafford's best-known institutions' 1910** 'The Old Curiosity Shop' on the corner of Bath Street and Albion Place, Stafford, described as recently established in Aug 22 1891 (later, it may have moved and adjoined the High House). It closed in Dec 1910 on the retirement of its founder William Albert Marson (1840-1916), grocer at the High House from 1863. It was a 'landmark', a place of interest to townspeople and visitors alike (SA Dec 14 1910) (WSL M530. William

Marson's Scrapbook vol 2. pp154p,193). **First Stafford council houses At** Broadeye 1901 (SN May 4 2006 p13). **'one of the finest late Victorian buildings in Staffordshire', 'one of Britain's finest Victorian municipal buildings'** The County Buildings, Martin St, dated 1895 (SN Aug 31 2006 p17) (ES Sept 2 2006 p2). **Smallest Odeon cinema** Stafford Odeon, which Odeon's founder, Oscar Deutsch, called his drawing room cinema (ES Your Week Oct 7 2006 p9). **'one of the finest comprehensive leisure centres in the Midlands area' 1976** Riverside Recreation Centre, Stafford, opened July 1974, demolished 2008. It had swimming pools for teaching, main and diving, sports hall, climbing wall, squash courts, range area, sauna suite, amenity and committee rooms and licensed bar (Stafford Borough Offical Guide. 1976. pp52p,53p). **UK's 2nd oldest licensed inn, one of the AA's 1001 Great Family Pubs, National Pub Website of the Year 2002, Staffordshire Dining Pub of the Year 2003** The Holly Bush Inn at Salt, with origins thought to reach back to 1190, claimed as such by 1938 (book of the above title, 2005) (SA Nov 19 1938 p6p) (SN Oct 11 1958 p14p) (SVB p147) (Nicholson's Real Ale Guide to the Waterways. p138) (SN Jan 10 1997 p9ps) (The Good Pub Guide 2003) (E&S Feb 5 2003 p14p). **Oldest licensed premises in Staffordshire** Reputedly The Vine, Salter Street (Staffordshire County Guide 2006/7, advert). **1st ever 'Best Decorated Street' at Stafford Pageant** A tie between New Street and North Walls in 1935 (Stafford Pageant: The Exciting Innovative Years 1901-1952. Gordon Henry Loach. 2007).

St Mary's Church, Stafford.

6. Churches...

'The County's Church' St Mary's, St Mary's Grove, STAFFORD, as considered by Ven WA Parker, rector and archdeacon of Stafford, when appealing for restoration funds in 1947 (SA May 31 1947 p5 col 2); this church is **one of 23 such county dedications** (most common dedication in the county); **55th= oldest AP county church** dating from 1220. **One of the highest spires in England in C16** St Mary's parish church; but it fell in a storm in 1593 (NHS p369) (LGS p215). **Second longest church entry in Pevsner's 'Staffordshire'** St Mary's at 93 lines (BOE pp240-243). **First known dean of Stafford Collegiate Church** Robert 1159-1207. **Longest-serving dean** John Thrower, who served 57 years, 1467-1524. **Longest-serving rector of St Mary's** John Palmer, who served

52 years, 1587-1639. At BROADEYE St Bertelin's, 1900, closed 1920, demolished 1964 (Around Stafford. Roy Lewis. 1999. p87p). At FORE-GATE is Christ Church, Foregate Street, built 1837-39. **Only person in the world holding the appointment of 'churchwarden emeritus'** In 1958, Arthur Packman of Cannock Road, Stafford, churchwarden of Christchurch, 1921-56, became possibly the only person in the world to hold this title (SA & Chron Jan 1 1959 p1p). At HOPTON is St Peter, junction of Hopton, Hoptonhall, and Wilmorehill Lanes, built 1876. At LITTLEWORTH is St John the Baptist, Bedford Ave, built 1926-28. At SALT is St James the Great, junction of Trentfield Lane and Salt Road, built 1840-41. At WHITGREAVE is St John, built 1844. NON-CON-FORMIST Congregational church, Eastgate Street, Stafford, built 1966, replacing an earlier building in Martin Street. **Longest-serving organist in one Staffordshire church** Mr WT Edgar organist July 1 1888 to June 26 1938, with the exception of vacation Sundays and a short period of illness Mr Edgar officiated at nearly every service over the 50 years, a record probably unique, not only in the Congregational churches though-out the country, but in any denomination (SA June 25 1938 p5 col 6).

7. Education...

Earliest grammar school in Staffordshire Possibly Stafford Free Grammar School; documented 1473 (SKYT p66), if not Lichfield, re-putedly existing by 1440. **Worst headmaster of Stafford Grammar School** Rev George Norman, who held the job 1825-59, despite numer-ous complaints and attempts to get rid of him. He attended school for only three hours a day, refused to teach anything but the Classics, and used to send boys out to buy drink for him (So you think you know? Staf-ford. A quiz & miscellany. Francis Frith Collection. 2005. p18).

8. People...

Stafford's most famous old worthy St Bertram or Bertelin (c680-after c705), Mercian prince who renounced his heritage and built himself a hermitage on an island known as Betheney, which became the town of Stafford, and so he is considered the founding father of Stafford. He apparently ended his days in the Staffordshire Moorland foothills. The shrine in Ilam church is reputedly his, as was a preaching cross, discov-ered in 1954 on the site of the church of St Bertram behind St Mary's in Stafford. **'world's most famous fisherman', 'the father of Fly Fish-ing', one of the 'Seven sons of Staffordshire'** Izaak Walton, writer on angling, born in Stafford 1593 (AVH p55) (Staffordshire Handbook c1966 p25). **370th Lord Mayor of London** Sir Hugh Homersley, Staf-ford native, who served in 1627-8. **602nd Lord Mayor of London** Tho-mas Sidney, Stafford native, who served in 1853-4. **1st archbishop of the new Catholic Birmingham archbishopric** Edward Ilsley (d1926) of Stafford in 1911 (VCH vol 3 p115 note) (Birmingham News Dec 11 1926). **Youngest sergeant in the British Army to 1915** Perhaps James Fursey of 26 Backwalls, Stafford, when aged only 18, in the Army Serv-ice Corps 1915 (SA & Chron March 11 1965 p8). **1st Stafford Pageant Queen (or Pageant Rose Queen)** Miss Irene Bradshaw in 1918. The last to merely hold the Stafford Pageant Queen title, before the additional title of Miss Staffordshire was introduced, was Miss Majorie Davies in 1932, aged 18, of Acton Gate (Stafford Pageant: The Exciting Innovative Years 1901-1952. Gordon Henry Loach. 2007). **Last surviving Stafford Volunteer** Mr Betteridge, native of Stafford, who died 1948 aged 89 (SA July 17 1948 p4 col 1). **Youngest Governor in the Colonial Service 1956, last Governor of Malta, first Governor-General of Malta** Sir Maurice Henry Dorman (b c1914) of Stafford, grandson of WH Dorman, founder of the Stafford engineering firm. Governor of Sierra Leone 1956-; Governor-General of Sierra Leone 1961-62; Governor of Malta 1962-64; Governor-General 1964-71 (SA & Chron April 12 1962 p8 col 8) (Wikipedia 2008). **England's first 'Miss Rock 'n Roll'** Miss Jean Fox of Stafford, chosen on March 9 1957 for the Stafford Pageant Queen and Miss Staffordshire contest. Possibly, it transpired this was an erroneous claim, for it was not repeated in the Advertiser the following week (SA & Chron March 7 1957 p1. March 14 1957 p8p). **Miss Staffordshire 1958** Carreen Horne, aged 20, of 168 Oxford Gardens, Stafford (SN June 21 1958 p8p). **Miss Staffordshire 1959** Yolande Challinor of Salt, aged 16 (SN May 30 1959 p7p). **Miss World 1964 visits Stafford** When Ann Sidney of Poole, Dorset, attended a dance organised by the Stafford Pageant Committee at the Top of the World ballroom on Oct 29 1965 (SA & Chron July 1 1965 p1). **Strange but true!** Albert Huffen, ex-miner from Stafford, was sentenced 1982 to life imprisonment for killing his room mate because of his loud snoring (ES Your Week Feb 24 2007 p6).

First solicitor to claim fees for his work on his own case Geoffrey Robinson of Lloyd and Robinson, Stafford. In 1986 Trading Standards department alleged renovation treatment Robinson said had been done to a house in Castletown had not been done. Stafford Magistrates Court dismissed the case during committal proceedings to the Crown Court. Robinson was awarded costs and submitted a claim including £5,890 for his own work carried out before the case went to court. The clerk to Stafford, Stone, Eccleshall justices refused to pay that part of the claim from Central Funds because a layman would not have been able to claim for doing legal research himself. In early Nov 1987 it was ruled a solicitor was entitled to claim fees for his own work because he could have spent the time working for a client; thus a legal precedence was set (SN Nov 13 1987 p23). **UK's oldest and youngest recipients of keyhole surgery** Sidney Clews, 100, and Damian Peake, 24 days, at Stafford District General Hospital 1994 (ES Aug 3 1994 p3p). **Staffordshire General Hospital's 1st Millennium baby** Benjamin Yates of Hednesford at 3.25am Jan 1 2000 (E&S Jan 3 2000 p13). **Patrick, Earl of Lichfield's last official engagement** Opening of Stafford College arts department at Broad Eye, 2005 (SN May 18 2006 p3). **Number 10 in UK charts 1973, Number 3 in USA charts 1973** 'Couldn't Get it Right' consisting mainly of former King Edward VI School pupils (Stafford: A History & Celebration. Roger Butters & Nick Thomas 2005 pp111-112). **TV's 'Stars In Their Eyes Kids' winner 2006** Christopher Napier, aged 9, of Kingston Hill (ES March 21 2006 p6pc) (SN March 23 2006 p3pc). **Last resident of Tinkerborough rock caves** Miss Rachel Holford (SA Feb

STAFFORD PEOPLE - Dr Withering, after a portrait by Von Breda, Izaak Walton, William Salt.
Second row - William Horton, Peter Thorneycroft M.P., Richard Brinsley Sheridan M.P..
Bottom row - Miss Violet Charlesworth, David Blomeley (hero), William Albert Marson (trade).

10 1950) (WSL CB/ SALT/ 3). **Champion cake-maker 2007** Sue Walk-ers of Stafford (BBC 1 Midlands Today. July 30 2007). **Licensee of the Year 2008** Chris Lewis, 39, of The Swan Inn, Greengate Street, in the British Institute of Innkeeping awards (E&S March 19 2008 p7p). **Stafford's villainess** Miss Violet Charlesworth, born Stafford 1884, pretty-faced contrickster. After using supreme duplicity to climb socially, and exploit the illusion of her status, she and her mother were tried at Derby Assizes in Feb 1910. Both got five years imprisonment, which was later reduced to three years (SA Feb 12 1910 p7 col 1) (TB Oct 15 1998 p15p). **Stafford's bravest** Reg Jones of Stafford who rescued Harold Tyson, of about 9 years old, from the River Sow in c1929. He received the Royal Humane Society's Certificate (Staffordshire Weekly Sentinel April 27 1929 p4p). **Stafford's poorest** When St Mary's Collegiate Church, in the area of the present St Mary's, was mostly demolished 1736-38, a workhouse was established in some of the outbuildings. This remained in use until the poor were removed to the new Stafford Union Poor House at Marston, built 1837-8 (VCH vol 3 pp206,303-309. vol 6 p231). **Stafford's kindest** Sir Martin Noell (1614-65), a London merchant and financier, native of Stafford. By 1662 he had built a group of almshouses in Mill Street, Stafford. But died of plague before he could properly en-dow them. His family later gave the building to the borough authorities in trust, and it continues to house alms folk (VCH vol 6 p266). **Staffordian of 1906-2006 nominees** Ray Edensor, paramedic charity run-ner; Sir Stanley Clarke, property developer; William Henry Peach, shoe manufacturer and benefactor; Patrick, Earl of Lichfield; Gordon Loach, campaigner; Robert WV Robins (d1968), cricketer (SN June 22 2006 p8ps). **Staffordshire's 2nd wills proved in a civil District Probate Registry** Belong to John Wright of Stafford, a farmer, and a man from Berkswich, both proved on Jan 19 1858. Wills before Jan 12 1858 were proved in an ecclesiastical court. **Stafford's earliest recorded wills** Be-long to Richard Lees, Richard Sale, and Edward Wovall, all dated Oct 4 1550. **First person in the parish register** Margery daughter of Richard Drury baptised Oct 1 1559. **Choicest quotes** Daniel Defoe in his A Tour Through The Whole Island of Great Britain, 1724-6, "tis an old and indeed ancient town, and gives name to the county, but we thought to have found something more worth going so much out of the way in it'. John Betjamin, poet, after visiting the town in 1958, said "What I like about Stafford is that it is all there still, with only just a few accretions which need tidying up. All Stafford is there as it used to be.. And when the glorious time comes when there is going to be a by-pass so that you can shop at ease in the streets, then Stafford will be seen again." (SA & Chron March 6 1958 p10 cols 4-5).

9. War heroes...

Stafford's WW1 hero Pte A Horobin was among the first Stafford-ians to volunteer for service in WW1. He enlisted into the Coldstream Guards and fought at the Front from November 1914, taking part in the famous Christmas Day truce (info Nick Thomas). **Whitgreave's hero** Corp Charles Groves of the 1st Staffs Yeomanry, who received an

M.M. in 1919 for bravery in the field, rendering valuable assistance to one of his wounded comrades under shell fire in 1917 whilst advancing near Jerusalem (SA March 6 1920 p5p). **Staffordshire's last combat deaths in WW1** Perhaps Sgt Bert Robson of Tenterbanks, of North Staffs Regt, and L-Corp Arthur Stanton of Rowley Street, 8th North Staffs Regt, both killed on Nov 4 1918; another man from Penkridge also died on this day (SA Nov 30 1918 p5 col 5ps). **Croix de Guerre winner** L-Corp Henry John Mountford, 21, of South Backwalls, Stafford, in 1918 (SA March 2 1918 p4p). **Stafford's WW2 hero** James Malcolm S Poole, attended King Edward VI High School (where a commemorative plaque to him hung in the library). He was First Lieutenant on HMS Submarine Urge, which sank on May 6 1942 after possibly hitting a mine, whilst on patrol in the Mediterranean. He was awarded the Distinguished Service Cross in Dec 1941, and in Nov 1942 awarded posthumously a second DSO (bar) (Stafford At War. an SN publication. 1995 pp8, 13). **Staffordshire's last combat death in WW2** Possibly Sergt Henry Fellows, aged 26, of Water Street, Stafford, Royal Artillery, former English Electric Ltd employee, who died Aug 10 1945 from accidental shell wounds received in the Indian theatre of war. Another possibility is Pte Frank Hammersley of Haregate, Leek, Queen's Royal Regt, aged 20, killed in action in Burma; his parents received the news of his death in Sept 1945 (SA Aug 25 1945 p4 col 9. Sept 8 1945 p6 col 4). **Only Staffordian to have flown in Battle of Britain** David Blomeley (1916-1991), son of a Stafford headmaster. He fought with 151 Squadron, flying Hawker Hurricanes in defence of the BEF in France. He recorded his first 'kill' over Dunkirk on May 29 1940. He destroyed or damaged 10 German aircraft during 1940, finishing the War with 15 'kills' and the Distinguished Flying Cross. By late 1943 he was a Squadron Leader, flying Mosquitoes with 604 Squadron. In 1950 he served as a Vulcan bomber pilot in the Suez crisis (Stafford At War. an SN publication. 1995. p7p) (Stafford: A History & Celebration. Roger Butters & Nick Thomas 2005 p26). **Distinguished Flying Cross medalist** Squadron Leader Dennis Herbert (1922/3-2006) of Littleworth, who became a specialist navigator and helped to form the 623 Squadron (SN Aug 10 2006 p2p). **First in action in Korea battle** Fusilier WJ Cocklin of 27 Prospect Road, Coton, Royal Northumberland Fusiliers, when a convoy was attacked by three parties of Communists in early 1951 (SA Feb 2 1950 p5p).

10. People in politics...

First known by-election Took place some time between 1530 and 1532 at Stafford, when Sampson Erdeswick of Sandon was elected (SHC 1917-18 pp297-9, 303) (VCH vol 6 p237). **Staffordshire's most intellectual brilliant M.P.** Richard Brinsley Sheridan, according to George JS King in an SA General Election Supplement Oct 12 1951. It was as member for Stafford (1780-1806) that he delivered, in a debate on Warren Hastings, a speech lasting five hours, 40 minutes, which was, by common consent, one of the greatest in the annals of Parliament. When he resumed his seat it was said that the 'whole

House - the members, peers, and strangers - involuntarily joined in a tumult of applause, and adopted a mode of expressing their approbation, new and irregular in that House by loudly and repeatedly clapping their hands.' On one of his election visits he accosted one of the burgesses, a baker named Wright, and said "When I come to Stafford I always enjoy your excellent rolls for breakfast, and I promise you when I become Chancellor of the Exchequer I shall make you Master of the Rolls". At an election dinner in the town Sheridan proposed the toast: "May the manufactures of Stafford be trodden under foot by all the world". His son, Tom, was a candidate at one contest, and imitated his father, with the toast: "The craft of Stafford, and may every other craft go barefoot" (Wilks' Scrapbook, WSL D1863, newspaper cutting, vol 2 p20) ('Borough' Guide to Stafford. No. 84 in Borough Pocket Guides series. c1925. p40) (VCH vol 6 p217). **England's first Labour M.P., 1st President of the National Association of Miners** Alexander Macdonald (d1881), MP for Stafford in 1874, as the endorsed candidate of the Labour Representation League, thus making him, along with Thomas Burt, MP for Morpeth (1874), one of the first two overtly labour, albeit Liberal/ labour, members of parliament. He became President of the National Association of Miners when they formed in 1863 (DNB) (SA Feb 8 1947 p5 col 2. Feb 15 1947 p8 col 7) (SN April 4 1980 p8il). **108th Chancellor of the Exchequer** Peter Thorneycroft of Stafford who served between Jan 13 1957 and Jan 6 1958 (ES Your Week Jan 20 2007 p6). **Fancy that!** Ray Shenston was the only member of the English National Party (with only 1,000 members nationally at the time) to turn up to the Stafford branch AGM, which he had organised, on Feb 23-24 1980. He claimed severe weather had put people off (SN Feb 29 1980 p22). **The candidate who labelled his ballot paper "Soon to be unemployed"** Christopher David Teasdale, Independent, in the 1984 Stafford-by election, and received 220 votes (Wikipedia).

11. Religion...

Earliest ecclesiastical dedication to Thomas Becket Possibly St Thomas Becket Priory, to the E of Stafford, founded c1175~80 by Richard Peche, bishop of Lichfield, in memory of his friend, murdered 1170 (BOE p247). **First to apply for registration after the Test Act of 1672** Presbyterians of Stafford who registered a house for meetings 1672 (SKYT pp43,44-5) (VCH vol 6 p255) (Trinity Church, Stafford: A Short History. Hilma Wilkinson. 1991) (SIOT p12) (LOU p86). **John Wesley's least religious town** After he preached in Stafford on March 29 1785 he declared in his diary 'there are few towns in England less infected with religion than Stafford' (SLM Sept 1950) (SKYT p125). **First Sunday school in Stafford** Wesleyan meeting room in St Chad's Passage 1805 (VCH vol 6 pp253-4). **First and last Pleasant Sunday Afternoon meetings at Stafford** On Sunday Sept 22 1889 (formed at Congregational Church School, Martin Street), and Jan 22 1961 with the disbanding of the Pleasant Sunday Afternoon Society Brotherhood and Sisterhood (SA & Chron Feb 9 1961 p11 col 1). **First female archdea-**

con in the Diocese of Norwich Rev Jan McFarlane (b1965), appointed Archdeacon of Norwich in 2008, having served in the Stafford Team Ministry shortly after her ordination at Lichfield Cathedral in 1993 (SN June 26 2008 p11).

12. Welfare and society...

Earliest evidence of freemasonry in Stafford 1814 when the Lodge of Fortitude was constituted, but the records of the earlier years are incomplete and no lodge roll survives pre-1833 (An Attempt at Compiling a History of Freemasonry in Stafford. T Ward Chalmers. 1882) (SA March 4 1882 p2 col 7). **5th county mental asylum in England and Wales built** Stafford Mental Asylum, opened 1818 - the others were Nottingham (1812), Bedford (1812), Norfolk (1814), Lancaster (1816) (Wilks' scrapbook, D1863, newspaper cutting c1933, vol 2, p110). **No town in the kingdom with better institutions for the insane** Stafford, according to Dr Bell Fletcher at the AGM of the friends of the Birmingham and Midland Counties Middle-class Idiot Asylum at Knowle, Warws (which had potential to serve five Midland counties, including Staffordshire), held at the Shire Hall, Stafford, with reference to Stafford County Asylum, and the Coton Hill institution, on April 18 1874 (SA April 25 1874 p6 col 6). **When Napoleon's physician came to Stafford** On Aug 24 1826 Stafford County Asylum received a visit from Monsieur Ferrus: in 1837 the hospital received yet another distinguished French visitor, Monsieur le Dr Fairet, chief physician of the Salpetriere Hospital, Paris (Wilks' scrapbook, D1863, newspaper cutting c1933, vol 2, p110). **Staffordshire's earliest photographic scene** Perhaps Greengate St, Stafford, 1858; it is certainly Stafford's earliest (info Roy Lewis, 2006; reproduced in SSTY p78p). **Worst outbreak of Legionnaires' Disease ever to occur in UK, possibly in the world** At Stafford District General and Kingsmead Hospitals in Stafford in April 1985 with 101 suspected cases, 68 confirmed cases, 28 deaths (Stafford: A History & Celebration. Roger Butters & Nick Thomas. 2005. p26). **4th best place to buy property in Britain 2008** Stafford, according to The Property List TV programme on Channel Five, June 19 2008; Milton Keynes was top (SN June 19 2008 p24). **UK's only crime prevention centre** Stafford to 1996, when it moved to Yorkshire (info Carol Galpin). **1st probation service in the country to achieve a special excellence status** Stafford probation area (SN March 29 2007 p21).

13. William Salt Library...

Most comprehensive private collection of historical documents to 1863 Accumulated by William Salt, member of a wealthy banking family, and on which the William Salt Library, Eastgate Street, is based (SKYT p75). **'The foremost historical library for the county'** Claimed of the Library by the Official Guide to Stafford, 1958 (SA & Chron Oct 23 1958 p6 col 7). **One of William Salt's greatest buys** The Compton Census (1676), purchased 1844; still forms part of WSL (WSHL p32). **Most valuable item in the original collection** An extremely rare coin of Beornwulf; but sold in 1868 for £25 10s (WSHL p46). **Most treasured documents by its staff** Anglo-Saxon charters relating to the lands of Burton Abbey (info Dominic Farr). **First visitor to the library** John Kelsall, mayor of Stafford, Jan 20 1874 (WSHL p52). **First Librarian** TJ Mazzinghi (1873-93). **Longest serving Librarian** F(reddy) B. Stitt, 1957-85 (WSHL p64). **'Most exclusive tied cottage in Staffordshire'** Librarian's living quarters in the Library's upper rooms; but they were vacated in 1983 (WSHL p53).

14. Staffordshire Advertiser...

First offices of the paper At the rear of the George Inn, Stafford, one of the two adjoining hostelries which were taken down when the Guildhall and Market Hall were built (A Centenary History of the Staffordshire Advertiser 1795-1895. 1895 p10). **The first supplement** Appears on July 15 1813, and contained Lord Wellington's despatches announcing his great victory over the French at Vittoria (A Centenary etc. p13). **'The Father of the English Press'** James Amphlett, editor from 1804. Towards the end of his journalist career he edited a paper at Shrewsbury, where in 1860 he published a volume of rambling 'Reminiscences' styling himself as such (A Centenary etc. p12). **'larger circulation than any of the London daily papers, the *Times* alone excepted'** The paper in 1861 when it had a circulation of 6,500 copies weekly, which was greater than the combined circulation of all the journals in the counties respectively of Derby, Chester, Shropshire, Leicester, Gloucester, and Worcester (A Centenary etc. p20). **'the largest-sized newspaper on a single sheet at present published in the United Kingdom'** At the beginning of 1857 when the paper was enlarged, the increase being equivalent to 12 columns (A Centenary etc. p21). **First photographs** The paper was very late to publish photographs. The first was of a Sunbeam car in an advertisement, c1908. The first photograph relating to Staffordshire showed the Presentation of Colours to the 1st Battalion The South Staffordshire Regiment by George V at Gibraltar, Jan 31 1912, in the edition Feb 10 1912 p8. The first portrait (with others) in a feature spread was of the Earl of Lichfield (d1918), April 20 1912 p4. The North Midland Territorial Division summer camp in Rheidol and Ystwyth Valleys near Aberystwyth, was the first illustrated news story, on June 8 1912 p8. The first photographic property advertisement was for Moss Pit House, near Stafford, June 15 1912. The first news story portrait showed Peter Broughton-Adderley of Barlaston, Oct 5 1912. **First edition with front page news** Was Feb 2 1951; from Feb 3 1955 the paper was Staffordshire Advertiser and Chronicle. **First eight-unit broadsheet web-offset press in the world, first full-scale lithographic rotary press to be installed in the British Isles** The press belonging to Powysland Newspapers, Stafford, on which the Staffordshire Advertiser and Chronicle was printed from edition (Thursday) Feb 15 1962. The press was 66 feet long, 11 feet high in parts, and weighs 50 tons. When printing a 24-paper it used 70 miles of paper, a yard wide, every hour (SA & Chron Feb 15 1962 p1p). **Oldest surviving copy in private hands (nor in any private newspaper collection) by 1952** An edition of Jan 6 1801 discovered c1950 by Mr V Smith manger of George Newton, builders' merchants, Railway Wharf, Stafford, neatly folded in a drawer of a desk in the office, formerly used by the late Mr George Newton of Gnosall (SA Jan 17 1948 p5 col 2. May 2 1952 p5 col 6).

15. Trade...

'No provincial town, of the same extent, can boast of more handsome shops than Stafford, particularly those of the mercers and drapers' Stafford in 1845 when the streets were being repaired and the shop of Messrs Boulton, Talbot and Buxton was opened (SA Oct 4 1845 p3 col 4). **Last Cattle fair held in the main street** 1910, at the instigation of Alderman HJ Bostock the police removed the animals to Lammascote Farm, the owners eventually followed; there was talk of legal action against the Council, but it did not materialise (Edwardian Echo - publish by Stafford Independents Association Feb 27 1969, Horne's Scrapbook, No. 1, item 77). **'one of best-known and highly-respected tradesmen of the town'** 1910 William Albert Marson (1840-1916), grocer at the High House from 1863 until his retirement in 1910. He was the first Stafford tradesman to introduce the system of calling at private houses for orders (SA Dec 14 1910) (WSL M530. William Marson's Scrapbook vol 2. p193). **Stafford's first labour exchange** Was officially opened in Market Square, Stafford, on Nov 1 1910 (SA Nov 5 1910 p1 col 1). This was possibly Staffordshire's first labour exchange. **'Stafford's oldest tradesman' 1953, 1st chairman of the Old Stafford Society 1925** Philip Thomas Dale (1876-1953), shopkeeper, antiquarian and trustee of the Izaak Walton Trust. At the age of 13 he started work in the half-timbered bow-fronted ironmonger's shop at 11 Greengate Street, Stafford, which had been in his family for two generations (SA Nov 6 1953 p1 cols 3-4). **First pneumatic tyred farm tip cart built at Stafford** One of Messrs John Bagnall of the Borough Coachworks, South Walls, exhibited at the Smithfield on Feb 8 1933 (SA Feb 11 1933 p6 col 4). **'one of the most carefully guarded secrets of the war'** 'Pluto', the underwater fuel pipelines linking England with the continent laid towards the end of WW2, for which Messrs Dorman & Co. Ltd. of Stafford manufactured the Flexstel ball and socket joints; these were also fitted to flame-throwing tanks (SA Sept 22 1945 p5 cols 8&9). **Staffordshire's quaintest urban shop** CJ Williams' The County Fruit Store, thatched and dated '1610' in Mill Street. **First Stafford pet shop** F.(red) Mountford Pet Store, Eastgate Street, 1932-67 (SN March 16 2006 p8p). **First Stafford store to adopt self-service methods** International foodstore, Goalgate Street, 1953; or/ also The Maypole Dairy Company, Greengate Street, 1958 (SN May 18 2006 pp8,12). **Stafford's first help-yourself service cafeteria** Jenkinson's Cafe, Greengate Street, which opened on May 15 1958. It was owned by Mrs N Dean (SA & Chron May 15 1958 p11p). **First Stafford supermarket** Elmo's, on site of the Alexandra Hotel, 1964 (SN May 18 2006 pp12-13). **First Stafford shop with an escalator** Allied Carpets who opened in July 1978. **World's largest valves - goggle valves** Two made by GEC works, 1972 for Argentina (SN July 20 2006 p6). **First Stafford cinema** The Electric Picture Palace, Glover Street, July 1910 (SN May 4 2006 p13). **'one of the most efficient and modern medium-sized printing organisations in the United Kingdom' 1980 Hourds of Mill Street, Stafford (SN Sept 19 1980 p21). 'one of the best in Europe' The proposed £130 million super coal pit at Hopton according to National Coal Board area director Ray Hunter to Stafford Chamber of Commerce in 1980 (SN Jan 25 1980 p17. Feb 1 1980 p1 - in addition, there was a possible major oil field at Haughton). One of the 100 best employers in Europe 2006 Omicron, power system test equipment manufacturer, which has its UK base at Staffordshire Technology Park, Beaconside (SN June 8 2006 p24). AA Contractor of the Year 2008 Davies Motors (Stafford) Ltd, car breakdown recovery operator (SN April 24 2008 p71 advert). National home of the Electrical Insulation Association (EIA, 1911) Stafford in 2008.

16. Shoes...

Stafford's first boot and shoe factory The works of William Horton (d1832) in Mill Street, evidently when Richard Brinsley Sheridan was MP for Stafford 1780-1806 (VCH vol 6 p217). "May the trade of Stafford be trodden under foot by all the whole world" Richard Brinsley Sheridan, MP for Stafford, proposed this as a toast at an election dinner at Stafford (VCH vol 6 p217). Stafford's largest footwear firm c1850-1980, one of the first British manufacturers to install new sewing machine's capable of stitching leather Bostocks (Lotus from 1919) at Foregate, Marston (see), 1855, causing a workers' strike in protest (VCH vol 6 p218) (Lasting Impressions: Memories of Stafford's Shoe Making & Related Industries in the 20th Century. Chris Copp & others. 2006). Lotus' first shops Four retail shops opened in 1926 (Lasting Impressions etc). Closure of Stafford's last shoe factory Lotus, Dec 1988 (Stone & Eccleshall Gazette July-August 2006 p50). 'Made shoes for Queen Victoria', originated the Lotus welted Veldtshoen method of shoe manufacture William H Tooth (b1861), employed at Messrs Edwin Bostock & Co from 1874. When at Lotus in 1897 he was chosen to make the shoes presented to Queen Victoria from Stafford on the occasion of her Jubilee. In addition, he made shoes for the Chamberlain family and Sir Arthur Balfour. He retired 1931 as principal inspector at Lotus Ltd, Sandon Road, acclaimed as having 'technical knowledge, excellence of craftsmanship, and a devotion to duty which is rarely equalled in the industrial world' (SA Nov 14 1931 p4p). Last skittle competition between the Stafford branches of the British Boot & Shoe Institution and the Managers' and Foremen's Association 1958. For this competition a trophy was awarded (SN July 12 1958 p1op). The 'Princess Louise Boot' Was patent for ladies' boots by Thomas Turner, Stafford shoe manufacturer, in 1871. It was an ingeniously simple idea of exhibiting the clean fair stitch round the sole of the boot, so well executed by machinery as to deceive even a practised eye (SA Feb 11 1871 p4 col 5. July 29 1871 p7 col 6). Largest maker of wooden heels in the British Empire early 1930s Heels Ltd, later Heels (Stafford) Ltd, which began production in 1920; by late 1940s was producing some 400,000 dozen pairs a year (VCH vol 6 p218).

17. Sport (A-C)...

'Stafford's greatest sporting personality' 1960 WT Richardson (SA

& Chron Jan 7 1960 p1p). ANGLING **First person ever to win the T. Poulson Fishing cup three times** Mr H Shelley, a gas fitter with West Midland Gas Board at Stafford, in 1936, 1955, 1961 (SA & Chron Feb 2 1961 p16p). **National Championships 1969 11th** Charles Sutton, member of Izaac Walton AA. **National Championships 1971 5th** Dave Blackmore of the Trotters (Stafford) AA (SSTY p194 - in addition, National Championships 1967 or 1977 3rd Frank Holt of Stafford). ATHLETICS **Pedestrian feat** When a pedestrian called 'the Rabone Youth' walked seven miles in one hour, and again walked seven miles in the succeeding hour, making a total of 25 miles in three hours, over a ground from Gaol Square to Radford Bridge in Aug 1834 (SA Aug 15 1834). **'first of its kind to be held in the Midlands',** Wolverhampton-Stafford Road Race first held on March 17 1951, organised by Stafford Athletic Club, with 79 runners taking part, setting off from Goodyear Sports Ground, Wolverhampton at 3pm and concluding at 4.25pm at King Edward VI School, Stafford. The winner to take the Staffordshire Advertiser 'Trophy' was Jack Holden of Tipton Harriers in 1 hour 21 mins, 10 secs. The last man home was JM Bucknall. By 1953 the race had become so successful it ranked as a National event (SA March 9 1951 p1. March 16 1951 p1 cols 6-7. March 23 1951 p1ps. March 27 1953 p2p). **Midland Counties AAA general championship record for a mile** Mike Whittaker, aged 21, of Stafford AC when he achieved 4 mins 13.6 seconds at Perry Barr Stadium on June 19 1954 (SA June 25 1954 p3). **First Stafford and District Youth Clubs' cross country championship** Saturday March 1 1958, starting and finishing on Milford Common. Francis Shipley of Rising Brook Youth Club won the senior event, F Evans of Earl Street Youth Club won the junior event (SA & Chron March 6 1958 p14p). **Achieved six consecutive Huddersfield Marathons** Malcolm Mountford of Stafford AC in 1985 (SN April 10 2008 p81). **English Schools' track and Field Champion Long Jump bronze medalist 2008** Alice Lennox of Stafford, aged 17 (E&S Aug 7 2008 p18pc). BOWLS **British Crown Green Individual Merit bowling champion 1953, All-England bowls champion 1954** Bill Slater. See Marston.

BOXING **'was prepared to fight any man of his age, size and weight' despite being of Liliputian dimensions** Thomas Hodgson, alias 'Cupid', prize-fighter of Stafford in early C18. When aged 55 he stood just 5 feet, 1 inch high, and weighed 5 stone 11lb. He sold his wife in Stafford Market Square for 5s. 6d. in 1828 (Wilks' Scrapbook, WSL D1863, newspaper cutting. vol 2 p20). **Schoolboy Boxing Champion of Great Britain 8st, 4lb intermediate class 1948** DW Edesnor, pupil of King Edward VI School, Stafford (SA April 3 1948 p6p). **The first Stafford and District Amateur Boxing Club tourament** Saturday evening, April 5 1958 at Drill Hall, Newport Road, Stafford, a contest between Stafford A.B.C. and Stoke-on-Trent A.B.C.: Stoke won five of the seven contests, and were the winners (SA & Chron April 10 1958 p11p). CANOEING **Home of the West Midland Canoe School** Founded at the Recreation Department of North Stafordshire Polytechnic at Beaconside, Stafford,

1977. To 1980 its members had won 28 international medals (SN July 4 1980 p61). CRICKET **Stafford's oldest sporting club** Stafford Victoria Cricket Club, founded 1844 (Stafford: A History & Celebration. Roger Butters & Nick Thomas. 2005 p71). **Stafford Cricket Club's first professional** Peter Webb, aged 22, New Zealand Test Cricket batsman from Auckland, in 1980 (SN April 25 1980 p60p). **One of the youngest players to participate in international cricket** Chris Paget of Stafford, aged 16 when selected to play for Derbyshire Cricket Club First XI against the West Indies at Derby in Aug 2004 (BBC news Aug 4 2004). CYCLING **Mid. NCU Champion (0.25m) 1908, Mid. NCU Champion (25m) 1909, English NCU Champion (25m) 1909, Northern AAA Champion (5m) 1910, English AAA Champion (5m, 1m, and 0.5m) 1910, Northern Counties' Amateur Association Championship Sports 0.25m winner 1911, 1m winner 1911** Jack Harvey, landlord of the The Old Blue Posts Hotel, Martin Street, Stafford, in 1911-15 (SA June 10 1911 p6 col 7) (Around Stafford. Roy Lewis. 1999. p72p). **Stafford Road Club's first weekend run** Sept 25-26 1954 to Much Wenlock, Ironbridge, and Buildwas (SA Oct 1 1954 p3 col 3).

18. Sport (D-Z)...

FIRE FIGHTING **Mitchell Shield winners 1908, 1909, 1910, 1911** Stafford Fire Brigade. Four successive wins in this competition of the Midland District of the National Fire Brigade Union was considered a record (SA Aug 26 1911 p6 col 7). FOOTBALL **One of the oldest (football) clubs in the country** Stafford Rangers, founded 1876 (Stafford: A History & Celebration. Roger Butters & Nick Thomas 2005 p71). **First time Stafford Rangers won the Birmingham League** 1927, defeating Oakengates 1-4 (SN 50 years ago supplement Oct 1977 px). **First time Stafford Rangers won the Staffordshire Senior Cup** 1955, defeating Leek Town, at Marston Road, Stafford (SA & Chron April 21 1955 p12). **Stafford Rangers most successful decade** 1970s. **FA Trophy winners 1972, 1979** Stafford Rangers. **Northern Premier League (football) winners 1971, runners-up 1972, 1976** Stafford Rangers. **Players of more games (playing and winning) than any other club in the Preliminary Round of the FA Cup** Stafford Rangers in 1974-5 (Stafford: A History & Celebration. Roger Butters & Nick Thomas 2005 p97). HOCKEY **Played for England** Miss TJ Longwood of Stafford, selected 1927 for an international against the South Africans (SN 50 years ago supplement Oct 1977 px). **Played for Ireland** Robin Bailey of Stafford when they lost to England in the triple crown 1961 (SA & Chron April 20 1961 p18p). HORSE RIDING **Horse of the Year Show 1978 3rd, Junior European Championships Nations Cup team event winners 1978** Jill Kelly of Hopton (b1960) on 'Pepper Pot', she was also a member of the British team that won the Junior European Championships in 1978 (SN Aug 21 2008 p74). ICE-SKATING **British Amateur Skating Champions 1958** Clive Preston of Stafford, and his partner Miss Joan Loudwell (SA & Chron 22 1959 p14 6). MARKSMANSHIP **Artillery record** Corp Walter George Anthony, of Tenterbanks, of C Battery 232nd Brigade, RFA, set a new record for firing rounds on an 18 pounder gun in 5 minutes, when he fired 111 rounds at the battle of Gommecourt, July 1 1916, beating the previous record of 23 rounds. He was awarded one week's leave and 100 francs (SA March 8 1919 p3 col 6p). **Darts marathon record** When Ian Concar, Arthur Candlin jnr, Alan Burton and John Hupka smashed the previous best by 48 hours, completing 216 hours (9 days) non-stop playing in 1972 at the New Inn, Stafford (Essence of the Orient restaurant in 2008). Their total score was 2,827,688, with a total of 174,861 darts thrown. Money raised went to the intensive care unit of Staffordshire General Infirmary (SN June 1 2008 p81p). **Overall class A trophy winner 1988-2008, British record in 50 lb English longbow** Mike Willrich of Stafford at the British National Archery Flight Championships. In 2008 he came 1st in Unlimited Flight Bow (class B), 517 yds 8 in, Unlimited Target Bow (class A), 556 yds 3, and took the British record in the 50 lb English longbow with 248 yds 2 ft 5 in (SN Aug 28 2008 p68pc). **Overall class A trophy winner 1997-2008** Janice Willrich of Stafford, wife of above, at the British National Archery Flight Championships. In 2008 she came 1st in 35 lb English longbow (222 yds 6 in), 50 lb English longbow (244 yds 2.9 feet), Unlimited longbow (all class D), 236 yds, and 50 lb Target Bow (class A), 392 yds 12 in (SN Aug 28 2008 p68pc).

MOTOR SPORT **Staffordshire's first motorcar hill-climb competition** Possibly that at Weston Bank on June 8 1907. This was Mid-Staffordshire Automobile Club's first motorcar hill-climb competition. The total distance was about 800 yards; the steepest gradient was 1 in 7. Mr FA Boulton of Oakamoor entered the most powerful car, a 40-h-p, Daimler, and accomplished the feat in the quickest time of 48.1 seconds, winning the challenge cup. Stile Cop was the venue the following year on May 23 1908. On June 14 1913 Mid-Staffordshire AC hosted an inter-club contest there when a Mr HG Day of Derby and N.S. A.C., in a 15 h.p. Talbot, won first place and highest merit for fastest time (SA June 15 1907 p4 col 5. May 9 1908 p2 col 4. May 13 1908. May 23 1908 p4. June 21 1913 p8 col 1) The Club's first motorcycle hill-climb competition was perhaps that held at Satnall Hill, Milford, Berkswich, see. Their first motorcycle reliability trail took place on Saturday May 20 1911. The course was from Stafford to Gnosall, Newport, Market Drayton, Whitmore, Trentham, Stone, Sandon, Eastgate Street, Stafford (55 miles); Mr C Fowke in a 3.5 hp Triumph and sidecar won first prize, a silver medal (SA May 27 1911 p7 col 1). **'the second battle of Hopton Heath'** An autocross meeting on Hopton Heath on April 8 1962. This was perhaps Stafford and District Car Club's 2nd Autocross meeting (the first being at Bradley in 1961); other contestants were the English Electric (Stafford) Motor Cycle and Car Club, and Rugeley and District Motor Club. The first battle of Hopton Heath was a battle in the Civil War 1643 (SA & Chron April 12 1962 p15ps). RUGBY **First Staffordian to have gained a Rugby international 'cap'** DS Wilson of Stafford (b1927), who was selected to play for England against France at Twickenham on Feb 28 1953 (SLM March 1953 pp5p). WEIGHT LIFTING **World All-Round Weightlifter 1992** David Horne of Littleworth, Stafford (TB Oct 1993 p15p).

19. The area...

Stafford is the **county's 36th largest parish**, consisting of 6,945 acres, and is the **parish of the county town; extremist length** 6.6m, making it **11th longest parish in the county; extremist width** 6m, making it **15th= widest parish in the county**. **Geology** HOPTON and COTON - Keuper Sandstones (Hopton Heath), Bunter (Blackheath-Hopton village), Keuper Marls (E fringe); SALT and ENSON - Keuper Marls (Enson hamlet, Sandonbank), Keuper Sandstones (Salt village, Heath), Bunter (Trent valley); STAFFORD - Keuper Marl (ancient borough), Alluvium (Sow valley); TILLINGTON, WHITGREAVE - Keuper Marls (all). **Epicentre of one of the biggest earthquakes ever recorded in UK** Stafford on 14 January 1916 (So you think you know? Stafford. A quiz & miscellany. Francis Frith Collection. 2005. p22). **Highest point** 449 feet on Hopton Heath. **Lowest point** 239 feet by the Sow below Kingston Hill. **One of the 'few towns of any size in the whole of Europe that have what is virtually a primeval swamp within a hundred yards of their Civic Centre'** Stafford in proximity to King's Pool marsh (MR2 p285). Stafford St Mary & St Chad was **12th most-populated Staffordshire parish in 1801** with 4,821 people; **14th in 1811** with 5,831; **13th in 1821** with 6,896; **12th in 1831** with 8,326; **13th in 1841** with 10,474; **13th in 1851** with 11,970; **16th in 1861** with 12,861; **18th in 1871** with 14,050; **18th in 1881** with 16,368; **18th in 1891** with 16,248; **18th in 1901** with 16,795.

20. RAF Stafford...

Gardening Trophy winners 1955 RAF Stafford with its 115-acres farm, situated by the station. This, the highest gardening award in the service, was awarded to the RAF by the American Air Force. By 1955 the station held three of the main gardening trophies in the previous rounds of this competition - the 40 Group and Maintenance Command trophies (SA & Chron Nov 24 1955 p1). The **'first permanent church to be built on a RAF station since WW2'** St Chad's church, RAF Stafford, Hopton, dedicated on Feb 3 1961 (SA & Chron Feb 9 1961 p13). **RAF's only selection centre in the British Isles for specialist recruits** RAF Stafford from May 31 1964. In addition, at the time RAF Stafford was one of the biggest maintenance units in the country (SA & Chron May 14 1964 p1). **Last day of RAF Stafford** The closure parade took place on March 30 2006 (ES March 30 2006 p5).

The huntsman spectre rides over Chartley Moss.

Stowe-by-Chartley
1. Did you know that...

Stowe-by-Chartley's top folklore A ghostly apparition of a huntsman with a pack of hounds has often been seen riding over Chartley Moss. Over the centuries many people have been lost in the moss. A bulldozer and a railway engine are believed to have sunk into it. **What Stowe-by-Chartley is famous for** Chartley Moss. The **name Stowe first appears** in 1199. **Parish's smallest cottage** Percy Ratcliffe's Cottage Back Lane, Hixon, only 16 feet by 12 feet, demolished in 1986 (info Hixon Local History Society). **Unique derivations for surnames** Grindley will be from Grindley, and Hix, Hix(s)on, Hickson will be from Hixon, both in this parish (PDS). **'Staffordshire's worst rail disaster'** When a Manchester to London express train collided at 80 mph with a heavy goods vehicle carrying a 120-tonne, 148 feet long, industrial electric transformer at Hixon level crossing at 12.30pm on Jan 6 1968. Eleven people were killed and 45 injured. The impact tore up 120 yards of track, derailed the engine, overturned 8 of the 12 coaches, tossed the load on to the track side and virtually sliced the transporter in half (ES Jan 2 2008 p17ps). **Hixon Heirloom** Shire stallion bay, foaled 1906, advertised for stud in 1908. It won first prize at Ashbourne 1906; the only time it was shown. Also belonging to the late Thomas Appleby of Ivy House, Hixon, there was Hixon Flora, winner of numerous First and Champion prizes (SA May 16 1908 p8 col 7). **Staffordshire County Show Best Farm 1948** Appears to have been a smallholding at Lea Heath run by VB Brown, in the small farm category, of under 80 acres; 1948 was the first year of this prize (SA July 24 1948 p5 col 7). **Staffordshire's last school built in the county's rural school reorganisation scheme** Hixon County Secondary School, which cost over £100,000, completed summer 1958 in one year (a national record), with formal handing over the keys ceremony in May 1959. There were a total of 8 Staffordshire rural secondary schools built under the scheme, initiated by the Minister of Education c1955 (SA & Chron June 4 1959 p4p. Nov 12 1959 p7). **Best UK Family Business 2008** Jesse Brough Metals International of Hixon, founded 1979, named by Coutts Family Business awards, with a turnover of £5m to £25m, they refine aluminium and recycle aluminum waste (The Birmingham Post June 12 2008 p23). **Staffordshire's saddest roadside accident** Cousins, aged six and nine, who were killed by a car careering off the A518 NE of Chartley as they took a birthday card to their aunt at a nearby garage, Dec 13 1986; two handmade crosses still (2006) mark the site (StE pp238-9). **Staffordshire Best Kept Village Stafford District winner (small village category) 1994, 1995, 1996, 1998, 1999, 2001, 2002, 2004, 2005, 2006** Stowe-by-Chartley. **First pub in North Staffordshire to secure a 24-hour licence** Green Man Inn, Lea Road, Hixon, Nov 2005 (ES April 15 2006 p15). **(Staffordshire) Pub of the Year 2006** Bistro le Coq at Stowe-by-Chartley judged by Staffordshire Good Food Awards (SLM Dec 2006 p100).

2. Churches...

At Stowe-by-Chartley is St John the Baptist, **one of 11 such county dedications** (of AP churches); **23rd= oldest county church** dating from the C12 or roughly 1150. **Stowe-by-Chartley's most famous old worthy** Walter Devereux (1490-1558), who has the most imposing monument in the church, an alabaster tomb, which he designed himself. It shows him in his Garter collar, his head on a plumed helmet; his wives wearing close-fitting hats, and six daughters and six sons round the tomb; one, Sir William, was the father of Queen Elizabeth's celebrated favourite Robert Devereux. Walter Devereux succeeded to Chartley Hall in Chartley Holme, and the barony of Ferrers, in 1501. He was Constable of Warwick Castle; Knight Garter 1523; fought against the French, 1544; Viscount Hereford, 1550. **Only memorials by Sir Edward Lutyens in Staffordshire** Those to William La Touche Congreve (d1916), and Sir Walter Norris Congreve (d1927) (BOE p270). The former, erected on Nov 3 1918 (SA Nov 9 1918 p5), may be the **first WW1 memorial erected to an individual in a Staffordshire church** and reads:- 'In thankful remembrance of William La Touche Congreve, eldest son of Gen. Sir Walter Congreve, V.C. of Congreve and Chartley, in this county, who, serving the King in the Rifle Brigade, by the age of 25 had attained the Victoria Cross, the Distinguished Service Order, the Military Cross, the Legion d'Honneur, and Beevet Majority. He fell in the battle of the Somme, July 26 1916, and is buried at Coebee. His life was fine, his career brilliant, his death glorious. *Non moritus cujus fama civit.*' At HIXON is St Peter, Church Lane, was built 1848.

3. The area...

Stowe is the **county's 49th largest parish**, consisting of 5,120 acres; **24th closest parish to the county town**, 4.1m ENE; **extremist length 4m; extremist width** 4.5m. **Parish's chief settlement** Hixon, is a large, growing dormitory village, Stowe-by-Chartley is a small (stagnant by contrast) village. **Geology** ALL - Keuper Marls. But **Staffordshire's only place where alabaster is found other than Tutbury** Stowe (MR p309). **Highest point** 564 feet N of Chartley Holme. **Lowest point** 249 feet by the Trent near Wychdon Lodge. **Britain's largest Schwingmoor bog, one of only two of its type in Britain** Chartley Moss. It is 14 metres deep with a raft of mainly peat 3 metres thick floating on top, covering 25 ha of land (Geographical Magazine. 65 (4) April 1993 pp17-19) (ES July 14 1995) (TRTC p188) (Staffs Wildlife Trust no 102 April 2008 p 16-17). Stowe-by-Chartley was **75th most-populated Staffordshire parish in 1801** with 696 people; **68th in 1811** with 853; **59th in 1821** with 1185; **59th in 1831** with 1283; **64th in 1841** with 1267; **64th in 1851** with 1269; **66th in 1861** with 1267; **70th in 1871** with 1267; **71st in 1881** with 1268 **75th in 1891** with 1043; **78th in 1901** with 934.

4. People...

Stowe's heroes Victor Antcliff and David Gregory of Drointon who risked their lives to save Raymond Cole from the burning wreckage of the Vickers Viscount which crashed at Chartley Moss on Feb 25 1994, which killed the pilot. The main part of the plane landed upside down and on fire in woodland near the moss. Alerted by the noise of the crash and a glow in the sky, the two men made their way in the darkness to where they could hear Mr Cole crying for help. Having pulled him to safety, they returned to see if they could help the pile who was showing no signs of life. In 1996 they were presented with the Queen's Commendation for Bravery (SLM July/Aug 1996 p15p). **Stowe's villain** John Oakley, whose burial is recorded in Stowe parish register on March 28 1784. The register goes on to record he was executed at Stafford for horse stealing. **Hixon's hero** Wilmot Martin (1875-1963) alias the 'Staffordshire Harry Lauder' (see Worston). **Hixon's WW1 hero** CQMA Frank Middleton, 1st Batt North Staffs, born Hixon, died of wounds Flanders Oct 24 1917, awarded the D.C.M., and the M.M. (Oct 1916) (ELSONNS p91). **Hixon's WW1 heroine** Miss H Morrough (1872-1938) of Hixon awarded personally by George V the Royal Red Cross in recognition of valuable services with the Armies in the field as a member of The Territorial Force Nursing Service attached to 2nd Western General Hospital, Manchester, and in France since 1915. In addition, she was awarded the Mons Star, the Territorial Nursing Service Medal, the Victory Medal, and the General Service Medal (SA Feb 2 1918 p3 col7p. Nov 5 1938 p4p). **Hixon's child hero** Mavis Watson, 14, of Hixon who saved her friend Lilian Bob, 12, of Smithy Lane, Hixon from drowning in the canal at Pasturefields; both were attending Colwich Secondary Modern School (SA &C July 21 1955 p5p). **Hixon's heroine** Phyllis Gray who was galvanised to help immediately after the Hixon level crossing disaster on Jan 6 1968, putting her skills as a Red Cross volunteer into action. She is reported to have remained at the scene until the afternoon of the following day, not taking a meal because she hadn't felt like one (SN Sept 4 2008 p6). **Hixon's bravest** Betsy Green, 57 year old lollipop lady of The Croft, who risked her own life and injured herself to save a mother and her 7 year old daughter from being hit by a car in Church Lane in Dec 1986. She received a Certificate of Appreciation from Staffordshire Police (SN Dec 25 1987 p10p). **First Staffordshirians to appear on Independent Television talking about their job** Possibly Mr and Mrs Harry Elsmore, level crossing keepers at old Hixon station, dismantled by 1958, in c1958 (SN Nov 8 1958 p14p). **First woman newsreader for Association Television** Miss Patricia Cox, who opened Hixon Flower

Show on Aug 4 1958. She was the first woman newsreader of Midlands I.T.A. (SN Aug 9 1958 p8p). **'Dairy Maid of South Staffordshire' 1960' 'Dairy Princess of Stoke-on-Trent' 1960** Miss Gillian Derricott (b1939) of Stowe-by-Chartley, attended Staffordshire Farm Institute, Rodbaston, 1956-57. When holder of the latter title she was one of the 16 finalists at the national Dairy Queen awards 1960 in London (SA & Chron May 19 1960 p5p. Aug 4 1960 p4p). **Stowe's kindest** John Tooth of Drointon according to a benefactions board in the church, gave 1692, 12s. to the poor of Stowe, from rental on land in Drointon township; 12s. was still being distributed in the 1830s to six poor widows, 2s. a piece. **Stowe's poorest** Stowe overseers' accounts show materials were needed for the fabric of a poor house in the parish 1761; and payment was made to Crouch workhouse in 1775, and 1777 (D14/A/PO/1); whilst its churchwardens' accounts tell of payment for ale to workmen when repairing the workhouse 1804-5 (D14/A/PC/1). From 1837 the poor could be housed at Stafford Union workhouse at Marston. **Stowe's earliest recorded wills** Belong to Richard Mason and Ralph Smyth, both dated April 24 1532. **First person in the parish register** John H _____ buried, baptised? 1574. **Choicest quote** Edmund Craik in his Memories of Hixon, 2002, says The shop was demolished and its rubble used as hard core for the Aerodrome 'There was a blacksmith's shop at Amerton on the corner of the Amerton to Shirleywich Lane run by Mr Edwards, but it was empty and derelict before the War when they started to build Hixon Aerodrome.'

SUBJECT INDEX *Sta to Sta*

Teddesley Hall.

Teddesley Hay
1. Did you know that...

Teddesley Hay's top folklore According to tradition Sir Edward Littleton used the treasure found at Pillaton Hall (a hoard of coins behind an oak casement in a chimney breast, found between 1742 and 1749) to finance the original building of Teddesley Hall, c1750. In addition, a chalice dating from 1525 also found at Pillaton Hall, stood on the mantelpiece in the study of the hall. Since the 1950s it has been at the Victoria and Albert Museum. **What Teddesley Hay is famous for** Teddesley Hall when occupied by the 1st Baron Hatherton in the earlier C19. The **name Teddesley Hay first appears** in 1236 for Teddesley, 1252 for Teddesley Hay. **Deldon Trophy winner 1960** 'Proud of Upend', a miniature bull terrier belonging to Mrs Barbara Butler of Bednall Head Farm. The award is for Best Bitch of the Year presented by the Miniature Bull Terrier Club at Crufts. Since it was founded in 1952 it had been won by Mrs Butler four times - her 'Champion Fury of Upend' winning thrice, and her 'Champion Willing of Upend' winning once (SA & Chron Feb 18 1960 p8p).

2. Teddesley Hall and the Littletons...

'one of the ugliest houses and one of the finest parks in England' Masefield on the Littleton's seat (LGS p105), the hall is certainly not attractive from the front view (SA April 30 1932 p9 col 1). **First overshot water mill of its kind in Midlands** Built at Home Farm in 1820 (but rivalled by one at White Barn Farm, Colwich). A successive iron wheel for it was claimed to be the largest in the country (IAS p200) (BERK2 p105) (MR2 p247). **Largest rickyard in the country** Claimed by Lord Hatherton for his Teddesley estate in the 1840s (BERK2 p106). **'amongst the oldest holdings in this County'** Teddesley Home Farm, one of the few remaining 'home-farms' (1951), on the estate of Lord Hatherton. In the earlier 1940s its acreage was stated to be 760, making it one of Staffordshire's largest farms (SLM Feb 1951 p26). The LITTLETON who: could be said to be **Teddesley Hay's most famous old worthy** Edward John Littleton (formerly Walhouse) (1791-1863), English country gentleman and politician. Through his uncle Sir Edward Littleton he inherited Teddesley Hall, 1815. He loved Teddesley, describing it as "one of the strongest passions I possess". He was M.P. for Staffordshire 1812-32. For the Liberals he held South Staffordshire 1832-4, 1835, when created Baron Hatherton. He was Lord Lieutenant of Staffordshire 1854, and was buried at Penkridge. The Hatherton Diaries (2003), are his published diaries and cover 1817 to 29th June 1862 for which day he simply wrote "A Bad night." Another entry, August 22 1831, could be said to be the **choicest quote** for Teddesley 'At 11 o' Clock Mr Leigh the Clergyman of Bilston came, and accompanied me to shoot Black game, on the Teddesley Hills, above the Reservoir. Killed 26'; was **'the most handsome lady in England'** Hyacinthe Littleton, society hostess, wife of Edward John Littleton (d1863), 1st Baron Hatherton, daughter of Richard, Marquess of Wellesley, niece of the Duke of Wellington (BERK2 p110 il). **'a gentleman without any previous military knowledge, being placed straight away at the head of a regiment'** Edward Richard Littleton, Lord Hatherton (1815-88), when the Marquis of Anglesea, then Lord Lieutenant, sent for him in the earlier 1850s and asked him to raise the 2nd Staffordshire Regt to fight in the Crimea. However, he did have the aid of his 2nd in command, Lieut-Col Dyott, who had considerable military experience (SA April 7 1888 p5 col 5). **Nurse probationer** Hon Edith Littleton, daughter of Lord and Lady Hatherton of Teddesley Hall who was awarded this title in recognition of meritorous work for nursing service in English and French hospitals from 1915 (London Gazette) (SA Jan 18 1918 p5 col 2).

3. People...

Staffordshire's first death due to overexertion on a bicycle Perhaps John Jones, 57, a bricklayer, living at Boscamoor, who collapsed riding a bicycle through Teddesley Park in summer 1897. A post mortem showed a ruptured blood vessel at the base of his skull, perhaps caused by overexertion. He had only been riding a bicycle for about two months (SA July 31 1897 p7 col 5). **Parents who lost three sons in WW1** Mr and Mrs T Dawson of Lordswood. Their eldest son L-Corp Thomas William, Rifle Brigade, was killed in action on May 9 1915; L-Corp Harry, second son, Queen Victoria's Rifles, went missing in 1917, and was reported dead on June 28 1917; Pte Edward John, third son, former servant at Teddesley Hall, Durham Light Infantry, was killed in action on July 19 1918, *see illustration above* (SA Aug 17 1918 p3 cols 3&4p).

First chairman of Staffordshire branch of the NFU Alderman John Edward Gold (1879-1954) of Teddesley Home Farm, the branch formed in 1919 (SA Sept 24 1954 p1 col 4). **First fatality in Cannock Chase Lido** Keith James Bloor, aged 18, of Streets Lane, Landywood, on Aug 10 1935. The lido was at Pottal Pool (LiMe Aug 16 1935 p5 col 2). **Staffordshire Agricultural Society's Champion Farmer of Staffordshire 1961** Ethan Buxton of Teddesley Home Farm (SA & Chron Aug 10 1961 p1p). **Teddesley Hay's poorest** From 1858 Teddesley Hay was in Penkridge Union, renamed Cannock Union from 1870s. From 1858 its poor could be sent to Brewood workhouse; from 1872 to the new Union workhouse on Wolverhampton road, Cannock.

4. The area...

Teddesley Hay is the **county's 18th largest parish** (extra parochial - so no church), consisting of 9,024 acres; **21st= closest parish to the county town**, 4m SSE; **extremist length** 1.9m; **extremist width** 3.1m. **Parish's chief settlement** None, save the compact estate settlement of Teddesley Home Farm. **Geology** BANGLEY Park-Wellington Belt - Keuper Marls; SW - Keuper Sandstones; TEDDESLEY Hall, Park and the E - Bunter. **Highest point** 729 feet on Berkswich boundary. **Lowest point** 252 feet by the Penk on Penkridge boundary. Teddesley Hay was **147th most-populated Staffordshire parish in 1801** with 50 people; **147th in 1811** with 59; **149th in 1821** with 43; **148th in 1831** with 50; **150th in 1841** with 61; **144th in 1851** with 109; **144th in 1861** with 117; **144th in 1871** with 128; **144th in 1881** with 130; **144th in 1891** with 115; **143rd in 1901** with 125.

SUBJECT INDEX *Sta to Sta*

Beppo the Clown.

Tillington
1. Did you know that...

Tillington's top folklore According to Sir Walter Chetwynd author of A History of Pirehill Hundred, written in the later C17, Tillington received its name because it was a place of note for husbandry and tillage, but a more likely explanation is the first part is from the personal name Tilla, Tylla or Tylli. **What Tillington is famous for** Tillington Hall Hotel, a popular venue for parties. The **name Tillington first appears** in Domesday Book, 1086. **British Champion Golden Retriever 1931, Crufts International Challenge Cup for best Golden Retriever 1932** Kelso of Aldgrove, belonging to Miss EL Mottram, younger daughter of TB Mottram of Brookfield House, Tillington; by 1933 she was residing at Albro, St John, Yorks. At Crufts in 1932 he also won five challenge certificates (SA Jan 28 1933 p4p). **Only Staffordshire school with an open-air theatre 1960** At Stafford North County Secondary School, Holmcroft, created in an old marl hole in the school grounds. The new school (later amalgamated and became Graham Balfour High School) was due to open in Jan 1960 (SA & Chron Sept 25 1958 p8il. Aug 25 1960 p1p). **School that piloted a language lab' for the country for primary school children** Graham Balfour School using their £4,000 booths for 20 pupils in the French dept. The primary schools chosen were Doxey Primary School, John Wheeldon School, Silkmore School, The Leasowes School, St John's School, Littleworth and the St Leonard's schools (SA & Chron Dec 5 1963 p6). **First car accident on first stretch of motorway in Staffordshire** Occurred a week before opening day (Aug 2 1962) of the Stafford by-pass, when motorist Terence James Francis Snow, aged 21, of Holmlea, Wheel Field, Codsall, and his passenger, Keith Cahill, aged 19, of Low Hill, Bushbury, turned on to the link road in error when he reached the Redhill roundabout at Stone Road, Stafford. The car collided with a heap of tar-macadam and overturned. They were unhurt (SA & Chron Aug 2 1962 p1 col 6).

2. Church...

At Holmcroft is St Bertelin, Holmcroft Road, **only such county dedication** (for AP churches); **the last AP county church built** dating from

1956 (Around Stafford. Roy Lewis. 1999. p87).

3. The area...

Tillington is the **county's 138th largest parish** (extra-parochial), consisting of 977 acres; **4th closest parish to the county town**, 0.4m NNW; **extremist length** 1.7m, making it **29th= shortest parish in the county**; **extremist width** 1.6m, making it **27th= narrowest parish in the county**. **Parish's chief settlement** The former fragmented collection of farms amounting to Tillington, and lands Holmcroft, and Trinity Fields are all now north Stafford suburbs. **Geology** Keuper Marls. **Highest point** 354 feet W of Marstongate Farm. **Lowest point** 246 feet by The Darling brook. Tillington was **153rd most-populated Staffordshire parish in 1801** with 29 people; **156th= in 1811** with 20; **151st in 1821** with 39; **150th in 1831** with 42; **151st in 1841** with 55; **149th in 1851** with 62; **147th in 1861** with 79; **145th in 1871** with 97; **129th in 1881** with 271; **104th in 1891** with 490; **98th in 1901** with 536.

4. People...

Tillington's most famous old worthy Rev Thomas Alleyn (d1558), whose estates included nearly 700 acres at Tillington. He left his estates in trust to Trinity College, Cambridge, with directions to found three free grammar schools - at Uttoxeter, Stone, and Stevenage, Herts. All three schools were founded and still bear his name (SIS p35). Trinity Fields district in Tillington takes its name from the Trinity College estate. **The seven soldier sons** The sons of Mr & Mrs ET Powner of 24 Alliance Street, Tillington, who all served in WW1: Joseph (the eldest) was of the 6th N. Staffs Regt (Territorials); Thomas of the King's Royal Rifles; 23-year old twins Sidney and Harry, both of the King's Shropshire Light Infantry (Harry, a Sgt, was killed in action 1918); Albert, a Pte of the N. Staffs Regt; Bert, a Pte in the King's Shropshire Light Infantry; D____, a Pte of the Durham Light Infantry (SA Oct 19 1918 p6). **'Stafford's Mr. Show Biz'** Charles John 'Jonny' Newbold, alias 'Beppo the Clown', of 6 Sayers Road, Holmcroft, stuntman, and then clown with Bertram Mills' Circus by 1952 when he saved two people from drowning whilst he was taking a walk between shows at Nottingham. Attended Corporation Street and Dartmouth Street Schools. After his marriage in 1961 Newbold lived at Brereton (SA May 14 1954 p1p. SA & Chron April 6 1961 p1p). **Stafford's only female taxi driver 1968** Gwendolyne Hall (b1913) of Stone Road, Trinity Fields, who did not learn to drive until she was 39 (SA & Chron Jan 4 1968 p9p). **Tillington's saddest** Leona Vandenborr (or Van den Borr), aged 5, of Belgium, who fell from a London-Liverpool express train passing through Tillington. She was travelling with her mother, a native of Lovi Gilly near Charleroi, to join her father working at the Minto Mines in Canada. The mother was unable to stay after the inquest, and the lack of family attending the little girl's funeral aroused a good deal of sympathy so a public subscription was got up which paid for a memorial to Leona erected in the borough cemetery (SA May 9 1908 p4 col 7. June 27 1908 p4 col 5). **Tillington's heroine** Miss Nora Wright, daughter of Col CH Wright of Tillington Hall, actively associated with V.A.D. work at Stafford, was one of a party of 50 Red Cross nurses from Staffordshire who went to France in May 1915. Invalided out of the war in 1916 she returned in May 1917, and was mentioned in Sir Douglas Haig's despatch of April 7 1918 (SA June 1 1918 p4 col7p). **Tillington's poorest** From 1858 the poor could be housed at Stafford Union workhouse at Marston. **Choicest quote** Joan Rogers in her private thesis 'A History of Eccleshall Road', 1985, writes 'the road running from Stafford to Eccleshall is now a wide, modern highway busy with traffic, but it was once a quiet country road and before that possibly little more than a track.'

SUBJECT INDEX *Sta to Te*

Mary Queen of Scots leaves Tixall, passing in front of Tixall Hall Gatehouse.

Tixall
1. Did you know that...

Tixall's top folklore Mary, Queen of Scots, was kept prisoner at Tixall Old Hall for two weeks between Aug 8 and 28 1586, so her apartments at Chartley (Old) Hall could be searched to implicate her in the Babington Plot. On leaving the hall, she is supposed to have disappointed the poor, who accosted her for alms, saying "Alas, I have nothing for you; I am a beggar too; all is taken from me" (SA Feb 8 1947 p5 col 2). The **name Tixall first appears** in Domesday Book, 1086. **What Tixall is famous for** Mary Queen of Scot's incarceration at Tixall Old Hall. **Staffordshire's most spurious evidence which led to conviction and execution** The heresy evidence of Stephen Dugdale, a steward of Lord Aston of Tixall Old Hall, at the trial in the Popish Plot, 1680; Lord Stafford was executed. **Smallest house in Staffordshire** Perhaps Tixall gatehouse, or bottle lodge (Staffordshire County Guide 2006/7 p98p). **'Barnfields Right Sort', 'Barnfields Prince'** Shire stallions of Barnfields Shire Horses of Tixall, foaled in 1901 and 1900 respectively, toured in 1904 to impregnate local mares (SA April 30 1904 p8 col 7). **Unique on a 'narrow' canal** Tixall Wide where sailing craft is allowed to move freely (Down the Trent: Francis Frith's Photographic Memories. Michael Taylor. 2001 p41). **Staffordshire Best Kept Village Stafford District winner (small village category) 2003, 2004, 2007** Tixall.

2. Church...

At Tixall is St John the Baptist, **one of 11 such county dedications** (of AP churches); **17th last AP county church built** dating from 1849. **In the churchyard** Chest tomb to Richard Biddulph (d1627), aged 82, he was servant to four Lord Astons at Tixall Hall. The tomb was restored by the later owners of Tixall (FSP p97).

3. The area...

Tixall is the **county's 109th largest parish**, consisting of 2,369 acres; **8th closest parish to the county town**, 1.8 ESE; **extremist length** 2.7m; **extremist width** 2.6m. **Parish's chief settlement** Tixall, a small village, veering between pretty and eerie. **Geology**

SOW confluence - Alluvium; SOW valley - Bunter; TIXALL village and centre - Keuper Sandstones; TIXALL Hall, Park - Keuper Marls. **Highest point** 426 feet at Upper Hanyards. **Lowest point** 236 feet by the Sow at Shugborough. Tixall was **133rd most-populated Staffordshire parish in 1801** with 198 people; **133rd in 1811** with 206; **137th in 1821** with 198; **137th in 1831** with 176; **135th in 1841** with 209; **135th in 1851** with 221; **129th in 1861** with 289; **132nd in 1871** with 256; **135th in 1881** with 226; **138th in 1891** with 212; **138th in 1901** with 187.

4. People...

Tixall's most famous old worthy Sir Walter Aston (1584-1639), eldest son of Sir Edward (d1597) of Tixall Old Hall, created a baronet in 1611; 'distinguished' Ambassador to Spain 1620-1625, and again 1635-38; created Baron Aston of Forfar in the Scottish peerage in 1627; justice of the peace 1604-24. He encouraged the poet Michael Drayton, and Fletcher dedicated his pastoral play The Faithful Shepherdess to him, describing Aston as 'that noble and true lover of learning' (SHC 1912 p327) (KES p208). **Worst Briton of the C17** Titus Oates, 'architect' of the Popish Plot (see above), as polled by BBC History Magazine, late 2005. **Shook hands with Louis XVIII** Sir Thomas Hugh Clifford (assumed the surname Constable from 1821) (1762-1823) asked the King to dine twice when he was in exile at Bath in 1813. On their final departure the King complained to Sir Thomas he probably would be unable to shake his hand owing to gout in his fingers. However, the King said "Put your hand into mine, and let me try". Sir Thomas did so, and his Majesty gave it a gentle squeeze, and said adieu (SA March 15 1823 p3 col 1). **'great gambler and best whist player of his time'** Granville Leveson-Gower (1773-1846), politician, ambassador, and peer. He rented Tixall Hall from Sir Thomas Hugh Clifford in 1808 (SHC 1933 pp9-10). **First novel by Georgiana Fullerton** 'Ellen Middleton' (1844); Fullerton was Granville Leveson-Gower's daughter; she was born at Tixall Hall, 1812. **Inventor of the steel-headed rail, and the curvilinear slotting machine** Francis William Webb (d1906), civil engineer mainly for railway locomotives, second son of William Webb, rector of Tixall (1831-1883), was born at Tixall Rectory in 1836. He patented more than 75 inventions between 1864 and 1903 (DNB) (A History of Tixall. volume 1: Tixall's Churches. Anne Andrews. 1995 pp59-68). **Stafford borough's first electrical engineer** Richard Edwin Meade (d1954), former Mayor, Gaol Square Garage proprietor, of Marsh Rise, Tixall (SA & Chron March 17 1955 p5 col 4). **Tixall's poorest** From 1858 the poor could be housed at Stafford Union workhouse at Marston. **Tixall's earliest recorded will** Belongs to John Hatton, and is dated April 18 1554. **First person in the parish register** Edward Robins buried March 1669. **Choicest quote** Michael Drayton, poet, who, as Arthur Mee says, makes Tixall Old Hall live on by a couplet in his Polyolbion:

> 'Among the better souls, the Astons' ancient seat,
> Which oft the Muse hath found her safe and sweet retreat.'

(KES p208).

5. Tixall Old Hall Gatehouse...

'one of the fairest pieces of work made in late times' Sampson Erdeswick on the C16 Tixall Old Hall gatehouse, **'one of the purist examples of early renaissance architecture in England'** Bannister-Fletcher (HAH pp78-79). **'the most ambitious gatehouse in England'** Pevsner (BOE p283).

SUBJECT INDEX *Te to UK*

*Selina,
Countess of
Bradford and
Disraeli.*

Weston-under-Lizard
1. Did you know that...

Fancy that! Disraeli gave Selina, 3rd Countess of Bradford, a yellow parrot, which one day in 1903 laid an egg, an unusual feat for a cock bird. After laying eggs for the next 23 days it died. **Weston-under-Lizard's top folklore** That the Lizard part of the name is from 'lazar', a leper, and that there was once a leper colony on Lizard Hill, which is in Shropshire. **What Weston-under-Lizard is famous for** Weston Park. The **name Weston-under-Lizard first appears** in 1081 as Weston; c1255 for Weston under Brewood; 1340 for Weston-under-Lizard. **Very curious and rare plant** Moor balls were found briefly in the C18 by White Sitch pool (SHOS vol 1 part 1 p102). **Derby winner 1892** 'Sir Hugo' owned by Lord Bradford (SLM Winter 1954 pp9,26). **The parish that wanted to leave Staffordshire** Weston-under-Lizard, along with Blymhill, petitioned in 1926 to be incorporated in Shifnal RD and in Shropshire, as recommended in the Boundaries Commission report of 1888 (SA May 15 1926 p7). **Weston-under-Lizard's villainess** Mary Hand, of Beighterton, the delivery of whose bastard child was at the great expense of the parish. In Weston parish accounts it is recorded for 1774-5 'Extraordinary Expenses att ending the Prosecution of Mary Hand of Beighton for the provider of a Bastard Child. Paying the Surgeon, Coroner, sending her to Goal & expenses at the assizes...£7.4.0' (SRO D1050/4/1). In 2008 Beechcroft, Weston-under-Lizard was the **national home of the Group Travel Organisers Association** (GTOA, 1992) for group travel organisers and travel trade suppliers; and Men of Stones (MOS, 1947) who advocate the use of stone and natural building materials/ craftsmanship in limestone belt. **Weston's poorest** There is no record of a workhouse in the parish accounts. But charity money was distributed to 33 parishioners by the minister Rev G Bridgeman in 1822, and in the early years of the C19 soldiers with their families passing on Watling Street were relieved by the constable (SRO D1050/4/1). **Weston-under-Lizard's earliest recorded will** Belongs to John and Constance Milton (Mitton?), and is dated July 11 1551. **First person in the parish register** Richard Lewis, son of Richard Lewis and Margaret, baptised Jan 19 1652.

2. Church...

At Weston-under-Lizard is St Andrew, **one of 3 such county dedications** (of AP churches); **88th= oldest AP county church** dating from the C14 or roughly 1350. **Earliest and only medieval wooden effigy in Staffordshire** A knight, c1300, believed to be Sir Hugh de Weston (d1305) (VCH vol 4 p171) (BAST vols 69-71 p27). **Weston-under-Lizard's longest-serving vicar** Roger de Aston, who served 59 years, 1381-1440.

Weston Park Hall.

3. Weston Park & The Westons & Bridgemans...

1st Staffordshire property featured in Country Life magazine Weston Park, on Nov 27 1897 pp592-594, volume ii. The article is by John Leyland. **Only Staffordshire property that inspired PG Wodehouse** Weston Park is possibly the model for the estate of Blandings Castle in his novels (Channel Four Dec 28 2002) (Daily Telegraph Sept 5 2003 p13). **Some of the finest trees in England** Those in the park at Weston Park (SA Oct 1 1904 p4 col 4). **Largest and one of the earliest oriental plane tree in the country** That at Weston Park, in the middle of the lawn on the lowest terrace with a circumference of 23 feet and a height of 70 feet; its branches span a circumference of more than 130 yards (The Trees of Great Britain and Ireland. Elwes and Henry. vol 6. 1913 il) (SST il on front cover) (NSJFS 1969 p133) (WPG p27). **First County Landowners' Association Game Fair held at Weston Park** July 21-22 1961. This was the 4th fair of the Association; the 1st was held at Stetchworth Park, Newmarket, 1958; the 3rd at Castle Howard, Yorks (SA & Chron Feb 16 1961 p8 cols 5-6). **Venue for world leaders for 24th G-8 (Group of Eight) Summit** The Orangery at Weston Park on May 16 1998, although the summit was principally at Birmingham. **Greatest distance covered by a model steam locomotive in 24 hours** Is 167.7m (269.9km) by the 18.4cm 7.25 gauge 'Peggy,' on Weston Park Railway in Weston Park in 10 shifts between June 17 and 18 1994 (GBR 1996 p125). **Staffordshire's biggest music festival** The V Festival held annually from 1999 at Weston Park; 150,000 attended in 2006; the same number in 2008 (ES March 21 2006 p6. Aug 26 2006 p11) (Daily Telegraph Aug 18 2008 p10p). The WESTON who was: the **earliest-known prisoner in Stafford Gaol** Hugh de Weston, accused with Henry der Mer of the murder of William, son of John Gille. Hugh was released by letter close in 1235 as it appeared that they had been accused out of hatred and malice; Hugh, son of John, was in possession of the manor in 1227 (SHC vol xx, vol II new series p16) (The Old Gaol at Stafford 1185-1793. AJ Standley, part 1, p1).

The MYTTON who could be said to be **Weston-under-Lizard's most famous old worthy**, was **first Englishwoman to draw architectural plans, only woman who designed a church in Staffordshire in C18** Dame Elizabeth Mytton (1631-1705), heiress, who married Sir Thomas Wilbraham. She rebuilt (1671) Weston Hall in a Renaissance style on strict Palladio principles, a building "remarkably advanced for its period"; she later rebuilt Weston church, 1700-01 (BOE p29), and her copy of an early (1663) translation of Palladio's 'First Book of Architecture' with her own notes and costings clearly visible in the margins was long kept at the hall. Lely painted her in c1662 (St-p). The BRIDGEMAN who was: **Lord Chief Baron and Lord Keeper of the Great Seal, 'a mighty able man', 'he did wholly rip up the unjustness of the war against the King'** Sir Orlando Bridgeman (1609-1674), born Exeter, great-great-grandfather of Sir Henry Bridgeman (d1800). The first quote on him is from Samuel Pepys, the second refers to his time as Lord Chief Baron 1667-72. In such a position he was effectively Lord Chancellor, and would have been 142nd Lord Chancellor, but was denied the title. He presided at the trial of the regicides (SA Oct 1 1904 p4 col4) (Weston Park guide, 1974) (DNB); **Weston's kindest, benefactress of schooling at Brocton and Forebridge** Dorothy Bridgeman (d1697), second wife of Sir Orlando Bridgeman (d1674), whom she married in 1647 (VCH vol 5 pp10,11); **55th bishop of Sodor and Man** Henry Bridgeman (1615-1682), younger brother of Sir Orlando Bridgeman (d1674), serving 1671-83 (DNB); **first owner of Weston** Sir Henry Bridgeman (1725-1800), great-grandson of Dame Elizabeth Mytton, who succeeded to the estate in 1762; **Surveyor of the Royal Parks to George II** George Bridgeman (1727-1767), younger brother of Sir Henry (b1725); Pope had originally introduced his name into his "Epistle on Taste' as a perfect judge of landscape gardening, but omitted it at his own request (SHC 1899 p266); **witnessed the supposed secret marriage between George, Prince of Wales, and Maria Fitzherbert** Orlando Bridgeman (1762-1825), son of Sir Henry (d1800), created Earl of Bradford (second creation) (SOP p166); **they died in a tragic fire accident at the hall** Lucy Caroline (b1826) and Charlotte Anne (b1827), two of the 2nd Earl of Bradford's five daughters, burnt to death when Lady Lucy's dress caught fire from a candle, and Lady Charlotte in her efforts to save her also caught fire. They lingered for several days, Charlotte passing away on Nov 26 1858, and Lucy on Dec 3 1858. The stained glass windows in the N aisle of Blymhill church are to their memory (SHC 1899 pp287-288); **made considerable alterations at Weston** Orlando George Charles Bridgeman (1819-1898), 3rd Earl of Bradford; **close friend of prime minister Benjamin Disraeli** Selina Louisa Forester (1819-1894), daughter of Cecil Weld, 1st Lord Forester, married Orlando George (d1898), becoming 3rd Countess of Bradford. There was preserved at the hall a selection of

1,100 letters written by Disraeli to Selina, between 1873 to 1881. And in the **choicest quote** on the parish, he writes to her from Whitehall gardens on March 14th 1877: '...I have now been in London since the 14th of October - never away for a moment except that short though sweet visit to Weston; and for that I got scolded - "surprised to find Lord Beaconsfield out of town, etc."' (The Letters of Disraeli to Lady Bradford and Lady Chesterfield 1876-1881. Ed by Marquis of Zetland. vol 11. p108); **expert in peerage law** Charles George Orlando Bridgeman (1852-1933), younger son of Rev Hon George Bridgeman. Barrister, archaeologist, contributor to the Staffordshire Historical Collections. Buried Blymhill (SHC 1933 pp18-9).

4. The area...

Weston-under-Lizard is the **county's 107th largest parish**, consisting of 2,438 acres; **60th closest parish to the county town**, 10m SW; **extremist length** 2.9m; **extremist width** 3.4m. **Parish's chief settlement** Weston-under-Lizard, an estate village partly aligned along Watling Street. **Geology** WESTON Hall, Park (West Park) - Keuper Sandstones; WESTON Park (East Park), Beighterton - Keuper Marls; WOODLANDS, White Sitch and W - Bunter. **Highest point** 469 feet on Blymhill boundary at Park Pales. **Lowest point** 282 feet feet at Weston Old Mill on the Shrops border. Weston-under-Lizard was **142nd most-populated Staffordshire parish in 1801** with 101 people; **126th in 1811** with 275; **127th in 1821** with 296; **131st in 1831** with 257; **127th in 1841** with 297; **132nd in 1851** with 248; **132nd in 1861** with 275; **126th in 1871** with 325; **116th in 1881** with 384; **122nd in 1891** with 316; **123rd in 1901** with 301.

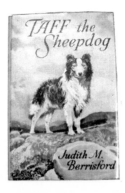

Weston-upon-Trent
1. Did you know that...

Model for Taff in 'Taff, the Sheepdog' Taff, a Welsh collie, belonging to Mr TH Tavernor of Outwoods Farm, Weston, was the model for the hero in the best-selling children's book of the above title by Judith M Berrisford of Stafford, published 1949 (SA Oct 29 1949 p5p). **Weston-upon-Trent's top folklore** The ghost of a man named Preston Moore was seen in a lane in Weston-upon-Trent in c1860 very shortly after he had died. The **name Weston-upon-Trent first appears** in Domesday Book, 1086 ad Weston; 1293 as Weston-upon-Trent. **What Weston-on-Trent is famous for** Salt production. **Earliest recorded site of successful saltworking in Staffordshire** At Brinepits, later called Shirleywich (SPJD p73). **Staffordshire Best Kept Village County Village of the Year 2002**; **winner (large village category) 1998, 2002, 2005, 2006, 2007, 2008**; **winner (medium village category, and last ever winner in this category 1987) 1970, 1971, 1972, 1973, 1974, 1976, 1977, 1978, 1982, 1983, 1987**; **Stafford District winner (large village category) 1987, 1992, 1993, 1995, 1998, 2001, 2002, 2003, 2005, 2006, 2007, 2008** Weston upon Trent; in 1977 when it won the medium catagory for the seventh time in eight years, it became the most successive best-kept village winner ever (ES Oct 12 2002 p21). **When Weston was called 'Weston-under-water'** In autumn 1968 Gayton Brook burst its banks flooding Spencer Close area, Abbeylands, and the Village Stores (times gone by. Spring 2007 p11). **One of the best village greens in Staffordshire 1973** Weston-upon-Trent. Before Queen Elizabeth II's visit to Shugborough on 25 May 1973, Weston village school lobbied the Lord Lieutenant of Staffordshire to try and persuade the royal party to make a slight detour through Weston village. In a letter to the Lord Lieutenant the School said 'The Village Green is a very good example of its kind and considered to be one of the best in Staffordshire' (Weston PC correspondence D1383/6). **Tim Cockin's biggest cartographical blunder** He neglected to show the 'panhandle' of Weston's original boundary stretching beyond Salt along the Trent Valley in his Old Parish Boundaries of Staffordshire: Pirehill (2005).

2. People...

Weston-upon-Trent's most famous old worthy Sir Robert Shirley (1650-1717), prolific peer and salt extractor. Succeeded to Chartley Hall, Chartley Holme, 1656. In the later 17th Century he exploited the salt reserves at Brinepits, Weston parish, later called Shirleywich. The works declined in the 19th Century and had ceased by 1901. Shirley, created Lord Ferrers in 1677, and 1st Earl Ferrers in 1711, is claimed to have fathered 57 children. **First deputy-clerk, and first returning officer of Staffordshire County Council** Isaac Edward Everett (1844-1904), solicitor at Messrs Hand, Blakinton, Everett, and Hand, of Abbeylands, in 1889. He was also one of the founders of the Staffordshire Farmers' Association (SA March 26 1904 p4 col 5). **Strange but true!** What was believed to be a fireball in a thunderstorm struck the house of Hu and Beatrice Jones in Ferrers Rd, Weston, whilst they were asleep in the early hours of May 8 1976. Their upstairs toilet had been blasted out onto the landing. They, nor their children, Moira 8, and Grant 5, were hurt (SN May 14 1976 p13). **Weston's villain** Stephen Maddocks (b1835), convicted in 1863 of setting fire to a stack of hay and sentenced to four years prison. He was freed in 1866, but 10 days later set fire to a barn. On Oct 15 1867 he set fire to a certain barn at Weston-upon-Trent, and was sentenced to 10 years prison at the Staffordshire Winter Assizes 1867 (SA Dec 21 1867 p6 col 4). **Weston's most-travelled, 'Fairy Godmother Shaw'** Miss Annie Shaw (d1937), born in the 1850s, who had practically lived all her life at The Wellyards, Weston. She was fond of travel and devoted several months of the year to this pursuit, visiting in her lifetime nearly all the countries of Europe, including Iceland. Ever since Miss Shaw bequeathed a considerable sum of about £15,000-£17,000 for the church and village of Weston she had been known by Weston as 'Fairy Godmother Shaw'. Miss Shaw had lived modestly and had not previously made any large benefactions (SA Oct 9 1937 p4 col 5. Jan 1 1938 p6 col 3) (The Venture: Magazine for Staffordshire Women March 1948 pp6-8). **Miss Staffordshire 1965** Patricia Wright of Station House, Weston, aged 15, she was then working as an assembly worker. It was during Patricia's 'reign' Stafford Pageant and Carnival Committee, Miss Staffordshire contest organisers, heard news of another Miss Staffordshire contest, organised by the Tipton Community Association in the south of the county. Patricia's father threatened to take his daughter to Tipton to declare her the real 'Miss Staffordshire' (SN June 11 1965 p15p) (SA & Chron Oct 14 1965 p1). **Weston's kindest** According to the benefactions board in the church Mrs Elizabeth Palin in 1782 left 10L to the poor of the parish to be laid out in bread for them every Christmas Eve; by the 1830s it was being distributed on Christmas Day. Miss Moore of Wychdon, who paid for the school building (built on land donated by Earl Ferrers) 1870, and all of the enlargement and restoration of the parish church, 1872 (SA Dec 10 1870 p4 col 7. June 1 1872 p5 col 3). **Weston's poorest** From 1837 the poor could be housed at Stafford Union workhouse at Marston. **Weston's earliest recorded will** Belongs to George

Boghay, and is dated Nov 3 1540 (this excludes unspecified Westons, elsewhere in Lichfield diocese). **First person in the parish register** William Lowe buried April 14 1573. **Choicest quote** Weston W.I. in The Venture Magazine for Staffordshire Women, March 1948, describe their village thus: "Weston is a typical mid-Staffordshire village where times seems to be at standstill, and the peace and quiet is reminiscent of the 'early Sunday morning feeling,"

3. The area...

Weston-upon-Trent is the **county's 144th largest parish**, consisting of 831 acres; **19th= closest parish to the county town**, 3.8m NE; **extremist length** 2.5m; **extremist width** 2.15m. **Parish's chief settlement** Weston-upon-Trent, a pretty village with a large Green. **Geology** WESTON village and Trent valley - Alluvium; N fringe - Keuper Marls. **Highest point** 298 feet near Wadden Farm. **Lowest point** 246 feet by the Trent at Shirleywich. Weston-upon-Trent was **120th most-populated Staffordshire parish in 1801** with 306 people; **117th in 1811** with 394; **113th in 1821** with 442; **97th in 1831** with 587; **102nd in 1841** with 562; **100th in 1851** with 570; **107th in 1861** with 502; **105th in 1871** with 495; **102nd in 1881** with 528; **108th in 1891** with 453; **112nd in 1901** with 401.

4. Church...

At Weston-upon-Trent is St Andrew, **one of 3 such county dedications** (of AP churches); **55th= oldest AP county church** dating from 1220. **4th oldest church bell in Staffordshire** No. 2 bell at Weston, bearing the inscription 'Ave Maria Mater Dei, miserere mei' but bearing no date or name (SA July 17 1953 p4 col 4) if coeval with No. 3 bell at Milwich, according to Charles Lynam in his Church Bells of Staffordshire 1889, placing it after those at St Chad's Lichfield, Farewell, and Milwich. If those at St Chad's, Lichfield, and Farewell post-date the Weston bell then the Weston bell would be Staffordshire's 2nd oldest bell.

The 'Staffordshire Harry Lauder' was born at Worston Mill House.

Worston
1. Did you know that...

Worston's most famous worthy Wilmot Martin (1875-1963), MBE, the 'Staffordshire Harry Lauder,' touring musician, was born at Worston Mill House, the son of a corn miller. He is buried at Hixon where he spent most of his life, passing away at his home there, 'The Wee Hoose Mang the Heather'. Hixon Village Hall has (2008) an oil painting of him and framed photographs of his touring troupe of musicians who in 42 years raised £25,000 for charity (SA & Chron April 11 1963 p7 col 1) (info Hixon Local History Society). Worston is the **county's 164th largest parish/ 6th smallest parish**, consisting of 172 acres. **14th= closest parish to the county town**, 3.5m NW; **extremist length** 0.7m, making it **6th= shortest parish in the county**; **extremist width** 0.7m, making it **7th= narrowest parish in the county**. The **name Worston first appears** in 1227. **Geology** ALL - Keuper Marls. **Highest point** 298 feet N of Worston. **Lowest point** 275 feet by the Sow, S of Worston. **Worston's top folklore** Worston Mill is said to be haunted by the ghost of 'George', someone associated with the mill who hung himself. **'one of the few mills in Staffordshire which are still working' 1956** Worston Mill (SA & Chron Aug 2 1956 p6 col 9). **'Staffordshire's best kept secret'** The Mill at Worston, restaurant, according to their own advert in The Stone & Eccleshall Gazette. Dec 2007 p20. **Worston's poorest** From 1858 the poor could be housed at Stafford Union workhouse at Marston. Worston was **156th most-populated Staffordshire parish in 1801** with 23 people; **155th in 1811** with 23; **156th= in 1821** with 23; **154th in 1831** with 25; **160th in 1841** with 23; **161st in 1851** with 17; **160th in 1861** with 17; **165th in 1871** with 5; **165th in 1881** with 7; **162nd in 1891** with 15; **158th in 1901** with 23.

SUBJECT INDEX *Wi to Wo*

*A Yarlet Hall Prep
School boy.*

Yarlet
1. Did you know that...

Yarlet is the **county's 159th largest parish**, consisting of 400 acres; **14th= closest parish to the county town**, 3.5m N; **extremist length** 0.6m, making it **5th shortest parish in the county**; **extremist width** 1.1m, making it **11th narrowest parish in the county**. The **name Yarlet first appears** in Domesday Book, 1086. **Geology** ALL - Keuper Marls. **Highest point** Yarlet Hill at 440 feet. **Lowest point** 282 feet on Enson Lane. **Yarlet's top folklore** There was for the folk of North Staffordshire the expression to go 'over Yarlet Hill,' which meant to go for trial or imprisonment at Stafford, as the main road from the north to Stafford passed over Yarlet Hill. **Yarlet's villains** John Betley of Combermere, Cheshire, aged 29, John Biddle of London, aged 45, and Richard Ellis of Hanford, Staffordshire, aged about 27, who robbed and murdered Thomas Ward, an attorney of Stafford, at the foot of Yarlet Hill by a brook. All three were executed at Stafford on March 20 1793 (Crime broadsheets in the WSL). **Yarlet's saddest** Arthur Bruce of Woodseaves, unemployed labourer aged 35, who was carol singing at Yarlet on Boxing Day 1932 when he was knocked down by a car travelling from Stafford to Stone. He died the next day in Stafford General Infirmary (SA Jan 2 1932 p9 col 6). **'one of the leading preparatory school headmasters of his day'** Rev Walter Earle (b1839), headmaster of Yarlet Hall School 1873-87. When he began the school in 1873 he instigated a wider range of activities for the boys than was to be found in the schools of most of his contemporaries. Although, innovative, he was very severe and loathed by some. After another headship to 1902 he retired to Reigate, where he was still living in 1922 (The Yarlet Story. Nigel Harris. 1993. p7). **Miss Yarlet 1937** Miss Marion Bailey. **Miss Yarlet 1938** Miss Betty Groves of The Lodge (SA April 2 1938 p9 col 4. April 23 1938 p10p). **First winners of the Staffordshire under-13s Cricket Cup** Yarlet Hall School in 1973; subsequently they won in 1980, 1982, 1986-91. **Under-11 national cricket champions 1984** Yarlet Hall School (The Yarlet Story. p67). **Yarlet's poorest** From 1858 the poor could be housed at

Stafford Union workhouse at Marston. Yarlet was **151st= most-popu-lated Staffordshire parish in 1801** with 33 people; **151st in 1811** with 33; **152nd in 1821** with 33; **157th in 1831** with 21; **159th in 1841** with 24; **158th in 1851** with 22; **158th in 1861** with 21; **162nd in 1871** with 11; **146th in 1881** with 117; **153rd in 1891** with 59; **149th in 1901** with 82. **Choicest quote** Oliver Davies in The Yarlet Story, p89, is accredited with this poem referring to Yarlet. It has perhaps apocalyptical resonance for children starting the autumn term at the now co-educational Yarlet Hall School:-

> O, hips and haws are scarlet,
> And all my time's my own,
> So I will go to Yarlet
> Or maybe into Stone,
> For Autumn is the season
> And golden is the morn,
> And clearly shows the reason
> That ever I was born.
>
> In robes of red and yellow
> The tall trees are arranged,
> Then come forth every fellow
> And come forth every maid
> Come Jonathan and Charlotte,
> Come Timothy and Joan,
> And take a walk to Yarlet,
> Or maybe into Stone.

SUBJECT INDEX *Wo to Z*

Also by MALTHOUSE PRESS

The Staffordshire Encyclopaedia. Hardback. 2000. ISBN.
0-9539018-0-7
The Staffordshire Encyclopaedia. Paperback. 2006. ISBN.
0-9539018-0-7
Old Parish Boundaries of Staffordshire: Pirehill. 2005.
ISBN. 0-9539018-1-5
Map of Staffordshire. Biographical County Maps.
2006. ISBN. 0-9539018-2-3
Staffordshire Moorlands. Did You Know That... No. 2 in
series. 2007. ISBN. 978-953-9018-24-3
The Autobiography of Thomas Newton.... etc. Life of
Walsall saddlery manufacturer. The Pocket series. 2008.
ISBN. 978-953-9018-3-8
The Natural History of Staffordshire. Robert Plot. 1686.
The Pocket series. 2009. ISBN 978-0-953918-7-6
Staffordshire The Black Country. Did You Know That...
No. 5 in series. 2008. ISBN. 978-953-9018-4-5

For more details contact Malthouse Press, Grange Cottage,
Malthouse Lane, Barlaston, Staffordshire, ST12 9AQ. Telephone (01782) 372067. Email: Timcockin@yahoo.com

Lightning Source UK Ltd.
Milton Keynes UK
UKOW051043131211

183690UK00001B/18/P